THE R

THE REDS

DAY-TO-DAY LIFE AT ANFIELD

RICHARD LERMAN AND DAVID BROWN

MAINSTREAM
PUBLISHING

EDINBURGH AND LONDON

First published in Great Britain in 1998 by
MAINSTREAM PUBLISHING COMPANY (EDINBURGH) LTD
7 Albany Street
Edinburgh EH1 3UG

ISBN 1 84018 037 4

A catalogue record for this book is available from the British Library

Typeset in Times
Printed and bound in Great Britain by Butler & Tanner Ltd

But for a disagreement over a planned rent increase by John Houlding, Everton might never have moved out of Anfield and Liverpool would therefore never have been formed. As it was, Everton departed to set up on the other side of Stanley Park, leaving John Houlding with a ground but no name (Everton took that with them as well) and no team. After legal steps to try and retain the name Everton failed, Houlding was left with little option other than to start from scratch. That the team he assembled should become one of the best in Europe adds further spice to an already interesting tale.

The usual football club history book is laid out chronologically from past to present, developing chapter by chapter the story of the journey to prominence (or in some cases oblivion) and the characters that shaped the destiny of the club and the team.

Alternatively, a player by player analysis or a who's who will attempt to list, in alphabetical order, all or sometimes just the key participants who have taken part in the building of the organisation or the events on the field.

We believe that *The Reds* introduces a third, and new, concept to the study of Football clubs.

Simply, by using a diary format, we have attempted to catalogue the important events, the landmarks along the way for both the club and its players and the highs and lows as they occurred on a day-to-day basis from formation to the present.

Obviously in a topic as large as the one we have attempted to cover there will be a debate about what material should be included and what should be left out. It would not have been practical to have included details of every player that has ever worn the red shirt of Liverpool. We have had to establish criteria that only those who have played a minimum number of games, or have been recognised for some other aspect of their career, be included. If, as we suspect, this has led to the omission of many fine players who for one reason or another did not make it into these pages, we apologise to them, their families and their supporters.

It has not been our policy to be contentious; we have desired to present a factual account of the history of this great club and, in so doing, some subjective decisions have had to be made. However, if any reader should consider we have made a glaring omission or a factual inaccuracy, we should be glad to address these matters with correspondence via our publisher, so that we might include any changes in a future edition of this book.

Finally, it has been our privilege to work on this subject matter. As the European success of the 1970s and 1980s begins to fade a little in the memory, the current side being assembled at Anfield is undoubtedly one worthy of the name Liverpool Football Club, and we suspect it will not be too long before the glory days are back at Anfield!

THE AUTHORS

This is the first time that the authors, Richard Lerman and David Brown, have worked together. This book, and three other titles from the same partnership, form part of a series on football that Mainstream Publishing are issuing where the material is organised in diary format.

Richard Lerman is married with three sons (all keen football enthusiasts) and lives in north London.

David Brown is married with two daughters (who care more for music than football) and lives in Kent.

Both men travel the length and breadth of Great Britain and Europe in pursuit of their obsession with football and are avid collectors of football memorabilia and statistics.

ACKNOWLEDGEMENTS

Authors Richard Lerman and David Brown would like to thank the following who have helped us in the research and for providing us with the material to make this book possible: Jim Gardiner, Les Gold, and Andrew Miller.

We would also like to thank the many readers of *Boot Magazine*, which specialises in football memorabilia (6 Denmark Road, London, N8 0DZ) who have provided us with material for this publication. The photographs in this book have been supplied by Wellard Huxley Promotions, Bob Bond and John Allen (proprietor of *The Football Card Collector Magazine*, PO Box 21709, London E14 6SR).

Last but not least, we would very much like to thank Graham Betts for his efforts in organising this project together with all the staff at Mainstream Publishing.

JANUARY 1ST

1894	Arsenal	H	League Division 2	2–0
1895	West Bromwich Albion	H	League Division 1	4–0
1896	Manchester City	H	League Division 2	3–1
1897	Bolton Wanderers	A	League Division 1	4–1
1898	West Bromwich Albion	H	League Division 1	1–1
1900	Sunderland	A	League Division 1	0–1
1901	Stoke City	H	League Division 1	3–1
1903	West Bromwich Albion	H	League Division 1	0–2
1904	Nottingham Forest	H	League Division 1	0–0
1906	Stoke City	H	League Division 1	3–1
1907	Bolton Wanderers	A	League Division 1	0–3
1908	Nottingham Forest	H	League Division 1	0–0
1909	Sunderland	A	League Division 1	4–1
1910	Arsenal	H	League Division 1	5–1
1912	Bradford City	H	League Division 1	1–0
1913	Newcastle United	A	League Division 1	0–0

Elisha Scott made his debut in goal shortly after his arrival from Belfast.

1914	Bradford City	H	League Division 1	0–1
1920	Manchester United	H	League Division 1	0–0
1921	Aston Villa	A	League Division 1	4–1
1924	Chelsea	H	League Division 1	3–1
1926	Aston Villa	H	League Division 1	3–1
1927	Bolton Wanderers	A	League Division 1	1–2
1934	Newcastle United	A	League Division 1	2–9
1935	Middlesbrough	A	League Division 1	0–2
1938	Chelsea	H	League Division 1	2–2
1948	Charlton Athletic	H	League Division 1	2–3
1949	Sunderland	A	League Division 1	2–0
1955	Derby County	H	League Division 2	2–0
1960	Hull City	A	League Division 2	1–0
1966	Manchester United	H	League Division 1	2–1
1972	Leeds United	H	League Division 1	0–2
1974	Leicester City	H	League Division 1	1–1
1977	Sunderland	H	League Division 1	2–0
1983	Notts County	H	League Division 1	5–1
1985	Watford	A	League Division 1	1–1
1986	Sheffield Wednesday	H	League Division 1	2–2

Whilst most of the 39,000 that attended the game settled into their seats, those already in their places were stunned to see the visitors take the lead inside a minute through a Carl Shutt header from a corner, their only corner of the game. In the first half Liverpool produced possibly the worst 45 minutes of football of their season. Ian Rush, who was going through his worst-ever non-scoring sequence for the club, continued to miss chances galore. All was to change just five minutes into the second half when, after good work from Whelan, Rush controlled the ball with one foot before shooting with the other to score a priceless goal to the relief of almost the entire ground. Liverpool were awarded a penalty shortly afterwards and Jan Molby stepped up only to see his spot-kick brilliantly turned away by Hodge, who had saved his previous four penalties. Paul Walsh, who had come on as substitute, scored with his first touch of the game to give the Reds the lead, but the joy was short-lived as Gary Thompson equalised almost immediately for the visitors. Champions Everton moved into second place on goal difference from Liverpool, and both were still five points behind leaders Manchester United.

1987	Nottingham Forest	A	League Division 1	1–1
1988	Coventry City	H	League Division 1	4–0
1989	Manchester United	A	League Division 1	1–3
1990	Nottingham Forest	A	League Division 1	2–2
1991	Leeds United	H	League Division 1	3–0
1992	Sheffield United	H	League Division 1	2–1
1994	Ipswich Town	A	Premier League	2–1
1996	Nottingham Forest	H	Premier League	4–2
1997	Chelsea	A	Premier League	0–1

JANUARY 2ND

1893	Fairfield	A	Lancashire League	4–1
1897	Sheffield United	H	League Division 1	0–0
1899	Sheffield United	A	League Division 1	2–0
1909	Chelsea	A	League Division 1	0–3
1911	Sunderland	A	League Division 1	0–4
1915	Notts County	A	League Division 1	1–3
1922	Newcastle United	A	League Division 1	1–1
1926	Leicester City	H	League Division 1	0–3
1928	Burnley	H	League Division 1	2–2
1932	Newcastle United	H	League Division 1	4–2
1937	Charlton Athletic	H	League Division 1	1–2
1939	Middlesbrough	A	League Division 1	0–3
1954	Bolton Wanderers	H	League Division 1	1–2
1965	Blackpool	A	League Division 1	3–2
1971	Aldershot	H	FA Cup 3rd round	1–0
1978	Middlesbrough	H	League Division 1	2–0

Kevin Kewley made his one and only appearance as a substitute. Possibly it will go down in history as the shortest playing career for the club. He obviously didn't impress too much as his contract was cancelled two weeks later.

| 1982 | Swansea City | A | FA Cup 3rd round | 4–0 |

Ian Rush scored two of the goals along with one each from centre halves Hansen and Lawrenson

| 1984 | Manchester United | H | League Division 1 | 1–1 |
| 1995 | Norwich City | H | Premier League | 4–0 |

JANUARY 3RD

1903	Blackburn Rovers	A	League Division 1	1–3
1914	Sunderland	A	League Division 1	2–1
1920	Sheffield United	A	League Division 1	2–3
1925	Arsenal	H	League Division 1	2–1
1931	Middlesbrough	H	League Division 1	3–1

Not surprisingly Gordon Hodgson scored two of the goals in this victory.

1948	Stoke City	H	League Division 1	0–0
1953	Stoke City	A	League Division 1	1–3
1959	Sunderland	H	League Division 2	3–1
1970	Southport	A	Friendly	1–0
1976	West Ham United	A	FA Cup 3rd round	2–0
1981	Altrincham	H	FA Cup 3rd round	4–1

Non-League Altrincham put up a brave performance but surrendered to two goals in each half.

1983	Arsenal	H	League Division 1	3–1
1987	West Ham United	H	League Division 1	1–0
1989	Aston Villa	H	League Division 1	1–0
1993	Bolton Wanderers	A	FA Cup 3rd round	2–2
1998	Coventry City	H	FA Cup 3rd round	1–3

JANUARY 4TH

| 1896 | Rotherham United | A | League Division 2 | 5–0 |

George Allan scored a hat-trick in this game. It was one of four he netted during the season.

| 1902 | Stoke City | H | League Division 1 | 7–0 |

Andy McGuigan became the first Liverpool player to score five goals in a game. He was to make only 31 appearances in total for the club, scoring 14 times.

1913	Bradford City	H	League Division 1	2–1
1930	Everton	A	League Division 1	3–3
1936	Everton	A	League Division 1	0–0
1947	Chelsea	A	League Division 1	1–3
1958	Southend United	H	FA Cup 3rd round	1–1
1964	Derby County	H	FA Cup 3rd round	5–0

Alf Arrowsmith scored four goals and Roger Hunt got the other in this comprehensive demolition of Derby.

1969	Doncaster Rovers	H	FA Cup 3rd round	2–0
1975	Stoke City	H	FA Cup 3rd round	2–0
1986	Norwich City	H	FA Cup 3rd round	5–0

Second Division leaders Norwich arrived on snow covered Merseyside for the Cup game, and probably wished they hadn't bothered. After Liverpool's recent run of form without a victory in six games there was always going to be a backlash and today was the day. A game totally dominated by the home side saw MacDonald, Walsh, McMahon, Whelan and John Wark score the five goals that provided a safe journey into the next round.

| 1994 | Manchester United | H | Premier League | 3–3 |
| 1997 | Burnley | H | FA Cup 3rd round | 1–0 |

JANUARY 5TH

| 1874 | Archie Goldie was born in Ayrshire. After starting out with Clyde he joined Liverpool in 1895. He was to go on and make 130 appearances for the club helping them to the Division Two title in 1896. |

| 1895 | Sheffield Wednesday | A | League Division 1 | 0–5 |
| 1907 | Blackburn Rovers | H | League Division 1 | 0–2 |

1924	West Ham United	A	League Division 1	0–1
1929	Aston Villa	H	League Division 1	4–0
1935	Arsenal	H	League Division 1	0–2

Contrary to reports Arsenal full-back Eddie Hapgood scored the rebound from his penalty kick with his head and not directly from the spot.

1946	Chester City	H	FA Cup 3rd round	2–1
1952	Wolves	H	League Division 1	1–1
1957	Southend United	A	FA Cup 3rd round	1–2

1957 David Fairclough was born in Liverpool.

1974	Doncaster Rovers	H	FA Cup 3rd round	2–2
1980	Grimsby Town	H	FA Cup 3rd round	5–0
1982	West Ham United	H	League Division 1	3–0
1985	Aston Villa	H	FA Cup 3rd round	3–0
1991	Blackburn Rovers	A	FA Cup 3rd round	1–1

JANUARY 6TH

1894	Rotherham United	A	League Division 2	4–1
1906	Blackburn Rovers	A	League Division 1	0–0
1912	Manchester City	A	League Division 1	3–2
1923	Chelsea	H	League Division 1	1–0
1934	Sheffield United	A	League Division 1	2–2
1951	Norwich City	A	FA Cup 3rd round	1–3
1962	Chelsea	H	FA Cup 3rd round	4–3
1968	West Bromwich Albion	H	League Division 1	4–1
1973	West Ham United	A	League Division 1	1–0
1984	Newcastle United	H	FA Cup 3rd round	4–0
1990	Swansea City	A	FA Cup 3rd round	0–0
1992	Crewe Alexandra	A	FA Cup 3rd round	4–0
1996	Rochdale	H	FA Cup 3rd round	7–0
1997	Middlesbrough	A	League Cup 5th round	1–2

JANUARY 7TH

1893	Heywood Central	A	Lancashire League	2–1
1899	Sunderland	H	League Division 1	0–0
1905	Chesterfield	H	League Division 2	6–1
1911	Blackburn Rovers	H	League Division 1	2–2
1922	Sunderland	A	FA Cup 1st round	1–1
1928	Aston Villa	A	League Division 1	4–3
1933	Newcastle United	H	League Division 1	3–0
1939	Luton Town	H	FA Cup 3rd round	3–0
1950	Blackburn Rovers	A	FA Cup 3rd round	0–0
1956	Accrington Stanley	H	FA Cup 3rd round	2–0

Billy Liddell scored both goals in the victory.

| 1961 | Coventry City | H | FA Cup 3rd round | 3–2 |
| 1967 | West Ham United | H | League Division 1 | 2–0 |

Peter Thompson scored both goals in the game inside three minutes of each other.

| 1970 | Coventry City | A | FA Cup 3rd round | 1–1 |

| 1978 | Chelsea | A | FA Cup 3rd round | 2–4 |

Not one of the best performances of the season by far, Kenny Dalglish and Craig Johnston scoring the consolation goals for a Liverpool side completely outplayed.

1989	Carlisle United	A	FA Cup 3rd round	3–0
1995	Birmingham City	A	FA Cup 3rd round	0–0
1998	Newcastle United	A	League Cup 5th round	2–0

JANUARY 8TH

| 1898 | Blackburn Rovers | A | League Division 1 | 1–2 |
| 1910 | Chelsea | H | League Division 1 | 5–1 |

James Stewart scored a hat-trick and Jack Parkinson scored the other two goals. Jack went on to score thirty goals in the season.

1921	Manchester United	H	FA Cup 1st round	1–1
1927	Bournemouth	A	FA Cup 3rd round	1–1
1938	Crystal Palace	A	FA Cup 3rd round	0–0
1949	Nottingham Forest	A	FA Cup 3rd round	2–2
1955	Lincoln City	A	FA Cup 3rd round	1–1
1958	Southend United	A	FA Cup 3rd round replay	3–2
1966	Arsenal	A	League Division 1	1–0

Ron Yeats scored in the last two minutes of the game to ensure Liverpool came away from Highbury with the two points.

1972	Leicester City	A	League Division 1	0–1
1974	Doncaster Rovers	A	FA Cup 3rd round replay	2–0
1977	Crystal Palace	H	FA Cup 3rd round	0–0
1983	Blackburn Rovers	A	FA Cup 3rd round	2–1
1991	Blackburn Rovers	H	FA Cup 3rd round replay	3–0
1994	Bristol City	A	FA Cup 3rd round	1–1 abd

JANUARY 9TH

1895	Derby County	A	League Division 1	1–0
1897	Wolves	A	League Division 1	2–1
1904	Sheffield Wednesday	A	League Division 1	1–2
1909	Blackburn Rovers	H	League Division 1	1–1
1915	Stockport	H	FA Cup 1st round	3–0
1932	Everton	A	FA Cup 3rd round	2–1
1937	Grimsby Town	A	League Division 1	1–2
1946	Chester City	A	FA Cup 3rd round	2–1
1954	Bolton Wanderers	A	FA Cup 3rd round	0–1
1960	Leyton Orient	H	FA Cup 3rd round	2–1

1962 Ray Houghton was born in Glasgow. Started his career at West Ham but never made it into the first team and moved across London to Fulham on a free transfer in the summer of 1982. Played nearly 150 games for Fulham before being sold to Oxford United for £150,000 in the summer of 1985 where he spent 2 years and never missed a game. He also helped them to their 3–0 League Cup triumph in 1986 over QPR.

1963	Wrexham	A	FA Cup 3rd round	3–0
1965	West Bromwich Albion	A	FA Cup 3rd round	2–1
1968	Ferencvaros	H	European Fairs Cup 3rd round 2nd leg	0–1

1971	Blackpool	H	League Division 1	2–2
1988	Stoke City	A	FA Cup 3rd Round	0–0
1990	Swansea City	H	FA Cup 3rd round replay	8–0

Ian Rush scored a hat-trick in the club's record victory in the competition.

| 1993 | Aston Villa | H | Premier League | 1–2 |

JANUARY 10TH

1914	Barnsley	H	FA Cup 1st round	1–1
1970	Stoke City	A	League Division 1	2–0
1976	Ipswich Town	H	League Division 1	3–3
1979	Southend United	A	FA Cup 3rd round	0–0
1981	Aston Villa	A	League Division 1	0–2
1983	Tranmere Rovers	A	Friendly	3–1

1991 Jimmy Carter was signed from Millwall for £800,000. The tricky winger who had played over 100 games for Millwall joined in a shock move after he was reportedly being tipped to join his old manager George Graham at Arsenal.

| 1998 | Wimbledon | H | Premier League | 2–0 |

JANUARY 11TH

| 1896 | Arsenal | H | League Division 2 | 3–0 |

One of the few occasions these two teams have met in the Second Division. Jimmy Ross grabbed two of the goals.

1902	Everton	A	League Division 1	0–4
1908	Derby County	H	FA Cup 1st round	4–2
1922	Sunderland	H	FA Cup 1st round replay	5–0
1930	Cardiff City	H	FA Cup 3rd round	1–2
1936	Swansea Town	H	FA Cup 3rd round	1–0
1947	Walsall	A	FA Cup 3rd round	5–2
1950	Blackburn Rovers	H	FA Cup 3rd round replay	2–1
1958	Fulham	H	League Division 2	2–1
1964	Chelsea	H	League Division 1	2–1
1969	West Bromwich Albion	H	League Division 1	1–0
1975	Derby County	A	League Division 1	0–2
1977	Crystal Palace	A	FA Cup 3rd round replay	3–2

Two second half goals from Steve Heighway saw Liverpool through to the next round after Crystal Palace fought very hard in both the first game and this replay.

1987	Luton Town	A	FA Cup 3rd Round	1–0
1992	Luton Town	H	League Division 1	2–1
1995	Arsenal	H	League Cup 5th round	1–0
1997	West Ham United	H	Premier League	0–0

JANUARY 12TH

1895	Nottingham Forest	H	League Division 1	5–0
1907	Birmingham	H	FA Cup 1st round	2–1
1921	Manchester United	A	FA Cup 1st round replay	2–1
1924	Bradford City	H	FA Cup 1st round	2–1
1927	Bournemouth	H	FA Cup 3rd round replay	4–1

| 1929 | Bristol City | A | FA Cup 3rd round | 2–0 |
| 1935 | Yeovil & Petters | A | FA Cup 3rd round | 6–2 |

After the first 45 minutes it would have been questionable who were the League team and who were the non-League team. Going into the second half level Liverpool soon showed their class and scored four goals in the first nine minutes.

1938	Crystal Palace	H	FA Cup 3rd round replay	3–1
1952	Workington	H	FA Cup 3rd round	1–0
1955	Lincoln City	H	FA Cup 3rd round replay	1–0
1957	Doncaster Rovers	H	League Division 2	2–1
1970	Coventry City	H	FA Cup 3rd round replay	3–0
1971	Manchester City	H	League Division 1	0–0
1974	Birmingham City	H	League Division 1	3–2
1980	Southampton	H	League Division 1	1–1
1982	Barnsley	H	League Cup 5th round	0–0
1986	Watford	A	League Division 1	3–2

On another horrific day in terms of weather conditions, Liverpool produced one of their best displays of the season to overcome a very determined Watford side. Paul Walsh who was still preventing Kenny Dalglish from picking himself, was even talked about England selection again, two years after winning the last of his four caps, stole the show again with two goals and Ian Rush sealed the points in a pretty one-sided game, even though the scoreline suggested otherwise.

| 1988 | Stoke City | H | FA Cup 3rd round replay | 1–0 |
| 1991 | Aston Villa | A | League Division 1 | 0–0 |

JANUARY 13TH

1894	Rotherham United	H	League Division 2	5–1
1900	West Bromwich Albion	H	League Division 1	2–0
1906	Leicester Fosse	H	FA Cup 1st round	2–1
1912	Leyton	H	FA Cup 1st round	1–0
1923	Arsenal	H	FA Cup 1st round	0–0
1926	Southampton	H	FA Cup 3rd round replay	1–0
1934	Fulham	H	FA Cup 3rd round	1–1
1951	Derby County	A	League Division 1	2–1
1962	Norwich City	H	League Division 2	5–4

In a season where 99 goals were scored this scoreline was no surprise to the crowd. It was the fifth occasion (they did it once more) of the season that they had netted five in a home game.

| 1973 | Burnley | A | FA Cup 3rd round | 0–0 |

1984 Former Hibernian, Liverpool and Scotland goalkeeper and President of the Scottish Football Association Tommy Younger died aged 54.

1990	Luton Town	H	League Division 1	2–2
1993	Bolton Wanderers	H	FA Cup 3rd round replay	0–2
1996	Sheffield Wednesday	A	Premier League	1–1

JANUARY 14TH

| 1893 | West Manchester | A | Lancashire League | 0–0 |
| 1899 | Wolves | A | League Division 1 | 0–0 |

1911	Gainsborough Trinity	H	FA Cup 1st round	3–2
1933	West Bromwich Albion	A	FA Cup 3rd round	0–2
1939	Charlton Athletic	A	League Division 1	3–1
1950	Bolton Wanderers	A	League Division 1	2–3
1961	Brighton & Hove Albion	A	League Division 2	1–3
1967	Sheffield Wednesday	A	League Division 1	1–0
1978	West Bromwich Albion	A	League Division 1	1–0
1981	Manchester City	A	League Cup semi-final 1st leg	1–0
1984	Wolves	H	League Division 1	0–1
1986	Tottenham Hotspur	A	Screen Sport Super Cup 2nd round 2nd leg	3–0

1987   More cup woe for Luton. Having been thrown out of the League Cup for refusing to admit visiting supporters to their ground, they landed in further trouble with the FA following their non-appearance in Liverpool for an FA Cup replay. Bad weather had affected the entire country but Liverpool's pitch was playable and Luton were informed that the match was going ahead. However, the Hatters left it too late to make their travel arrangements and advised Liverpool that they would not be able to fulfil the fixture. Liverpool asked the FA to throw Luton out of the cup but the Hatters survived the threat, forced another replay, and won 3-0 on their way to the semi-finals.

| 1989 | Sheffield Wednesday | A | League Division 1 | 2–2 |

1992   Gary Ablett was sold to neighbours Everton after spending nearly 9 years at Anfield. The cultured defender played 135 games and scored 1 goal.

| 1995 | Ipswich Town | H | Premier League | 0–1 |

JANUARY 15TH

1910	Bristol City	A	FA Cup 1st round	0–2
1913	Bristol City	H	FA Cup 1st round	3–0
1914	Barnsley	A	FA Cup 1st round replay	1–0
1921	Sunderland	H	League Division 1	0–0
1927	Manchester United	A	League Division 1	1–0
1938	Charlton Athletic	A	League Division 1	0–3
1949	Nottingham Forest	H	FA Cup 3rd round replay	4–0

After Bob Paisley's 90th-minute equaliser in the first game Liverpool made no mistake in this replay running out comfortable winners in the end. Three second half goals put an end to the determination of a strong Forest side.

1959	Worcester City	A	FA Cup 3rd round	1–2
1966	West Bromwich Albion	H	League Division 1	2–2
1972	Oxford United	A	FA Cup 3rd round	3–0

Two goals in the last ten minutes from Keegan and Alec Lindsay saw Liverpool into the fourth round against Leeds.

1977	West Bromwich Albion	H	League Division 1	1–1
1983	West Bromwich Albion	A	League Division 1	1–0
1994	Oldham Athletic	A	Premier League	3–0

JANUARY 16TH

1881   Tommy Fairfoul was born. Tommy started his career with Kilmarnock before moving to Third Lanark in 1906 before arriving at Liverpool in 1913.

| 1897 | Stoke City | H | League Division 1 | 1–0 |

1904	Sunderland	H	League Division 1	2–1
1909	Lincoln City	H	FA Cup 1st round	5–1
1915	Sunderland	H	League Division 1	2–1
1926	West Ham United	A	League Division 1	2–1
1932	Aston Villa	A	League Division 1	1–6
1937	Norwich City	A	FA Cup 3rd round	0–3
1954	Preston North End	A	League Division 1	1–2
1960	Sheffield United	H	League Division 2	3–0
1965	Sheffield Wednesday	H	League Division 1	4–2
1971	Crystal Palace	A	League Division 1	0–1
1973	Burnley	H	FA Cup 3rd round replay	3–0
1982	Wolves	H	League Division 1	2–1
1985	Juventus	A	European Super Cup	0–2
1988	Arsenal	H	League Division 1	2–0
1993	Wimbledon	A	Premier League	0–2

JANUARY 17TH

1903	Stoke City	A	League Division 1	0–1
1914	Everton	H	League Division 1	1–2
1920	Sheffield United	H	League Division 1	2–0
1923	Arsenal	A	FA Cup 1st round replay	4–1

Only the second time these two clubs had met in the competition with the same result as the first ten years earlier.

1925	Manchester City	A	League Division 1	0–5
1931	Huddersfield Town	A	League Division 1	1–2
1934	Fulham	A	FA Cup 3rd round replay	3–2

Tiny Bradshaw scored in the last minute of normal play to force the game into extra time. Syd Roberts then scored the winner with just two minutes remaining to see Liverpool go through to play Tranmere in the next round.

1948	Burnley	A	League Division 1	0–3
1953	Manchester City	H	League Division 1	0–1
1970	West Bromwich Albion	H	League Division 1	1–1
1976	Sheffield United	A	League Division 1	0–0
1978	Wrexham	A	League Cup 4th Round	3–1
1979	Southend United	H	FA Cup 3rd round replay	3–0
1981	Norwich City	A	League Division 1	1–0
1984	Sheffield Wednesday	A	League Cup 5th round	2–2
1987	Manchester City	A	League Division 1	1–0
1998	Leicester City	A	Premier League	0–0

JANUARY 18TH

1908	Bolton Wanderers	H	League Division 1	1–0

Jimmy Harrop made his debut.

1913	Manchester City	A	League Division 1	1–4

1913 Bill Lacey made his debut for Ireland in the 0–1 defeat by Wales in Belfast. He went on to win 12 caps in his career.

1930	West Ham United	A	League Division 1	1–4

1936	Grimsby Town	A	League Division 1	0–0
1947	Bolton Wanderers	H	League Division 1	0–3
1958	Middlesbrough	H	League Division 2	0–2
1961	Peter Beardsley was born in Newcastle upon Tyne.			
1964	West Ham United	A	League Division 1	0–1
1967	Leicester City	A	League Division 1	1–2
1969	Chelsea	A	League Division 1	2–1
1975	Coventry City	H	League Division 1	2–1
1983	West Ham United	H	League Cup 5th round	2–1
1986	West Ham United	H	League Division 1	3–1

A game of two halves. West Ham, pushing hard for second place themselves, came to Anfield and for the opening 45 minutes looked very comfortable indeed. But that all changed in the second half when Liverpool were awarded a dubious penalty, even by Dalglish's own admission, when Martin was adjudged to have tripped Walsh. Jan Molby promptly smashed home the kick, which left the West Ham players still arguing with the officials which resulted in Ray Stewart being sent off. From then on it was all one-way traffic with Rush and Walsh scoring to put the match beyond doubt, even though the Hammers got a consolation goal through Dickens. Nigel Clough scored a last-minute winner at Old Trafford for Nottingham Forest and Everton won which meant that both Merseyside clubs were within two points of the leaders.

1992	Oldham Athletic	A	League Division 1	3–2

Mickey Thomas scored his first goal for the club.

1995	Birmingham City	H	FA Cup 3rd round replay	1–1
1997	Aston Villa	H	Premier League	3–0

JANUARY 19TH

1901	Everton	H	League Division 1	1–2
1907	Sunderland	A	League Division 1	5–5
1924	Manchester City	A	League Division 1	1–0
1929	Leicester City	A	League Division 1	0–2
1930	Geoff Twentyman was born in Carlisle.			
1935	Portsmouth	A	League Division 1	2–1
1952	Sunderland	A	League Division 1	0–3
1957	Stoke City	A	League Division 2	0–1

1969 Steve Staunton born in Dundalk. Signed by Liverpool from Dundalk for £20,000 in 1986 he was a member of the side that won the FA Cup in 1989 and League title in 1990, but he was unable to command a regular place in the side and was surprisingly sold to Aston Villa for £1.1 million in 1991. He went on to prove the bargain of the decade, helping Villa win the League Cup in 1994 and 1996 but returned to Liverpool on a free transfer in 1998. He has won over 70 caps for the Republic of Ireland.

1974	Stoke City	A	League Division 1	1–1
1980	Coventry City	A	League Division 1	0–1
1982	Barnsley	A	League Cup 5th round replay	3–1
1985	Norwich City	H	League Division 1	4–0
1991	Wimbledon	H	League Division 1	1–1
1994	Bristol City	A	FA Cup 3rd round	1–1

JANUARY 20TH

1900	Everton	A	League Division 1	1–3
1906	Sunderland	H	League Division 1	2–0
1912	Everton	H	League Division 1	1–3
1923	Middlesbrough	A	League Division 1	2–0
1934	Aston Villa	H	League Division 1	2–3
1951	Everton	H	League Division 1	0–2
1962	Scunthorpe United	A	League Division 2	1–1
1968	Southampton	H	League Division 1	2–0
1973	Derby County	H	League Division 1	1–1
1984	Aston Villa	A	League Division 1	3–1
1990	Crystal Palace	A	League Division 1	2–0

1995   After 14 years magnificent service to the club Steve Nicol was given a free transfer and joined Notts County. Steve had made 431 appearances and scored on 46 occasions and is in the top 20 of the all-time appearance table for Liverpool. He won 4 Championships in 1984, 1986, 1988 and 1990, 3 FA Cup winners' medals in 1986, 1989 and 1992. He was part of the European Cup winning team in 1984 as well as being capped 27 times by Scotland. At the age of 34 Steve returned to Premiership Football with Sheffield Wednesday.

1996	Leeds United	H	Premier League	5–0

It's always nice to destroy local rivals Leeds and a second half blitz with four goals scored ensured a comprehensive victory. Neil Ruddock and Robbie Fowler scored two with Stan Collymore getting the other.

1998	Newcastle United	H	Premier League	1–0

JANUARY 21ST

1899	Everton	H	League Division 1	2–0
1905	Lincoln City	H	League Division 2	1–1
1911	Nottingham Forest	A	League Division 1	0–2
1922	Huddersfield Town	A	League Division 1	1–0
1925	Aston Villa	A	League Division 1	4–1
1928	Sunderland	H	League Division 1	2–5
1933	Aston Villa	A	League Division 1	2–5
1939	Stockport County	H	FA Cup 4th round	5–1
1950	Birmingham City	H	League Division 1	2–0

1954   Phil Thompson was born in Liverpool. He joined the club as an apprentice in 1971 where he was to stay for 15 years.

1956	Leicester City	H	League Division 2	3–1
1961	Ipswich Town	H	League Division 2	1–1
1967	Southampton	H	League Division 1	2–1
1978	Birmingham City	H	League Division 1	2–3
1986	Ipswich Town	H	League Cup 5th round	3–0
1987	Everton	A	Littlewoods Cup 5th Round	1–0

Having met in the FA Cup final the previous season, Everton were paired with Liverpool again in the Littlewoods Cup fifth round at Goodison Park. A crowd of 53,323 (the last time Goodison Park witnessed a crowd above 50,000 for the visit of Liverpool) saw a bruising game in which little quarter was expected or given. A clash between Gary Stevens and Jim Beglin left the Liverpool player with a broken leg, but the incident affected Stevens for the rest of the game. With seven minutes left and a replay looking the likeliest outcome, Ian Rush struck to win the tie for Liverpool.

| 1989 | Southampton | H | League Division 1 | 2–0 |

JANUARY 22ND

1878 Bill Goldie was born in Ayrshire. Like his younger brother Archie, Bill started his career with Clyde before joining the ranks at Anfield in 1898. He made over 150 appearances for the club helping them to the Division 1 title in 1901. He left the club in 1904 to join Fulham where he helped them become Southern League Champions in 1906 and 1907.

1898	Sunderland	A	League Division 1	0–1
1910	Blackburn Rovers	A	League Division 1	1–1
1921	Sunderland	A	League Division 1	1–2
1927	Derby County	H	League Division 1	3–2
1938	Sheffield United	A	FA Cup 4th round	1–1
1949	Bolton Wanderers	A	League Division 1	3–0
1955	Blackburn Rovers	H	League Division 2	4–1
1966	Chelsea	H	FA Cup 3rd round	1–2

1971 Stan Collymore born in Cannock. After failing to make the grade with Wolves Stan rebuilt his career with non-League Stafford Rangers and cost Crystal Palace a fee of £100,000 when he signed in 1991. Palace got their money back when they sold him to Southend and it was here that his career took off. A £2 million fee took him to Nottingham Forest in 1993 and he developed into a highly feared striker. Liverpool paid £8.5 million for him in 1995 but he failed to settle on Merseyside, refusing to move nearer the club's training facilities and frequently falling foul of disciplinary measures. At the end of the 1997–98 season he was sold again, this time to Aston Villa for £7 million.

| 1972 | Wolves | A | League Division 1 | 0–0 |

Peter Thompson played what was to be his last game for the club even though he didn't leave for Bolton Wanderers until nearly a year later. He won two Championship medals and one FA Cup winners' medal in his eleven years at Anfield playing 404 games and scoring 58 goals.

1977	Norwich City	A	League Division 1	1–2
1980	Nottingham Forest	A	League Cup semi-final 1st leg	0–1
1983	Birmingham City	H	League Division 1	1–0
1993	Shelbourne	A	Friendly	2–1
1994	Manchester City	H	Premier League	2–1

JANUARY 23RD

| 1904 | West Bromwich Albion | A | League Division 1 | 2–2 |

Jimmy McDougal was born.

| 1909 | Bradford City | A | League Division 1 | 2–0 |
| 1915 | Sheffield Wednesday | A | League Division 1 | 1–2 |

1919 Robert (Bob) Paisley was born in Bishop Auckland. Although the Second World War cost him his best years as a player, he still made 252 appearances for Liverpool between 1946 and his retirement in 1953. However, as a player he is best remembered for a game he didn't play in – despite scoring in Liverpool's semi-final win against local rivals Everton, he was dropped for the 1950 FA Cup final against Arsenal, which Liverpool lost 2–0 (although he did win a winners' medal in the FA Amateur Cup with Bishops Auckland). Upon his retirement as a player he joined the famous 'boot-room' coaching staff, taking over as manager of Liverpool from Bill Shankly in 1974. It was felt that Shankly, one of Liverpool's most charismatic and successful managers of all time, would be a tough act to follow, but Bob Paisley surpassed all expectations and remains the most successful manager in the history of the English game. He won an astonishing six League titles, the European Cup three times, the League/Milk Cup three times in succession (on the final occasion, Paisley's last season as manager, the team sent him up to collect the trophy from the Royal Box at Wembley), six FA Charity Shields and the UEFA and European Super Cups once each. The one domestic trophy to elude him during his reign as manager was the FA Cup – the competition obviously didn't agree with him! He handed over the reins to Joe Fagan in 1983 and immediately took up a seat on the board of directors, a position he held until 1992 when ill-health forced his retirement. He was awarded the OBE for his services to football.

1926	Arsenal	H	League Division 1	3–0
1932	Chesterfield	A	FA Cup 4th round	4–2
1937	Everton	H	League Division 1	3–2
1954	Tottenham Hotspur	H	League Division 1	2–2
1960	Middlesbrough	A	League Division 2	3–3
1971	Swansea Town	H	FA Cup 4th round	3–0
1982	Sunderland	A	FA Cup 4th round	3–0
1988	Charlton Athletic	A	League Division 1	2–0

JANUARY 24TH

1909	Vic Wright was born in Walsall. Joined the club in March 1934.			
1914	West Bromwich Albion	A	League Division 1	1–0
1920	Bolton Wanderers	A	League Division 1	3–0
1925	Bury	H	League Division 1	4–0
1931	Aston Villa	H	League Division 1	1–1
1948	Manchester United	A	FA Cup 4th round	0–3

Although this was a 'home' FA Cup tie for United, Old Trafford was still not ready for use due to redevelopment and so the tie was switched to Everton's Goodison Park ground, a crowd of 74,000 saw United win 3–0.

1953	Portsmouth	A	League Division 1	1–3
1959	Newcastle United	H	Friendly	2–2
1970	Wrexham	H	FA Cup 4th round	3–1
1976	Derby County	A	FA Cup 4th round	0–1
1981	Everton	A	FA Cup 4th round	1–2
1987	Newcastle United	H	League Division 1	2–0
1995	Everton	H	Premier League	0–0

1996   Nigel Clough was sold to Manchester City for £1.5 million. Nigel never really settled in during his two years at Anfield. He managed to make only 40 appearances in total scoring nine goals.

JANUARY 25TH

1896	Lincoln City	H	League Division 2	6–1
1902	Everton	H	FA Cup 1st round	2–2

The very first FA Cup meeting between Liverpool and Everton. With so much at stake it was no surprise the game ended in a draw.

1908	Birmingham City	A	League Division 1	1–1
1913	West Bromwich Albion	H	League Division 1	2–1
1930	Manchester United	H	League Division 1	1–0

Thomas 'Tiny' Bradshaw made his debut.

1936	Arsenal	H	FA Cup 4th round	0–2
1939	Bolton Wanderers	H	League Division 1	1–2
1947	Grimsby Town	H	FA Cup 4th round	2–0
1958	Northampton Town	H	FA Cup 4th round	3–1

Liverpool's biggest crowd of the season 56,939 saw goals from Billy Liddell, Louis Bimpson and an own goal give victory.

1964	Port Vale	H	FA Cup 4th round	0–0
1969	Burnley	H	FA Cup 4th round	2–1
1975	Ipswich Town	A	FA Cup 4th round	0–1
1984	Sheffield Wednesday	H	League Cup 5th round replay	3–0
1994	Bristol City	H	FA Cup 3rd round replay	0–1

One of the biggest shocks of the competition when Liverpool lost at home.

JANUARY 26TH

1907	Birmingham City	H	League Division 1	2–0
1924	Manchester City	H	League Division 1	0–0
1929	Bolton Wanderers	H	FA Cup 4th round	0–0
1935	Blackburn Rovers	A	FA Cup 4th round	0–1
1938	Sheffield United	H	FA Cup 4th round replay	1–0
1946	Bolton Wanderers	A	FA Cup 4th round	0–5

This is the club's record defeat in the competition, and probably one of the most forgettable in it as well.

1952	Aston Villa	H	League Division 1	1–2
1957	Bolton Wanderers	A	Friendly	3–5
1963	Burnley	A	FA Cup 4th round	1–1
1974	Carlisle United	H	FA Cup 4th round	0–0
1980	Nottingham Forest	A	FA Cup 4th round	2–0
1982	Notts County	A	League Division 1	4–0
1986	Chelsea	A	FA Cup 4th round	2–1

Liverpool arrived at Stamford Bridge to face bogie-team Chelsea. Knowing that their past three visits in the competition had ended in defeat, they were determined to right the record that had plagued them in the previous 20 years. A bright game was marred by a couple of unfortunate injuries to Kerry Dixon and Colin Lee, which left the Londoners with only 10 men for the last hour of the match. In the 47th minute, after another unfortunate ricochet off Craig Johnston, the ball fell to Ian Rush who gratefully drove it home from the edge of the box. Early in the second half Lawrenson seemingly put the game beyond Chelsea's reach with a goal that also had a bit of good fortune about it, as it squeezed under the keeper's body. Chelsea did rally and scored through

David Speedie with just over 20 minutes left, but Liverpool held on and showed that they were able to dig in and mix it as well as play the possession game.

1991	Brighton & Hove Albion	H	FA Cup 4th round	2–2
1994	Ronny Rosenthal was sold to Tottenham for £250,000.			
1997	Chelsea	A	FA Cup 4th round	2–4

JANUARY 27TH

1894	Grimsby Town	H	FA Cup 1st round	3–0

Liverpool's first game in the competition where they didn't have to qualify. Two goals from Harry Bradshaw and Joe McQue saw them into the next round.

1900	Stoke	A	FA Cup 1st round	0–0
1906	Birmingham City	A	League Division 1	0–1
1912	West Bromwich Albion	A	League Division 1	0–1
1923	Middlesbrough	H	League Division 1	2–0
1932	Leicester City	H	League Division 1	3–3
1934	Tranmere Rovers	H	FA Cup 4th round	3–1

Tranmere had originally been drawn at home in this fixture but because of the size of their ground decided to play at Anfield. It was a success in terms of a financial victory with over 61,000 in attendance, but it didn't work in terms of the playing side as Liverpool won the game.

1951	Charlton Athletic	A	League Division 1	0–1
1962	Oldham Athletic	A	FA Cup 4th round	2–1
1964	Port Vale	A	FA Cup 4th round replay	2–1
1968	Bournemouth	A	FA Cup 3rd round	0–0
1973	Wolves	A	League Division 1	1–2
1979	Bangor City	A	Friendly	4–0
1985	Tottenham Hotspur	H	FA Cup 4th round	1–0
1998	Middlesbrough	H	League Cup semi-final 1st leg	2–1

JANUARY 28TH

1893	Darwen	H	Lancashire Cup	1–0
1899	Blackburn Rovers	H	FA Cup 1st round	2–0
1905	Leicester Fosse	A	League Division 2	3–0
1911	Manchester City	H	League Division 1	1–1
1922	West Bromwich Albion	H	FA Cup 2nd round	0–1
1928	Cardiff City	A	FA Cup 4th round	1–2
1939	Leeds United	A	League Division 1	1–1
1950	Exeter City	H	FA Cup 4th round	3–1
1956	Scunthorpe United	H	FA Cup 4th round	3–3
1961	Sunderland	H	FA Cup 4th round	0–2
1967	Watford	A	FA Cup 3rd round	0–0
1978	Jamie Carrgaher was born in Bootle.			
1990	Norwich City	A	FA Cup 4th round	0–0
1994	Graham Souness was sacked as manager. Despite the FA Cup win his reign as manager			

had not matched the high standards he set as a player. He made excessive changes to the playing staff and the training programme etc and it was no real shock when he parted company with the club.

| 1995 | Burnley | A | FA Cup 4th round | 0–0 |

JANUARY 29TH

1898	Hucknall St John's	H	FA Cup 1st round	2–0
1921	Newcastle United	A	FA Cup 2nd round	0–1
1927	Southport	H	FA Cup 4th round	3–1
1938	Grimsby Town	A	League Division 1	0–0
1947	Everton	A	League Division 1	0–1
1949	Notts County	H	FA Cup 4th round	1–0
1955	Everton	A	FA Cup 4th round	4–0

72,000 fans packed into Goodison Park to watch Liverpool completely overrun the home side with a powerful display. This was the highest amount of spectators by nearly 22,000 to watch them during any one game in the season. John Evans scored two of the goals with Alan A'Court and Billy Liddell getting the others.

1966	Leicester City	H	League Division 1	1–0
1972	Crystal Palace	H	League Division 1	4–1
1974	Carlisle United	A	FA Cup 5th round replay	2–0
1977	Carlisle United	H	FA Cup 4th round	3–0
1983	Stoke City	H	FA Cup 4th round	2–0
1984	Brighton & Hove Albion	A	FA Cup 4th round	0–2
1989	Millwall	A	FA Cup 4th round	2–0
1992	Arsenal	H	League Division 1	2–0

JANUARY 30TH

| 1897 | Burton Swifts | H | FA Cup 1st round | 4–3 |
| 1902 | Everton | A | FA Cup 1st round replay | 2–0 |

Liverpool won 2–0 in the FA Cup first round replay at Goodison and thus won the very first clash between the two clubs in the competition.

1904	Small Heath	H	League Division 1	0–2
1909	Manchester United	H	League Division 1	3–1
1915	Sheffield United	A	FA Cup 2nd round	0–1
1926	Fulham	A	FA Cup 4th round	1–3
1929	Bolton Wanderers	A	FA Cup 4th round replay	2–5
1932	Everton	A	League Division 1	1–2
1937	Leeds United	H	League Division 1	3–0
1946	Bolton Wanderers	H	FA Cup 4th round	2–0
1960	Manchester United	H	FA Cup 4th round	1–3
1965	Stockport County	H	FA Cup 4th round	1–1
1968	Bournemouth	H	FA Cup 3rd round replay	4–1
1971	Arsenal	H	League Division 1	2–0

Arsenal suffered one of their rare defeats in what was to be their 'Double'-winning season. John Toshack scored after just three minutes and Tommy Smith added a second half penalty to reverse the same scoreline at Highbury the previous November.

1979	Blackburn Rovers	H	FA Cup 4th round	1–0
1982	Aston Villa	A	League Division 1	3–0
1991	Brighton & Hove Albion	A	FA Cup 4th round replay	3–2

1903	Sheffield Wednesday	A	League Division 1	1–3
1914	Gillingham	H	FA Cup 2nd round	2–0

Goals in the 81st and 83rd minutes saw Liverpool through their first tie in the competition.

1920	Luton Town	A	FA Cup 2nd round	2–0
1925	Bristol City	A	FA Cup 2nd round	1–0
1931	Chelsea	A	League Division 1	2–2
1948	Portsmouth	H	League Division 1	0–3
1953	Leeds United	A	Friendly	0–1
1959	Charlton Athletic	A	League Division 2	3–2
1970	Nottingham Forest	A	League Division 1	0–1
1976	West Ham United	A	League Division 1	4–0
1981	Leicester City	H	League Division 1	1–2

Liverpool lost at home in a First Division match for the first time in over three years, beaten by Leicester who were bottom of the League. Since losing 3–2 to Birmingham City on 28th January 1978, Liverpool had gone a record 85 home matches without defeat, comprising 63 League games, nine League Cup, six FA Cup, six European Cup and one Super Cup matches. Liverpool won 69 of the 85 encounters, scoring 213 goals and conceding only 35.

1988	Aston Villa	A	FA Cup 4th round	2–0
1990	Norwich City	H	FA Cup 4th round replay	3–1
1993	Arsenal	A	Premier League	1–0
1996	Aston Villa	A	Premier League	2–0
1998	Blackburn Rovers	H	Premier League	0–0

1896	Millwall	H	FA Cup 1st round	4–1
1900	Stoke	H	FA Cup 1st round replay	1–0
1902	Bury	A	League Division 1	0–0
1908	Brighton	H	FA Cup 2nd round	1–1
1913	Arsenal	A	FA Cup 2nd round	4–1

The first time these two great clubs had met in the FA Cup. Arthur Metcalfe scored a hat-trick as Liverpool eased into the third round.

1930	Grimsby Town	A	League Division 1	2–3
1933	Middlesbrough	H	League Division 1	1–3
1934	Leicester City	A	League Division 1	0–1
1936	West Bromwich Albion	A	League Division 1	1–6
1947	Leeds United	A	League Division 1	2–1
1958	Leyton Orient	A	League Division 2	0–1
1964	Sheffield United	H	League Division 1	6–1
1967	Watford	H	FA Cup 3rd round replay	3–1
1969	Sheffield Wednesday	H	League Division 1	1–0
1975	Arsenal	A	League Division 1	0–2
1983	Blackpool Select	A	Friendly	6–2
1984	Watford	H	League Division 1	3–0
1986	Ipswich Town	A	League Division 1	1–2

Ipswich, languishing in the bottom three of the table, should have been a reasonably comfortable match for the Reds but, as often is the case, the home team raised their game to fit the occasion. Ian Rush was absent through injury and, surprisingly, the manager, Kenny Dalglish, did not pick himself, opting for a more cautious approach by playing an extra midfielder (Sammy Lee) instead. The move backfired because Ipswich never looked like they were going to get beaten and it was a surprise when Ronnie Whelan opened the scoring with a rare Liverpool attack in the first period. The home side rallied in the second half and it was no more than they deserved when youngster Mitch D'Avray equalised and Wilson scored the winning goal. To make matters worse, Manchester United lost at West Ham and Everton beat Spurs to take over top spot in the league.

1992	Chelsea	H	League Division 1	1–2
1997	Derby County	A	Premier League	1–0

FEBRUARY 2ND

1895	Barnsley St Peter's	A	FA Cup 1st round	2–1
1901	Bolton Wanderers	A	League Division 1	0–1
1907	Oldham Athletic	A	FA Cup 2nd round	1–0
1914	Sheffield Wednesday	H	League Division 1	1–2
1924	Bolton Wanderers	A	FA Cup 2nd round	4–1
1929	Leeds United	A	League Division 1	2–2
1935	Leeds United	H	League Division 1	4–2
1938	Preston North End	H	League Division 1	2–2
1952	Wolves	H	FA Cup 4th round	2–1

61,905 attended the game which is the record attendance for the club at Anfield, with the restructuring and the abolition of terraces this is never likely to be beaten.

1957	Middlesbrough	H	League Division 2	1–2
1974	Norwich City	H	League Division 1	1–0
1982	Ipswich Town	A	League Cup semi-final 1st leg	2–0

Two goals inside a minute by Terry McDermott and Ian Rush set up Liverpool with a healthy lead after the first leg.

1985	Sheffield Wednesday	A	League Division 1	1–1

FEBRUARY 3RD

1894	Northwich Victoria	H	League Division 2	4–0
1900	Blackburn Rovers	H	League Division 1	3–1
1906	Barnsley	H	FA Cup 2nd round	1–0
1912	Fulham	A	FA Cup 2nd round	0–3
1923	Wolves	A	FA Cup 2nd round	2–0
1934	Tottenham Hotspur	H	League Division 1	3–1
1936	Harry Eastham joined the club from Blackpool where he started his career as an amateur.			
1951	Fulham	H	League Division 1	2–0
1962	Brighton & Hove Albion	H	League Division 2	3–1
1965	Stockport County	A	FA Cup 4th round replay	2–0
1968	Everton	A	League Division 1	0–1
1979	West Bromwich Albion	H	League Division 1	2–1
1990	Everton	H	League Division 1	2–1

| 1991 | Manchester United | A | League Division 1 | 1–1 |
| 1996 | Tottenham Hotspur | H | Premier League | 0–0 |

FEBRUARY 4TH

1899	Stoke City	H	League Division 1	1–0
1905	Everton	H	FA Cup 1st round	1–1
1911	Everton	A	FA Cup 2nd round	1–2

This was the fourth time Liverpool and Everton had been paired in the FA Cup, with 50,000 packing into Goodison for the derby game with extra flavour. Alex Young scored twice for Everton, with Parkinson netting for Liverpool.

1920	Bolton Wanderers	H	League Division 1	2–0
1922	Birmingham City	A	League Division 1	2–0
1925	Nottingham Forest	A	League Division 1	1–0
1928	West Ham United	H	League Division 1	1–3
1931	John Molyneux was born in Warrington.			
1933	Bolton Wanderers	A	League Division 1	3–3
1939	Everton	H	League Division 1	0–3
1950	Derby County	A	League Division 1	2–2
1956	Middlesbrough	A	League Division 2	2–1
1961	Scunthorpe United	A	League Division 2	3–2
1967	Sunderland	A	League Division 1	2–2
1973	Manchester City	H	FA Cup 4th round	0–0
1978	Coventry City	A	League Division 1	0–1
1984	Sunderland	A	League Division 1	0–0
1989	Newcastle United	A	League Division 1	2–2
1995	Nottingham Forest	A	Premier League	1–1

FEBRUARY 5TH

| 1898 | Sheffield United | H | League Division 1 | 0–4 |
| 1908 | Brighton | A | FA Cup 2nd round replay | 3–0 |

Jim Bradley scored two of the goals with Jack Cox getting the other. Bradley in his 169 appearances for the club only scored five goals so his effort in this game was quite phenomenal.

1921	Manchester United	A	League Division 1	1–1
1927	Arsenal	H	League Division 1	3–0
1938	Leeds United	H	League Division 1	1–1
1949	Everton	H	League Division 1	0–0
1955	Fulham	A	League Division 2	2–1
1966	Blackburn Rovers	A	League Division 1	4–1
1972	Leeds United	H	FA Cup 4th round	0–0
1974	Coventry City	H	League Division 1	2–1
1977	Birmingham City	H	League Division 1	4–1
1983	Luton Town	A	League Division 1	3–1
1986	Norwich City	A	Screen Sport Super Cup semi-final 1st Leg	1–1
1992	Bristol Rovers	A	FA Cup 4th round	1–1
1994	Norwich City	A	Premier League	2–2

FEBRUARY 6TH

1904	Blackburn Rovers	A	FA Cup 1st round	1–3

1908 Willie Steel was born in Lanarkshire. After a short trial period the right back joined Liverpool from St Johnstone in September 1931.

1909	Norwich City	H	FA Cup 2nd round	2–3
1915	Everton	A	League Division 1	3–1

1916 John Balmer was born in Liverpool. He joined the club at the age of 19.

1926	Everton	A	League Division 1	3–3
1932	Grimsby Town	A	League Division 1	1–5
1937	Birmingham City	A	League Division 1	0–5
1954	Burnley	A	League Division 1	1–1
1956	Scunthorpe United	A	FA Cup 4th round replay	2–1
1965	Aston Villa	A	League Division 1	1–0
1971	Leeds United	A	League Division 1	1–0
1982	Ipswich Town	H	League Division 1	4–0
1988	West Ham United	H	League Division 1	0–0
1993	Nottingham Forest	H	Premier League	0–0

FEBRUARY 7TH

1903	Manchester United	A	FA Cup 1st round	1–2

1904 Tiny Bradshaw was born in Renfrewshire. The strong centre half was bought from Bury in January 1930 for £8000.

1920	Blackburn Rovers	A	League Division 1	2–0
1923	West Bromwich Albion	H	League Division 1	2–0
1925	Everton	H	League Division 1	3–1
1927	Sheffield United	A	League Division 1	4–1
1931	Newcastle United	H	League Division 1	4–2
1948	Bolton Wanderers	A	League Division 1	0–3
1953	Middlesbrough	A	League Division 1	3–2

Alan A'Court made his senior debut for the club after joining from Preston Cables in September 1952.

1959	Bristol Rovers	H	League Division 2	3–2

1959 Sammy Lee was born in Liverpool.

1970	Leicester City	H	FA Cup 5th round	0–0
1973	Manchester City	A	FA Cup 4th round replay	0–2
1976	Leeds United	H	League Division 1	2–0
1978	Arsenal	H	League Cup semi-final 1st leg	2–1
1981	West Bromwich Albion	A	League Division 1	0–2
1984	Walsall	H	League Cup semi-final 1st leg	2–2

1992 Bob Paisley resigned from the Liverpool board owing to ill-health.

1995	Burnley	H	FA Cup 4th round replay	1–0
1998	Southampton	H	Premier League	2–3

FEBRUARY 8TH

1902	Southampton	A	FA Cup 2nd round	1–4
1905	Everton	A	FA Cup 1st round replay	1–2
1908	Sunderland	A	League Division 1	0–1

1913	Everton	A	League Division 1	2–0
1930	Leicester City	H	League Division 1	1–1
1936	Sunderland	H	League Division 1	0–3
1947	Derby County	H	FA Cup 5th round	1–0
1958	Charlton Athletic	H	League Division 2	3–1
1963	Drumcondra	A	Friendly	5–1
1964	Everton	A	League Division 1	1–3
1975	Ipswich Town	H	League Division 1	5–2

Goals by Toshack and Hall in the first eight minutes set up this easy victory.

| 1983 | Burnley | H | League Cup semi-final 1st leg | 3–0 |

Goals by Souness, Hodgson and a Phil Neal penalty gave Liverpool a strong first-leg lead as they tried to reach Wembley for the third year in succession.

| 1992 | Coventry City | A | League Division 1 | 0–0 |

FEBRUARY 9TH

1901	Notts County	A	FA Cup 1st round	0–2
1907	Arsenal	H	League Division 1	4–0
1921	Manchester United	H	League Division 1	2–0
1924	Bolton Wanderers	H	League Division 1	3–1
1929	Everton	H	League Division 1	1–2
1935	West Bromwich Albion	A	League Division 1	1–1
1952	Derby County	A	League Division 1	1–1
1957	Leicester City	A	League Division 2	2–3
1972	Leeds United	A	FA Cup 4th round replay	0–2
1980	Norwich City	A	League Division 1	5–3
1982	Ipswich Town	H	League Cup semi-final 2nd leg	2–2
1986	Manchester United	H	League Division 1	1–1

The day did not start well when a so-called Liverpool supporter sprayed a substance at the Manchester United players as they got off the team coach. To their credit the visiting players did not make much of the incident, in fact it seemed to make them more determined and for the first 20 minutes Liverpool hardly got out of their own penalty area. It was no shock, therefore, when Gibson put Manchester United in front. Further problems beset the home side, including the loss of Paul Walsh, who had been in fantastic form in the last few games, who had to go off with a serious ankle injury. However, Liverpool rallied and started to take control, and just before half-time substitute John Wark jabbed home the equaliser after Sammy Lee had hit an upright. Despite continuous second-half pressure, Liverpool couldn't find a way past the Manchester United defence, but they were extremely grateful in the end with a point.

| 1991 | Everton | H | League Division 1 | 3–1 |

FEBRUARY 10TH

1894	Preston North End	H	FA Cup 2nd round	3–2
1895	Barnsley St Peter's	H	FA Cup 1st round	4–0
1906	Derby County	A	League Division 1	3–0
1912	Blackburn Rovers	A	League Division 1	0–1

Kenny Campbell made his debut in goal.

| 1913 | Oldham Athletic | A | League Division 1 | 1–3 |

1923	West Bromwich Albion	A	League Division 1	0–0
1934	Everton	A	League Division 1	0–0
1951	Portsmouth	H	League Division 1	2–1
1962	Bury	A	League Division 2	3–0
1965	FC Cologne	A	European Cup 3rd round 1st leg	0–0
1973	Arsenal	H	League Division 1	0–2
1981	Manchester City	H	League Cup semi-final 2nd leg	1–1
1990	Norwich City	A	League Division 1	0–0
1993	Chelsea	A	Premier League	0–0

FEBRUARY 11TH

1893	Bury	A	Lancashire League	0–3
1899	Newcastle United	H	FA Cup 2nd round	3–1
1905	Leicester Fosse	A	League Division 2	2–0
1911	Sheffield Wednesday	H	League Division 1	3–0
1922	Birmingham City	H	League Division 1	1–0
1928	Portsmouth	A	League Division 1	0–1
1933	Everton	H	League Division 1	7–4

Liverpool sprung a surprise before the game, selecting a side that relied on youth as opposed to the seasoned professionals Everton had expected to be up against. A crowd of 50,000 were at Anfield for the game, with Everton taking the lead after eight minutes through Dixie Dean. It didn't take Liverpool long to equalise or then take the lead, with Everton's defence unable to cope with the speed of the Liverpool wingers, and Cresswell inadvertently helped on a free kick that led to Liverpool's third shortly before half-time. Everton got back into the game soon after the break, but that only seemed to inspire Liverpool to pull away again, scoring twice in a short spell through Barton and Taylor. Everton were still not finished and Dean scored his second of the game with a header to bring the score to 5–3, but Liverpool scored two more through Roberts and Barton who completed his hat-trick before Everton scored in the last minute to make the final result 7–4.

1939	Wolves	A	FA Cup 5th round	1–4
1950	Stockport County	A	FA Cup 5th round	2–1
1956	Plymouth Argyle	A	League Division 2	0–4
1961	Leyton Orient	H	League Division 2	5–0
1967	Aston Villa	H	League Division 1	1–0
1970	Leicester City	A	FA Cup 5th round replay	2–0
1972	Steve McManaman was born in Bootle.			
1984	Arsenal	H	League Division 1	2–1
1987	Southampton	A	Littlewoods Cup semi-final 1st Leg	0–0
1992	Bristol Rovers	H	FA Cup 4th round replay	2–1
1995	Queens Park Rangers	H	Premier League	1–1
1996	Queens Park Rangers	A	Premier League	2–1
1998	Michael Owen became the youngest player this century to play for England, when he played against Chile at Wembley.			

FEBRUARY 12TH

1898	Newton Heath	A	FA Cup 2nd round	0–0
1910	Everton	H	League Division 1	0–1

1921	Bradford City	H	League Division 1	2–1
1927	Everton	H	League Division 1	1–0
1938	Huddersfield Town	H	FA Cup 5th round	0–1
1947	Grimsby Town	H	League Division 1	5–0

Cyril Done scored a hat-trick, his second of the season and Joe Fagan scored the other two as Liverpool headed towards the top of the table.

1949	Wolves	A	FA Cup 5th round	1–3
1955	Swansea Town	H	League Division 2	1–1
1966	Sunderland	H	League Division 1	4–0

Roger Hunt scored a second half hat-trick in just 19 minutes.

1968	Chelsea	A	League Division 1	1–3
1972	Huddersfield Town	A	League Division 1	1–0
1975	Newcastle United	A	League Division 1	1–4
1980	Nottingham Forest	H	League Cup semi-final 2nd leg	1–1

A last-minute goal by supersub David Fairclough earned Liverpool the draw on the night, but it wasn't enough to see them through to the final.

1983	Ipswich Town	H	League Division 1	1–0
1985	Arsenal	H	League Division 1	3–0
1986	Queens Park Rangers	A	League Cup semi-final 1st leg	0–1
1989	Dundee	A	Friendly	3–1

FEBRUARY 13TH

| 1897 | West Bromwich Albion | A | FA Cup 2nd round | 2–1 |
| 1904 | Stoke City | H | League Division 1 | 0–0 |

Richard Edmed was born in Kent. Played for his local team Gillingham before moving to Liverpool in January 1926 for £1,800.

1909	Leicester City	H	League Division 1	4–1
1915	Chelsea	H	League Division 1	3–3
1926	Burnley	H	League Division 1	3–2
1929	Manchester United	H	League Division 1	2–3
1932	Grimsby Town	H	FA Cup 5th round	1–0
1937	Middlesbrough	H	League Division 1	0–2
1954	Charlton Athletic	H	League Division 1	2–3
1960	Plymouth Argyle	A	League Division 2	1–1
1963	Aston Villa	H	League Division 1	4–0
1965	Wolves	H	League Division 1	2–1
1971	Southampton	H	FA Cup 5th round	1–0
1979	Birmingham City	H	League Division 1	1–0
1982	Chelsea	A	FA Cup 5th round	0–2
1988	Watford	A	League Division 1	4–1
1993	Southampton	A	Premier League	1–2

FEBRUARY 14TH

1903	Notts County	A	League Division 1	2–1
1914	Bolton Wanderers	A	League Division 1	1–2
1920	Blackburn Rovers	H	League Division 1	3–0
1925	Newcastle United	H	League Division 1	1–1

| 1931 | Sheffield Wednesday | A | League Division 1 | 5–3 |
| 1948 | Newcastle United | A | Friendly | 3–0 |

1951 Kevin Keegan was born in Doncaster. He joined Scunthorpe in 1968 and made 120 appearances for them before being signed by Liverpool in May 1971.

1953	West Bromwich Albion	H	League Division 1	3–0
1959	Cardiff City	A	League Division 2	0–3
1978	Arsenal	A	League Cup semi-final 2nd leg	0–0
1981	Birmingham City	H	League Division 1	2–2
1984	Walsall	A	League Cup semi-final 2nd leg	2–0
1987	Leicester City	H	League Division 1	4–3
1994	Southampton	A	Premier League	2–4

1996 Bob Paisley died aged 77 in a local nursing home. He is the most successful manager in the club's history and his list of achievements that are likely to remain unrivalled reads six Championship wins, three League Cup wins, three glorious European Cup wins and one UEFA cup win, surprisingly he never managed to add the F.A.Cup to his list.

| 1998 | Sheffield Wednesday | A | Premier League | 3–3 |

FEBRUARY 15TH

1896	Wolves	A	FA Cup 2nd round	0–2
1902	Notts County	H	League Division 1	0–1
1908	Arsenal	H	League Division 1	4–1
1913	Sheffield Wednesday	H	League Division 1	2–1
1928	Derby County	A	League Division 1	3–2
1930	Birmingham City	A	League Division 1	0–1
1936	Birmingham City	A	League Division 1	0–2
1958	Scunthorpe United	A	FA Cup 5th round	1–0
1964	Arsenal	A	FA Cup 5th round	1–0
1969	Nottingham Forest	H	League Division 1	0–2
1983	Burnley	A	League Cup semi-final 2nd leg	0–1

Despite losing to a spirited Burnley side on the night Liverpool reached their third League Cup final in three years.

| 1986 | York City | A | FA Cup 5th round | 1–1 |

One year on from playing York at this stage of the competition and the same result. Jan Molby scored another penalty to rescue Liverpool from a very embarrassing defeat.

| 1995 | Crystal Palace | H | League Cup semi-final 1st leg | 1–0 |

FEBRUARY 16TH

1895	Nottingham Forest	H	FA Cup 2nd round	0–2
1897	Stoke City	A	League Division 1	1–6
1898	Newton Heath	H	FA Cup 2nd round replay	2–1
1907	Sheffield Wednesday	A	League Division 1	3–2
1924	Sunderland	A	League Division 1	0–0
1938	Everton	A	League Division 1	3–1
1952	Charlton Athletic	H	League Division 1	1–1
1957	Blackburn Rovers	A	League Division 2	2–2
1963	Wolves	H	League Division 1	4–1

1970	Newcastle United	H	League Division 1	0–0
1971	West Ham United	H	League Division 1	1–0
1974	Ipswich Town	H	FA Cup 5th round	2–0
1977	Manchester United	A	League Division 1	0–0
1980	Bury	H	FA Cup 5th round	2–0
1982	Swansea Town	A	League Division 1	0–2
1985	York City	A	FA Cup 5th round	1–1
1992	Ipswich Town	A	FA Cup 5th round	0–0

FEBRUARY 17TH

1900	West Bromwich Albion	A	FA Cup 2nd round	1–1
1906	Sheffield Wednesday	H	League Division 1	2–1
1912	Sheffield Wednesday	H	League Division 1	1–1

1917 Willie Fagan was born in Musselburgh. Willie started his career with his boyhood heroes Celtic before Preston North End signed him after he had scored nine goals in his 12 appearances in the League, for a fee reported to be in the region of £3,500 which at the time was a huge sum. A year later George Kay decided to splash out nearly £8,000 to bring him to Anfield.

1923	Blackburn Rovers	H	League Division 1	3–0
1934	Bolton Wanderers	H	FA Cup 5th round	0–3
1951	Bolton Wanderers	A	League Division 1	1–2
1962	Preston North End	H	FA Cup 5th round	0–0
1968	Walsall	A	FA Cup 4th round	0–0
1973	Manchester City	A	League Division 1	1–1

1988 Steve McMahon won the first of his 17 international caps in England's 0–0 draw with Israel in Tel Aviv.

| 1990 | Southampton | A | FA Cup 5th round | 3–0 |
| 1991 | Everton | H | FA Cup 5th round | 0–0 |

FEBRUARY 18TH

| 1893 | Nelson | A | Lancashire League | 3–2 |
| 1896 | Rotherham United | H | League Division 2 | 10–1 |

Liverpool's record victory in their League history and unlikely ever to be beaten. George Allan scored four of the goals, Malcolm McVean grabbed a hat-trick and Jimmy Ross scored a brace in this memorable game.

1899	Burnley	H	League Division 1	2–0
1911	Bristol City	A	League Division 1	1–1
1933	Leicester City	H	League Division 1	1–2
1939	Aston Villa	A	League Division 1	0–2
1950	West Bromwich Albion	H	League Division 1	2–1
1956	Manchester City	A	FA Cup 5th round	0–0
1961	Derby County	A	League Division 2	4–1
1967	Aston Villa	H	FA Cup 4th round	1–0
1976	Manchester United	A	League Division 1	0–0
1984	Luton Town	A	League Division 1	0–0
1986	York City	H	FA Cup 5th round replay	3–1

No repeat of the 7–0 victory of last year's replay but still a comfortable win with goals from Wark, Molby and Dalglish.

1989	Hull City	A	FA Cup 5th round	3–2
1996	Shrewsbury Town	A	FA Cup 4th round	4–0
1998	Middlesbrough	A	League Cup semi-final 2nd leg	0–2

FEBRUARY 19TH

| 1910 | Manchester United | A | League Division 1 | 4–3 |

United's first game at their brand new ground at Old Trafford. The honour of scoring the first goal at Old Trafford fell to Sandy Turnbull, but thereafter Liverpool ignored the script and ran out 4–3 winners!

1921	Bradford City	A	League Division 1	0–0
1927	Arsenal	A	FA Cup 5th round	0–2
1938	West Bromwich Albion	A	League Division 1	1–5
1949	Blackpool	H	League Division 1	1–1
1955	Huddersfield Town	H	FA Cup 5th round	0–2
1958	Doncaster Rovers	A	League Division 2	1–1
1964	Aston Villa	A	League Division 1	2–2
1966	Blackpool	H	League Division 1	4–1
1968	Walsall	H	FA Cup 4th round replay	5–2
1972	Sheffield United	H	League Division 1	2–0
1975	West Ham United	A	League Division 1	0–0
1977	Derby County	H	League Division 1	3–1
1980	Nottingham Forest	H	League Division 1	2–0

| 1992 | Rob Jones made his international debut in England's 2–0 victory over France at Wembley. He only managed to gain recognition on another five occasions. |

1994	Leeds United	A	Premier League	0–2
1995	Wimbledon	H	FA Cup 5th round	1–1
1997	Leeds United	H	Premier League	4–0

FEBRUARY 20TH

| 1897 | Harry Bradshaw became the first Liverpool player to have international recognition bestowed on him, when he played for England in their 6–0 victory over Ireland in Nottingham. |

1909	Arsenal	A	League Division 1	0–5
1926	Leeds United	A	League Division 1	1–1
1932	West Ham United	A	League Division 1	0–1
1935	Sheffield Wednesday	H	League Division 1	1–2

| 1951 | Phil Neal was born in Northants. He joined Northampton Town before moving to Anfield where he was to stay for 11 years. |

1954	St Mirren	H	Friendly	4–2
1960	Swansea Town	H	League Division 2	4–1
1962	Preston North End	A	FA Cup 5th round replay	0–0
1965	Bolton Wanderers	A	FA Cup 5th round	1–0
1971	Everton	A	League Division 1	0–0
1982	Coventry City	H	League Division 1	4–0
1983	Brighton & Hove Albion	H	FA Cup 5th round	1–2
1985	York City	H	FA Cup 5th round replay	7–0

| 1991 | Everton | A | FA Cup 5th round replay | 4–4 |

Everton and Liverpool put the uninspiring 0–0 draw of the first clash behind them with an unforgettable 4–4 draw that ebbed and flowed throughout. A crowd of 37,766 created a unique atmosphere that was more than matched by the play, with Liverpool taking the lead through Peter Beardsley but Everton equalising two minutes after the break. Twenty minutes from time an already exciting match moved up a gear, with Beardsley restoring Liverpool's lead, only for Sharp to capitalise on a clash between Bruce Grobbelaar and Steve Nichol for a simple tap-in. Ian Rush put Liverpool ahead for a third time; Tony Cottee equalised. John Barnes curled in a free-kick to seemingly put Liverpool into the sixth round, but Tony Cottee popped up again to bring Everton level for a fourth time with three minutes left on the clock. Shortly after match Kenny Dalglish announced his retirement as manager of Liverpool. As the football world was stunned, Dalglish stated he was in need of a complete rest from football and the enormous pressure it put him under (Howard Wilkinson of Leeds said, 'If he has resigned because of the pressures, the rest of us have no chance.'). He returned to the game a few months later as manager of Blackburn Rovers, then in the Second Division, and proceeded to gain promotion for them. Subsequently, with the use of Jack Walker's spending power, he guided Rovers to a Premiership title before again quitting in surprise circumstances. He later took over from Kevin Keegan at the underachieving Newcastle United.

| 1993 | Ipswich Town | H | Premier League | 0–0 |

FEBRUARY 21ST

| 1900 | West Bromwich Albion | H | FA Cup 2nd round replay | 1–2 |
| 1914 | West Ham | A | FA Cup 3rd round | 1–1 |

1917 Jim Harley was born in Fife. The flying full back who could play on either flank arrived at Liverpool in 1934. However, his career ended prematurely through injury in 1949. He played 133 games and won a Championship medal in 1947, he also played for Scotland during the war.

1920	Birmingham City	H	FA Cup 3rd round	2–0
1925	Birmingham City	H	FA Cup 3rd round	2–1
1931	Leeds United	A	League Division 1	2–1
1934	Chelsea	A	League Division 1	0–2
1948	Middlesbrough	H	League Division 1	0–1
1953	Newcastle United	A	League Division 1	2–1
1959	Huddersfield Town	H	League Division 2	2–2
1963	Burnley	H	FA Cup 4th round replay	2–1
1970	Watford	A	FA Cup 6th round	0–1
1976	Newcastle United	H	League Division 1	2–0
1979	Norwich City	H	League Division 1	6–0
1981	Brighton & Hove Albion	A	League Division 1	2–2
1987	Aston Villa	A	League Division 1	2–2

John Aldridge came on as substitute to make his League debut.

| 1988 | Everton | A | FA Cup 5th Round | 1–0 |

Liverpool arrived at Goodison Park top of the table and seemingly on their way to a second double of League and FA Cup within two years. Ray Houghton scored the only goal of the game in front of a crowd of 48,270 to put Liverpool into the quarter-finals.

FEBRUARY 22ND

1896	Grimsby Town	H	League Division 2	3–1
1902	Bolton Wanderers	A	League Division 1	0–1
1904	Middlesbrough	H	League Division 1	1–0
1908	Newcastle United	A	FA Cup 3rd round	1–3
1913	Newcastle United	H	FA Cup 3rd round	1–1
1914	Tom Bush was born in Salop.			
1930	Derby County	H	League Division 1	2–2
1936	Bolton Wanderers	H	League Division 1	1–1
1947	Huddersfield Town	H	League Division 1	1–0
1956	Manchester City	H	FA Cup 5th round replay	1–2
1958	Blackburn Rovers	A	League Division 2	3–3
1964	Birmingham City	H	League Division 1	2–1
1969	West Ham United	A	League Division 1	1–1
1975	Everton	H	League Division 1	0–0
1986	Everton	H	League Division 1	0–2

Apart from the fact it was the 134th Merseyside derby, the loss was a major blow to Liverpool's attempt to reach the summit of the League while inflicting a defeat on their challengers. For three-quarters of the game all was fine even though there had been no goals, but Liverpool had had the Champions on the rack. However, Bruce Grobbelaar decided that this was going to be one of those days when he had an erratic 15 minutes and basically cost Liverpool the game. Kevin Ratcliffe scored and then predator Lineker with his only real chance of the game scored his 30th goal of the season with a bit of clinical finishing. The win put Liverpool eight points behind their Merseyside rivals and five behind Manchester United who had a game in hand. The title looked a distance away now.

1992	Norwich City	A	League Division 1	0–3

1996 Jan Molby joined Swansea Town on a free transfer after nearly 12 years at the club. The Danish international who made 62 appearances for his country, was a stalwart in the midfield of the club in the mid-80s to the mid-90s. He played over 250 games and scored 60 goals. He won two Championship medals in 1986 and 1990, an FA Cup winners' medal in 1986 and 1992 as well as the League Cup in 1995. He has since moved into management.

1997	Blackburn Rovers	H	Premier League	0–0

FEBRUARY 23RD

1901	Sunderland	A	League Division 1	1–0
1907	Bradford City	H	FA Cup 3rd round	1–0
1924	Southampton	A	FA Cup 3rd round	0–0
1927	Leeds United	A	League Division 1	0–0

Dick Forshaw played his last game for the club. Forshaw was an ever present in the 1922 and 1923 Championship winning teams and in total played 287 games scoring 124 goals. He later joined Everton where he won another Division One Championship.

1929	Newcastle United	A	League Division 1	2–2
1935	Birmingham City	A	League Division 1	3–1
1952	Burnley	A	FA Cup 5th round	0–2

Jackie Balmer made his last appearance for the club. This great servant made his debut some 17 years earlier and despite great loyalty to the club was never a firm favourite with some of the Anfield crowd. He played 313 games scoring 111 goals, winning one Championship medal in 1947. He will be remembered most for his feat of scoring a hat-trick in three consecutive games during that championship-winning season.

1972	Ian Ross was sold by Liverpool to Aston Villa for £60,000. He scored four goals in 59 matches for the club.			
1974	Newcastle United	A	League Division 1	0–0
1980	Ipswich Town	H	League Division 1	1–1
1985	Stoke City	H	League Division 1	2–0
1991	Luton Town	A	League Division 1	1–3
1998	Everton	H	Premier League	1–1

FEBRUARY 24TH

1894	Bolton Wanderers	A	FA Cup 3rd round	0–3
1912	Bury	A	League Division 1	2–2
1923	Sheffield United	H	FA Cup 3rd round	1–2
1934	Sunderland	H	League Division 1	1–1
1937	Bolton Wanderers	A	League Division 1	1–0
1951	Stoke City	A	League Division 1	3–2
1954	Sheffield Wednesday	A	League Division 1	1–1
1962	Middlesbrough	H	League Division 2	5–1

Roger Hunt scored his third hat-trick of the season.

1965	Birmingham City	H	League Division 1	4–3

Ian Callaghan scored the winner in this seven-goal thriller with just two minutes to go.

1968	Leicester City	H	League Division 1	3–1
1973	Ipswich Town	H	League Division 1	2–1
1976	Arsenal	A	League Division 1	0–1
1979	Derby County	A	League Division 1	2–0
1996	Blackburn Rovers	A	Premier League	3–2

Michael Thomas scored with what was to be his only goal of the season plus two from Stan Collymore to give Liverpool the three points.

FEBRUARY 25TH

1893	Southport	H	Lancashire League	2–0
1898	Derby County	A	FA Cup 3rd round	1–1
1899	West Bromwich Albion	A	FA Cup 3rd round	2–0
1905	Grimsby Town	A	League Division 2	1–0
1914	West Ham	H	FA Cup 3rd round replay	5–1

Liverpool's biggest crowd of the season, 45,000, saw two goals from Billy Lacey and Tom Miller help put Liverpool into the quarter-final.

1922	Arsenal	H	League Division 1	4–0

Dick Forshaw scored a hat-trick with his last coming in injury time.

1928	Everton	H	League Division 1	3–3
1933	Portsmouth	A	League Division 1	1–2
1939	Wolves	H	League Division 1	0–2
1950	Middlesbrough	A	League Division 1	1–4
1956	West Ham United	A	League Division 2	0–2
1961	Lincoln City	H	League Division 2	2–0

1967	Fulham	A	League Division 1	2–2
1978	Manchester United	H	League Division 1	3–1
1984	Queens Park Rangers	H	League Division 1	2–0
1987	Southampton	H	Littlewoods Cup semi-final 2nd Leg	3–0

A comfortable victory saw Liverpool reach their sixth League Cup final in nine years.

1994	Coventry City	H	Premier League	1–0
1995	Sheffield Wednesday	A	Premier League	2–1

FEBRUARY 26TH

1910	Bradford City	H	League Division 1	1–0
1913	Newcastle United	A	FA Cup 3rd round replay	0–1
1920	Notts County	A	League Division 1	0–1

Kenny Campbell made his debut in goal for Scotland in their first international after the war, in the 1–1 draw with Wales in Cardiff.

1921	Huddersfield Town	H	League Division 1	4–1
1927	Newcastle United	H	League Division 1	1–2
1938	Wolves	H	League Division 1	0–1
1949	Newcastle United	A	Friendly	1–1
1962	Preston North End	Old Trafford		
		FA Cup 5th round 2nd replay		0–1
1966	Fulham	A	League Division 1	0–2
1972	Manchester City	H	League Division 1	3–0

Larry Lloyd scored his first-ever goal for the club after 37 minutes of this game. It was not to be a regular occurrence, he only managed four more in his Liverpool career, but still he was a great player.

1974	Southampton	H	League Division 1	1–0
1977	Oldham Athletic	H	FA Cup 5th round	3–1
1980	Wolves	A	League Division 1	0–1
1983	Manchester United	A	League Division 1	1–1
1992	Ipswich Town	H	FA Cup 5th round replay	3–2

FEBRUARY 27TH

1897	Nottingham Forest	H	FA Cup 3rd round	1–1
1904	Manchester City	H	League Division 1	2–2
1909	Notts County	H	League Division 1	1–1
1911	Newcastle United	H	League Division 1	3–0
1912	Alf Hanson was born in Bootle.			
1915	Burnley	H	League Division 1	3–0
1924	Southampton	H	FA Cup 3rd round replay	2–0
1926	Manchester City	A	League Division 1	1–1

The start of Gordon Hodgson's illustrious career at Anfield started as he made his debut.

1932	Chelsea	H	FA Cup 6th round	0–2
1937	Brentford	H	League Division 1	2–2

1948 Alec Lindsay was born in Bury 1948. Alec started his career with his local club before moving to Anfield in 1969 for £67,500.

1954	Aston Villa	A	League Division 1	1–2
1960	Brighton & Hove Albion	A	League Division 2	2–1

1965	West Ham United	A	League Division 1	1–2
1971	Wolves	A	League Division 1	0–1
1982	Leeds United	A	League Division 1	2–0
1988	Portsmouth	A	League Division 1	2–0
1991	Everton	A	FA Cup 5th round 2nd replay	1–0
1993	Sheffield Wednesday	A	Premier League	1–1

FEBRUARY 28TH

1903	Middlesbrough	A	League Division 1	2–0
1914	Oldham Athletic	A	League Division 1	2–2
1920	Notts County	H	League Division 1	3–0
1925	Sunderland	A	League Division 1	0–3
1931	Blackpool	H	League Division 1	5–2

1934 Ronnie Moran was born in Liverpool. He joined the club in 1952 and has been there ever since in various capacities.

1948	Chelsea	A	League Division 1	1–3
1953	Burnley	H	Friendly	3–2
1959	Leyton Orient	A	League Division 2	3–1
1970	Derby County	H	League Division 1	0–2
1976	Derby County	A	League Division 1	1–1
1979	Burnley	H	FA Cup 5th round	3–0
1981	Southampton	H	League Division 1	2–0
1987	Southampton	H	League Division 1	1–0
1995	Wimbledon	A	FA Cup 5th round replay	2–0
1996	Charlton	H	FA Cup 5th round	2–1
1998	Aston Villa	A	Premier League	1–2

FEBRUARY 29TH

1896	Burton Swifts	A	League Division 2	7–0

Frank Becton and Jimmy Ross scored a hat-trick apiece in one of the club's only five ever 7–0 League victories.

1908	Bristol City	H	League Division 1	3–1
1936	Aston Villa	A	League Division 1	0–3
1956	Leeds United	H	League Division 2	1–0
1964	Swansea Town	H	FA Cup 6th round	1–2
1992	Southampton	H	League Division 1	0–0

MARCH 1ST

1902	Manchester City	H	League Division 1	4–0
1913	Derby County	H	League Division 1	2–1
1924	Arsenal	A	League Division 1	1–3
1930	Manchester City	A	League Division 1	3–4
1947	Birmingham City	H	FA Cup 6th round	4–1
1952	Fulham	A	League Division 1	1–1
1958	Blackburn Rovers	A	FA Cup 6th round	1–2
1966	Honved	A	European Cup-Winners' Cup 2nd round 1st leg	0–0
1969	Leicester City	A	FA Cup 5th round	0–0

1975	Chelsea	H	League Division 1	2–2
1978	Benfica	A	European Cup 3rd round 1st leg	2–1
1980	Everton	A	League Division 1	2–1

Liverpool dominated the first half of the Merseyside derby, taking a two-goal lead through David Johnson and a Phil Neal penalty. Everton fought back in the second half, pulling one goal back from Peter Eastoe but were unable to force the equaliser. The 53,108 crowd included former Everton great Dixie Dean who sadly died soon after the final whistle.

| 1988 | CA Osasuna | A | Friendly | 2–0 |
| 1989 | Charlton Athletic | H | League Division 1 | 2–0 |

MARCH 2ND

1895	Derby County	H	League Division 1	5–1
1898	Derby County	H	FA Cup 3rd round replay	1–5
1901	Preston North End	A	League Division 1	2–2

Maurice Parry made his international debut for Wales in the 1–1 draw with Scotland.

1907	Manchester City	A	League Division 1	0–1
1912	Middlesbrough	H	League Division 1	1–1
1924	Lawrence Hughes was born in Liverpool. Started his career as an amateur with Tranmere before moving to Liverpool in 1943.			

1932	West Bromwich Albion	H	League Division 1	4–1
1935	Grimsby Town	A	League Division 1	2–3
1957	Fulham	A	League Division 2	2–1
1963	Leicester City	H	League Division 1	0–2
1968	Wolves	A	League Division 1	1–1
1974	Burnley	H	League Division 1	1–0
1977	St Etienne	A	European Cup 3rd round 1st leg	0–1
1983	Widzew Lodz	A	European Cup 3rd round 1st leg	0–2
1985	Nottingham Forest	H	League Division 1	1–0
1986	Tottenham Hotspur	A	League Division 1	2–1

For the fourth game running, Bruce Grobbelaar had a mad moment and gifted sorry Spurs an opener in the fourth minute. He palmed a Glenn Hoddle corner straight into the path of Chris Waddle who had no problem in finishing from one yard out. Maybe it was the curse of television with Bruce, but he seemed to save his worst moments for the cameras. This time the rest of the team responded and deservedly won the game 2–1, thanks to goals from Jan Molby and Ian Rush who scored his 20th of the season. Ray Clemence in the Spurs goal prevented a cricket score with an outstanding performance that the Anfield faithful and the Liverpool team had been used to over many years. For Spurs, Steve Perryman made his last-ever appearance at the end of a remarkable career with the north London club.

| 1997 | Aston Villa | A | Premier League | 0–1 |

MARCH 3RD

1894	Burton Swifts	H	League Division 2	3–1
1897	Nottingham Forest	A	FA Cup 3rd round replay	1–0
1900	Manchester City	H	League Division 1	5–2
1906	Manchester City	H	League Division 1	0–1
1923	Bolton Wanderers	H	League Division 1	3–0

1928	Bolton Wanderers	H	League Division 1	4–2
1934	Middlesbrough	H	League Division 1	6–2

Gordon Hodgson and ex Rangers star Sam English scored two goals in this rout over Middlesbrough. It was in stark contrast to a few weeks earlier when they lost to north-east rivals Newcastle 2–9.

1951	West Bromwich Albion	H	League Division 1	1–1
1955	Notts County	A	League Division 2	3–0
1956	Bury	H	League Division 2	4–2
1962	Walsall	A	League Division 2	1–1
1969	Leicester City	H	FA Cup 5th round replay	0–1
1970	Coventry City	A	League Division 1	3–2
1973	Everton	A	League Division 1	2–0
1976	Dynamo Dresden	A	UEFA Cup 4th round 1st leg	0–0
1979	Chelsea	A	League Division 1	0–0
1982	CSKA Sofia	H	European Cup 3rd round 1st leg	1–0
1984	Everton	A	League Division 1	1–1
1990	Millwall	H	League Division 1	1–0
1991	Arsenal	H	League Division 1	0–1
1996	Aston Villa	H	Premier League	3–0

Two goals from Robbie Fowler and one from Steve McManaman early in the first half secured the three points that kept Liverpool in third place in the League title race.

1998	Rangers	A	Friendly	0–1

MARCH 4TH

1893	Nelson	H	Lancashire League	3–0
1897	Wolves	H	League Division 1	3–0
1905	Blackpool	H	League Division 2	5–0
1911	Tottenham Hotspur	A	League Division 1	0–1
1922	Blackburn Rovers	A	League Division 1	0–0
1925	Southampton	A	FA Cup 4th round	0–1
1933	Arsenal	A	League Division 1	1–0
1939	Leicester City	H	League Division 1	1–1
1950	Blackpool	H	FA Cup 6th round	2–1

1951 Kenny Dalglish was born in Glasgow.

1953	Bolton Wanderers	H	League Division 1	0–0

1955 Joey Jones was born in Llandudno. Joey played for Wrexham where he won a Welsh Cup winners' medal in 1975 before his transfer immediately after the game to Liverpool in a fee in the region of £100,000.

1959 Tommy Bromilow died aged 64. The flying winger who starred in Liverpool's successive Championship-winning teams of 1922 and 1923, moved into coaching after his retirement. He had spells as manager of Burnley, Crystal Palace twice and Leicester.

1961	Portsmouth	A	League Division 2	2–2
1964	Sheffield Wednesday	A	League Division 1	2–2
1967	Stoke City	H	League Division 1	2–1

Emlyn Hughes made his debut for the club.

1972	Everton	H	League Division 1	4–0
1978	Chelsea	A	League Division 1	1–3

1981	CSKA Sofia	H	European Cup 3rd round 1st leg	5–1
1992	Genoa	A	UEFA Cup quarter-final 1st leg	0–2
1995	Newcastle United	H	Premier League	2–0

MARCH 5TH

1896	David Pratt was born in Fife. He was to make over 80 appearances for the club between 1922 and 1927.			
1910	Sheffield Wednesday	A	League Division 1	0–3
1921	Huddersfield Town	A	League Division 1	2–1
1927	Sheffield Wednesday	H	League Division 1	3–0
1932	Blackpool	A	League Division 1	2–2
1938	Leicester City	A	League Division 1	2–2
1949	Chelsea	A	League Division 1	1–2
1955	Stoke City	H	League Division 2	2–4
1958	Derby County	H	League Division 2	2–0
1960	Stoke City	H	League Division 2	5–1

Dave Hickson continued his fine run of form by scoring his seventh goal in five games.

1963	Ipswich Town	A	League Division 1	2–2
1977	Newcastle United	H	League Division 1	1–0
1983	Stoke City	H	League Division 1	5–1
1986	Queens Park Rangers	H	League Cup semi-final 2nd leg	2–2

Liverpool couldn't quite get the upper hand in this very hard fought semi-final. Once QPR had scored the away goal it was always going to be an uphill struggle despite goals from Steve McMahon and Craig Johnston.

| 1988 | Queens Park Rangers | A | League Division 1 | 1–0 |
| 1994 | Blackburn Rovers | A | Premier League | 0–2 |

MARCH 6TH

1905	George Latham made his debut in the 3–1 victory over Scotland in Wrexham. He went on to win eight caps in total.			
1915	Tottenham Hotspur	A	League Division 1	1–1
1920	Huddersfield Town	A	FA Cup 4th round	1–2
1926	Tottenham Hotspur	H	League Division 1	0–0
1948	Huddersfield Town	H	League Division 1	4–0

Albert Stubbins scored all four goals

1954	Huddersfield Town	H	League Division 1	1–3
1965	Leicester City	A	FA Cup 6th round	0–0
1971	Tottenham Hotspur	H	FA Cup 6th round	0–0
1976	Middlesbrough	H	League Division 1	0–2
1979	Coventry City	A	League Division 1	0–0
1982	Brighton & Hove Albion	H	League Division 1	0–1
1985	Austria Vienna	A	European Cup 3rd round 1st leg	1–1
1993	Manchester United	H	Premier League	1–2
1997	Brann	A	European Cup-Winners' Cup quarter-final 1st leg	1–1

Robbie Fowler scored the all-important away goal in this quarter-final.

MARCH 7TH

1871 Malcolm McVean was born in Jamestown, Dumbarton. Joined the club as 21 year old from Third Lanark in 1892.

1896	Burton Wanderers	A	League Division 2	1–2
1903	Newcastle United	H	League Division 1	3–0
1905	Bradford	A	League Division 2	4–2
1908	Notts County	A	League Division 1	2–2
1914	Queens Park Rangers	H	FA Cup 4th round	2–1
1928	Arsenal	A	League Division 1	3–6

Harry Chambers failed to score in his final game for the club before he signed for West Bromwich Albion. The big centre-forward had scored a total of 151 goals in 338 games for the club. He won two championship medals in 1922 and 1923.

1931	Manchester City	A	League Division 1	1–1
1936	Portsmouth	H	League Division 1	2–0
1953	Aston Villa	A	League Division 1	0–4
1959	Fulham	H	League Division 2	0–0
1964	Ipswich Town	H	League Division 1	6–0

A four-goal blitz in a 20-minute spell in the second half helped Liverpool towards their fourth game of the season when they had netted six times, coincidentally all of which were at Anfield.

1970	Leeds United	H	League Division 1	0–0
1973	Dynamo Dresden	H	UEFA Cup 4th round 1st leg	2–0
1984	Benfica	H	European Cup 3rd round 1st leg	1–0
1987	Luton Town	H	League Division 1	2–0
1998	Bolton Wanderers	H	Premier League	2–1

MARCH 8TH

1902	Wolves	A	League Division 1	1–3

Arthur Goddard started his long and distinguished career at Anfield.

1913	Tottenham Hotspur	A	League Division 1	0–1
1924	Newcastle United	A	FA Cup 4th round	0–1
1930	Portsmouth	H	League Division 1	2–0
1947	Blackburn Rovers	H	League Division 1	2–1
1950	Blackpool	H	League Division 1	0–1
1952	Middlesbrough	H	League Division 1	1–1
1958	Bristol Rovers	A	League Division 2	1–3
1966	Honved	H	European Cup-Winners' Cup 2nd round 2nd leg 2–0	
1975	Burnley	A	League Division 1	1–1
1978	Derby County	A	League Division 1	2–4
1980	Tottenham Hotspur	A	FA Cup 6th round	1–0
1986	Queens Park Rangers	H	League Division 1	4–1

Barely a week after being humbled by QPR in the Milk Cup, Dalglish picked himself and it was the transformation that made all the difference. From looking ordinary they now were back purring like a Rolls Royce and the early onslaught left the visitors dead and buried. Two goals by Steve McMahon and one each from Ian Rush and John Wark sealed the points that took Liverpool back into second place, five points behind reigning champions Everton.

| 1992 | Aston Villa | H | FA Cup 6th round | 1–0 |
| 1995 | Crystal Palace | A | League Cup semi-final 2nd leg | 1–0 |

MARCH 9TH

1901	Wolves	H	League Division 1	1–0
1907	Sheffield Wednesday	A	FA Cup 4th round	0–1
1908	Sheffield Wednesday	A	League Division 1	2–1
1912	Notts County	A	League Division 1	0–0
1929	Arsenal	H	League Division 1	2–4
1935	Preston North End	H	League Division 1	0–0
1957	Barnsley	H	League Division 2	2–1
1963	Arsenal	A	League Division 1	2–2
1968	Tottenham Hotspur	A	FA Cup 5th round	1–1
1974	Bristol City	A	FA Cup 6th round	1–0
1977	Tottenham Hotspur	A	League Division 1	0–1
1982	Stoke City	A	League Division 1	5–1

Scoring five goals in an away fixture doesn't happen that often and it's even rarer that five different players score. But this was one of those rare days as Terry McDermott, Kenny Dalglish, Graeme Souness, Sammy Lee and Ronnie Whelan hit the target. It was also Liverpool's eighth straight victory in a run that took them to the top of the table.

| 1991 | Manchester City | A | League Division 1 | 3–0 |

MARCH 10TH

1900	Sheffield United	A	League Division 1	2–1
1906	Southampton	H	FA Cup 4th round	3–0
1913	Blackburn Rovers	A	League Division 1	1–5
1915	Bradford City	A	League Division 1	2–3
1920	Sheffield Wednesday	H	League Division 1	1–0
1926	Manchester United	A	League Division 1	3–3
1928	Blackburn Rovers	A	League Division 1	1–2
1934	Blackburn Rovers	A	League Division 1	1–3
1937	Arsenal	A	League Division 1	0–1
1946	Jimmy Payne was born in Bootle.			
1951	Middlesbrough	A	League Division 1	1–1
1956	Barnsley	A	League Division 2	5–0
1962	Derby County	H	League Division 2	4–1
1965	Leicester City	H	FA Cup 6th round replay	1–0
1971	Bayern Munich	H	European Fairs Cup 4th round 1st leg	3–0
1973	Southampton	H	League Division 1	3–2
1979	Ipswich Town	A	FA Cup 6th round	1–0
1984	Tottenham Hotspur	H	League Division 1	3–1
1985	Barnsley	A	FA Cup 6th round	4–0

Ian Rush helped himself to a hat-trick and his seventh goal in the competition that season.

1987	Arsenal	A	League Division 1	1–0
1993	Queens Park Rangers	A	Premier League	1–0
1996	Leeds United	A	FA Cup 6th round	0–0

| 1997 | Newcastle United | H | Premier League | 4–3 |

For the second season running Newcastle suffered defeat by the same scoreline with the winning goal being scored in the last minute. This time Robbie Fowler heading the vital goal.

MARCH 11TH

1893	Bootle	A	Lancashire Cup	1–2
1899	Preston North End	A	League Division 1	2–1
1905	Doncaster Rovers	A	League Division 2	4–1
1907	Stoke City	A	League Division 1	1–1
1911	Middlesbrough	H	League Division 1	3–0
1922	Blackburn Rovers	H	League Division 1	2–0
1933	Manchester City	H	League Division 1	1–1
1939	Portsmouth	H	League Division 1	4–4
1950	Aston Villa	A	League Division 1	0–2
1961	Huddersfield Town	H	League Division 2	3–1
1967	Everton	A	FA Cup 5th round	0–1

Whilst over 64,000 people paid through the turnstiles at Goodison, back at Anfield a further 40,000 watched the game on closed circuit TV.

1970	Southampton	A	League Division 1	1–0
1972	Chelsea	A	League Division 1	0–0
1978	Leeds United	H	League Division 1	1–0
1980	Manchester City	H	League Division 1	2–0
1986	Watford	H	FA Cup 6th round	0–0

Watford came to defend and that's what they did, aided by some excellent goalkeeping from Tony Coton.

1989	Middlesbrough	A	League Division 1	4–0
1990	Queens Park Rangers	A	FA Cup 6th round	2–2
1992	West Ham United	H	League Division 1	1–0
1995	Tottenham Hotspur	H	FA Cup 6th round	1–2

MARCH 12TH

| 1898 | Notts County | H | League Division 1 | 2–0 |

Jack Cox made his debut for the club.

1904	Sheffield United	H	League Division 1	3–2
1910	Bristol City	H	League Division 1	0–1
1921	Middlesbrough	H	League Division 1	0–0
1923	Blackburn Rovers	A	League Division 1	0–1
1924	Bolton Wanderers	A	League Division 1	1–4
1927	Leicester City	A	League Division 1	2–3
1932	Sheffield United	H	League Division 1	2–1
1938	Sunderland	H	League Division 1	4–0
1949	Birmingham City	H	League Division 1	1–0
1955	Bury	A	League Division 2	4–3
1960	Portsmouth	A	League Division 2	1–2
1966	Tottenham Hotspur	H	League Division 1	1–0
1968	Tottenham Hotspur	H	FA Cup 5th round replay	2–1

| 1977 | Middlesbrough | A | League Division 1 | 1–0 |

1981 Bruce Grobbelaar was signed from Vancouver Whitecaps for £250,000.

| 1983 | West Ham United | H | League Division 1 | 3–0 |

MARCH 13TH

1897	Aston Villa	A	League Division 1	0–0
1909	Bristol City	H	League Division 1	1–2
1915	Manchester City	H	League Division 1	3–2
1920	Sheffield Wednesday	A	League Division 1	2–2

Elisha Scott made his debut in goal for Ireland in the 0–3 defeat by Scotland in Glasgow. His international career was to last for 16 years in which he was to win a total of 31 caps.

1926	Sunderland	A	League Division 1	2–3
1929	West Ham United	H	League Division 1	2–1
1937	Preston North End	H	League Division 1	1–1
1954	Sheffield United	A	League Division 1	1–3
1965	Sheffield Wednesday	A	League Division 1	0–3
1971	Coventry City	A	League Division 1	0–1
1973	Everton	A	Friendly	1–2
1976	Birmingham City	A	League Division 1	1–0
1979	Everton	H	League Division 1	1–1
1982	Tottenham Hotspur	Wembley	League Cup final	3–1

Just before the final the Football League announced they had concluded a sponsorship agreement with the Milk Marketing Board and that the League Cup would henceforth be known as the Milk Cup. This meant that the winners of today's match would collect two trophies from the Royal Box – the old (League Cup) and the new (Milk Cup). For much of the opening quarter of an hour it looked as though it could be Spurs collecting the silverware, as Steve Archibald latched onto a lofted pass from Glenn Hoddle, took advantage of a mix-up between Grobbelaar and Thompson and put Spurs ahead in the 11th minute. Liverpool pressed for much of the rest of the game and the Spurs defence appeared to be hanging on for dear life. Four minutes from the end Spurs worked another opening for Archibald, but with the Liverpool goal at his mercy he elected to wait for the ball to reach his favoured foot and in that split second the chance had gone. Barely a minute later the action swung back to the Spurs goalmouth and a momentary lapse of concentration allowed a cross from McDermott to reach Ronnie Whelan and he put the equaliser home with ease. The goal knocked Spurs out of their stride and fired up Liverpool and there was only ever going to be one winner in extra time, ten minutes from time Whelan knocked in his second of the game. A final effort from Ian Rush finally saw of the challenge from Spurs that ensured both trophies were going to Anfield rather than White Hart Lane. This was Spurs' first defeat in a domestic cup final (at the ninth attempt) and their first defeat at Wembley.

1988	Manchester City	A	FA Cup 6th Round	4–0
1993	Middlesbrough	A	Premier League	2–1
1994	Everton	H	Premier League	2–1
1996	Wimbledon	H	Premier League	2–2

MARCH 14TH

1906	Nottingham Forest	A	League Division 1	2–1
1908	Manchester City	H	League Division 1	0–1
1914	Burnley	A	League Division 1	2–5

1921 John Bamber and Tommy Bromilow both made their debuts for England in the 0–0 draw with Wales in Wrexham.

1925	Preston North End	A	League Division 1	0–4
1931	Derby County	H	League Division 1	0–0
1936	Huddersfield Town	A	League Division 1	0–1

Matt Busby made his debut.

1953	Sunderland	H	League Division 1	0–2
1964	Fulham	A	League Division 1	0–1
1970	Arsenal	A	League Division 1	1–2
1981	West Ham United	Wembley	League Cup final	1–1

Second appearance in a League Cup final and Liverpool were again held to a draw.

1987	Oxford United	A	League Division 1	3–1
1989	Luton Town	H	League Division 1	5–0
1990	Queens Park Rangers	H	FA Cup 6th round replay	1–0
1992	Crystal Palace	A	League Division 1	0–1
1995	Coventry City	H	Premier League	2–3
1998	Tottenham Hotspur	A	Premier League	3–3

MARCH 15TH

1892 After a meeting the majority of the Evertonians on the board of the club were forced to quit and leave Anfield, leaving owner John Houlding with an empty ground. In the following eight weeks Houlding along with a few of his supporters decided to form a new club which they did and called it the Liverpool Association and applied for membership to the Football League. The application was not greeted favourably and therefore had to be content with a place in the Lancashire League. They were to play their first game on September 1st 1892.

1902	Grimsby Town	A	League Division 1	1–1
1913	Middlesbrough	H	League Division 1	4–2
1924	Blackburn Rovers	H	League Division 1	0–0
1930	Bolton Wanderers	A	League Division 1	2–0
1939	Huddersfield Town	A	League Division 1	1–1
1947	Portsmouth	A	League Division 1	2–1
1950	Manchester United	A	League Division 1	0–0
1952	West Bromwich Albion	A	League Division 1	3–3
1958	Lincoln City	H	League Division 2	1–0
1969	Sunderland	A	League Division 1	2–0
1975	Sheffield United	H	League Division 1	0–0
1978	Benfica	H	European Cup 3rd round 2nd leg	4–1
1980	Bristol City	A	League Division 1	3–1
1986	Southampton	A	League Division 1	2–1

Grobbelaar this time wasn't entirely to blame for the second half goal he conceded but as with the game at Spurs the setback seemed to liven up the Reds and within the space of 10 minutes they had taken the lead through Ian Rush and John Wark. Liverpool now moved to within three points of leaders Everton who had a game in hand. Manchester United suffered a defeat at the hand of Queens Park Rangers to push them further back in the title race.

| 1997 | Nottingham Forest | A | Premier League | 1–1 |

MARCH 16TH

1893	Fairfield	H	Lancashire League	5–0
1901	Aston Villa	A	League Division 1	2–0
1907	Preston North End	A	League Division 1	1–3
1912	Tottenham Hotspur	H	League Division 1	1–2

Spurs won at Anfield. They would have had no way of knowing at the time, but this was the start of one of the longest runs in football – it took 73 years to the very day before another Spurs side could claim both points at Anfield. A crowd of 15,000 were in attendance.

1925	Sheffield United	A	League Division 1	1–0
1929	Birmingham City	A	League Division 1	0–0
1935	Wolves	A	League Division 1	3–5
1954	Carlisle United	A	Friendly	3–3
1957	Port Vale	A	League Division 2	2–1
1963	Arsenal	A	FA Cup 5th round	2–1
1968	Burnley	H	League Division 1	3–2
1970	Sheffield Wednesday	H	League Division 1	3–0
1971	Tottenham Hotspur	A	FA Cup 6th round replay	1–0
1974	Leeds United	H	League Division 1	1–0
1977	St Etienne	H	European Cup 3rd round 2nd leg	3–1
1983	Widzew Lodz	H	European Cup 3rd round 2nd leg	3–2
1984	Southampton	A	League Division 1	0–2
1985	Tottenham Hotspur	H	League Division 1	0–1

Garth Crooks' 70th-minute goal at Anfield enabled Spurs to win at Liverpool for the first time since 1912, perhaps the longest running losing streak in football (for many years Spurs have had to live with jibes that the Titanic was afloat the last time they won at Anfield). Rumour had it that the captain of the QE2 was quaking in his books when he listened to the football results that evening!

1988	Derby County	A	League Division 1	1–1
1991	Sunderland	H	League Division 1	2–1
1996	Chelsea	H	Premier League	2–0

MARCH 17TH

1894	Lincoln City	A	League Division 2	1–1
1900	Newcastle United	H	League Division 1	2–0
1906	Middlesbrough	H	League Division 1	6–1
1923	Manchester City	A	League Division 1	0–1
1928	Cardiff City	H	League Division 1	1–2
1934	Birmingham City	H	League Division 1	4–1
1951	Sheffield Wednesday	H	League Division 1	2–1
1956	Swansea Town	H	League Division 2	4–1
1962	Leyton Orient	A	League Division 2	2–2

1965 FC Cologne   H   European Cup 3rd round 2nd leg   0–0

As both games had ended without score a replay was scheduled for a week later with the proviso that a result will be attained.

1973 Stoke City   A   League Division 1   1–0

1976 Dynamo Dresden   H   UEFA Cup 4th round 2nd leg   2–1

1982 CSKA Sofia   A   European Cup 3rd round 2nd leg   0–2

1986 Watford   A   FA Cup 6th round replay   2–1

Liverpool left it late to force the game into extra time and set up a clash with Southampton in the semi-final. Jan Molby scored yet another penalty after Rush was brought down and it was Rush, who else, who rediscovered his goalscoring form with a vengeance, who got the winner. Everton were in the other semi-final so the possibility of the first ever Merseyside Cup final was still a reality.

MARCH 18TH

1893 South Shore   H   Lancashire League   4–1

1899 Sheffield United   Nottingham

     FA Cup semi-final   2–2

1905 Gainsborough T   H   League Division 2   6–1

Steve Raybould scored a hat-trick.

1911 Preston North End   A   League Division 1   1–2

1914 Chelsea   H   League Division 1   3–0

1922 Bolton Wanderers   H   League Division 1   0–2

1933 Leeds United   A   League Division 1   0–5

1936 Leeds United   H   League Division 1   2–1

1939 Arsenal   A   League Division 1   0–2

1950 Wolves   H   League Division 1   0–2

1961 Swansea Town   A   League Division 2   0–2

1967 Burnley   A   League Division 1   0–1

1971 Newcastle United   H   League Division 1   5–0

1978 Nottingham Forest   Wembley   League Cup final   0–0

This was the first time the club had appeared in the League Cup final.

1981 CSKA Sofia   A   European Cup 3rd round 2nd leg   1–0

1987 Queens Park Rangers   H   League Division 1   2–1

1989 Brentford   H   FA Cup 6th round   4–0

1990 Manchester United   A   League Division 1   2–1

1992 Genoa   H   UEFA Cup quarter-final 2nd leg   1–2

MARCH 19TH

1898 Bolton Wanderers   H   League Division 1   1–1

1904 Newcastle United   A   League Division 1   1–1

1910 Bury   A   League Division 1   2–1

1921 Middlesbrough   A   League Division 1   1–0

1924 Sunderland   H   League Division 1   4–2

1927 Blackburn Rovers   H   League Division 1   2–2

1932 Blackburn Rovers   A   League Division 1   3–1

1938 Brentford   A   League Division 1   3–1

1949 Charlton Athletic   A   League Division 1   1–2

1955	Lincoln City	H	League Division 2	2–4
1960	Huddersfield Town	H	League Division 2	2–2
1966	Everton	A	League Division 1	0–0

Nigel Clough was born in Sunderland. Son of one of the most famous managers of modern times, Brian, Nigel started his career at Nottingham Forest where he won two successive League Cup winners' medals in 1989 and 1990. He also gained international recognition when he played for England against Chile in the 0–0 draw at Wembley in 1989.

1975	Leicester City	A	League Division 1	1–1
1977	Middlesbrough	H	FA Cup 6th round	2–0
1980	Leeds United	H	League Division 1	3–0
1983	Everton	H	League Division 1	0–0
1994	Chelsea	H	Premier League	2–1
1995	Manchester United	H	Premier League	2–0

MARCH 20TH

1897	Aston Villa	Bramall Lane		
		FA Cup semi-final		0–3

The FA Cup semi-final draw had paired Villa with Liverpool, and quite by chance the two sides had met in the League the week before at Perry Barr and battled their way to a 0–0 draw. The cup, of course, was always going to be a different matter. For Villa, there was the added incentive of a possible domestic double, for they were already top of the League table and needed only two more points to confirm the trophy would remain their property for a further twelve months. But Liverpool had their own reasons for wanting to reach the FA Cup final, for having avoided Everton in the semi-final (they were drawn with Derby County) there was still the possibility of an all-Merseyside final for the first time. A crowd of more than 30,000 (including over 20,000 from Merseyside) watched as Liverpool performed heroically throughout, however Villa ran out easy winners 3–0 on the day. Whilst the double dream was still very much alive for Villa, the all-Merseyside final would have to wait another 89 years.

1909	Preston North End	A	League Division 1	0–2
1915	Middlesbrough	A	League Division 1	0–3

Walter Wadsworth made his League debut.

1920	Manchester City	H	League Division 1	1–0
1926	Huddersfield Town	H	League Division 1	1–2
1935	Everton	H	League Division 1	2–1
1937	Sheffield Wednesday	A	League Division 1	2–1
1948	Blackpool	H	League Division 1	2–0
1954	Chelsea	H	League Division 1	1–1
1959	Stoke City	H	League Division 2	3–4
1963	West Bromwich Albion	H	League Division 1	2–2

Chris Lawler made his first team debut in place of Gerry Byrne who was injured.

1964	Bolton Wanderers	H	League Division 1	2–0
1965	Fulham	H	League Division 1	3–2
1971	Derby County	H	League Division 1	2–0
1976	Norwich City	A	League Division 1	1–0
1979	Wolves	H	League Division 1	2–0

1982	Sunderland	H	League Division 1	1–0
1985	Austria Vienna	H	European Cup 3rd round 2nd leg	4–1
1988	Everton	A	League Division 1	0–1
1993	Everton	H	Premier League	1–0
1996	Leeds United	H	FA Cup 6th round replay	3–0
1997	Brann	H	European Cup-Winners' Cup quarter-final 2nd leg	3–0

MARCH 21ST

1896	Burton Swifts	H	League Division 2	6–1
1906	Notts County	A	League Division 1	0–3
1908	Preston North End	A	League Division 1	0–3
1914	Preston North End	H	League Division 1	3–1
1925	Burnley	H	League Division 1	3–0
1931	Leicester City	A	League Division 1	2–3
1936	Wolves	H	League Division 1	0–2
1953	Wolves	A	League Division 1	0–3
1970	Everton	H	League Division 1	0–2
1973	Dynamo Dresden	A	UEFA Cup 4th round 2nd leg	1–0
1981	Everton	H	League Division 1	1–0
1984	Benfica	A	European Cup 3rd round 2nd leg	4–1
1990	Tottenham Hotspur	A	League Division 1	0–1
1992	Tottenham Hotspur	H	League Division 1	2–1

1995 Republic of Ireland international Mark Kennedy was bought from Millwall for £1.5 million.

MARCH 22ND

1902	Newcastle United	H	League Division 1	0–1
1913	Notts County	A	League Division 1	0–3
1922	Arsenal	A	League Division 1	0–1
1924	Blackburn Rovers	A	League Division 1	0–0
1930	Aston Villa	H	League Division 1	2–0

John McKenna died aged 82. McKenna was the first man in charge of the club, even though he didn't have the title of manager, but he performed all the duties admirably. McKenna was responsible for bringing the majority of the players from Scotland who were to form part of the team in the early days of the club. He later became President of the club between 1909 and 1919.

| 1947 | Derby County | H | League Division 1 | 1–1 |

1949 John Toshack was born in Cardiff. Joined his local team before moving to Anfield in November 1970 for £110,000.

1952	Newcastle United	H	League Division 1	3–0
1958	Notts County	A	League Division 2	2–0
1975	Tottenham Hotspur	A	League Division 1	2–0
1977	Everton	A	League Division 1	0–0
1978	Nottingham Forest	Old Trafford	League Cup final replay	0–1
1980	Brighton & Hove Albion	H	League Division 1	1–0
1983	Brighton & Hove Albion	A	League Division 1	2–2

| 1986 | Oxford United | H | League Division 1 | 6–0 |

The only question after this game was how did Liverpool not reach double figures. From the moment Rush scored in the first minute there was only going to be one outcome. Further goals from Molby who got two with the obligatory penalty, Lawrenson and Whelan plus one more from Rush wrapped up the points. The biggest cheer of the afternoon came when the result from Kenilworth Rd was announced that Everton had been beaten, meaning the two clubs were joint level on 66 points with Everton still having a game in hand, suddenly talk of the 'Double' didn't sound as far-fetched as it seemed.

1987	Tottenham Hotspur	A	League Division 1	0–1
1989	Coventry City	A	League Division 1	3–1
1995	Tottenham Hotspur	A	Premier League	0–0

MARCH 23RD

1899	Sheffield United	Bolton	FA Cup semi-final replay	4–4
1901	Sheffield Wednesday	H	League Division 1	1–1
1903	Derby County	H	League Division 1	3–1
1907	Newcastle United	H	League Division 1	4–1
1912	Manchester United	A	League Division 1	1–1
1935	Huddersfield Town	H	League Division 1	3–2
1951	Charlton Athletic	H	League Division 1	1–0
1953	Chelsea	A	League Division 1	0–3
1957	Rotherham United	H	League Division 2	4–1
1960	Dundee	A	Friendly	0–1
1963	Burnley	A	League Division 1	3–1
1968	Sheffield Wednesday	A	League Division 1	2–1
1974	Wolves	A	League Division 1	1–0
1985	West Bromwich Albion	A	League Division 1	5–0
1991	Derby County	A	League Division 1	7–1
1993	Crystal Palace	A	Premier League	1–1
1996	Nottingham Forest	A	Premier League	0–1

MARCH 24TH

1894	Crewe Alexandra	H	League Division 2	2–0
1900	Aston Villa	A	League Division 1	0–1
1906	Preston North End	A	League Division 1	2–1
1913	Chelsea	H	League Division 1	1–2
1915	West Bromwich Albion	H	League Division 1	3–1
1923	Manchester City	H	League Division 1	2–0
1928	Sheffield Wednesday	H	League Division 1	0–4
1934	Leeds United	A	League Division 1	1–5
1951	Newcastle United	A	League Division 1	1–1
1956	Notts County	A	League Division 2	1–2
1961	Plymouth Argyle	H	League Division 2	1–1
1962	Preston North End	H	League Division 2	4–1
1965	FC Cologne	Rotterdam	European Cup 3rd round replay	2–2

In normal time Ian St John and Roger Hunt had given Liverpool hope of winning this replayed tie, however, the Germans fought back and squared the game. Extra time didn't produce any more goals so the match and a place in the semi-final against Inter Milan were to be decided by the toss of a coin. Unbelievably the first time it was thrown the coin stuck in the mud and had to be rethrown to which Liverpool called correctly and won through, to become only the second English club to reach that far in the competition.

1970	Ipswich Town	H	League Division 1	2–0
1971	Bayern Munich	A	European Fairs Cup 4th round 2nd leg	1–1
1973	Norwich City	H	League Division 1	3–1

1976 Phil Neal made his international debut for England in the 2–1 victory over Wales in Wrexham, Ray Kennedy scored one of England's goals.

| 1979 | Ipswich Town | H | League Division 1 | 2–0 |
| 1997 | Arsenal | A | Premier League | 2–1 |

MARCH 25TH

| 1893 | Rossendale United | H | Lancashire League | 2–1 |
| 1895 | Sunderland | H | League Division 1 | 2–3 |

Billy Dunlop made his debut at left back for the club after his transfer from Abercorn two months earlier for £35.

1899	Nottingham Forest	H	League Division 1	0–1
1905	Burton United	A	League Division 2	1–2
1908	Manchester United	H	League Division 1	7–4
1910	Sheffield United	H	League Division 1	0–0
1911	Notts County	H	League Division 1	2–1
1921	Tottenham Hotspur	H	League Division 1	1–1
1922	Bolton Wanderers	A	League Division 1	3–1
1933	Blackburn Rovers	H	League Division 1	2–2
1939	Brentford	H	League Division 1	1–0
1950	Everton	Maine Road		
			FA Cup semi-final	2–0

Although Everton had possession for much of the game, the lack of a proven goalscorer in their side proved their undoing, with countless chances being created but nobody on hand to turn them into goals. Liverpool on the other hand were able to take advantage of this with some excellent defending and ended up scoring through Bob Paisley and Billy Liddell and having another chance cleared off the line. Paisley was to be dropped for the final, whilst Everton would have to wait 16 long years before they were to visit Wembley again.

1967	Manchester United	H	League Division 1	0–0
1971	Southampton	A	League Division 1	1–0
1975	Newcastle United	H	League Division 1	4–0
1978	Wolves	A	League Division 1	3–1
1984	Everton	Wembley	League Cup final	0–0

The first-ever meeting in any competition between the two teams at Wembley and it turned out to be a damp squib. The conditions didn't help but as both teams were so determined not to lose it proved a stalemate.

MARCH 26TH

1898	Bury	A	League Division 1	2–0
1904	Aston Villa	H	League Division 1	1–1
1910	Tottenham Hotspur	H	League Division 1	2–0
1921	Blackburn Rovers	A	League Division 1	1–1
1927	Huddersfield Town	A	League Division 1	0–1
1932	Sunderland	H	League Division 1	1–2
1937	Manchester City	H	League Division 1	0–5
1938	Manchester City	H	League Division 1	2–0
1948	Sheffield United	H	League Division 1	4–0
1949	Stoke City	H	League Division 1	4–0
1955	Hull City	A	League Division 2	2–2
1966	Aston Villa	A	League Division 1	3–0
1983	Manchester United	N	League Cup final	2–1

1986 Kenny Dalglish was awarded the Freedom of Glasgow before the international between Scotland and Romania when Kenny won his 100th cap to join the exclusive club of centurions at international level.

1988	Wimbledon	H	League Division 1	2–1
1989	Tottenham Hotspur	A	League Division 1	2–1
1994	Arsenal	A	Premier League	0–1

MARCH 27TH

1897	Burnley	H	League Division 1	1–2
1899	Sheffield United	Fallowfield		
			FA Cup semi-final replay	1–0

The FA Cup semi-final second replay was abandoned at half-time because the crowd kept encroaching onto the field. At the time Liverpool were 1–0 ahead, although they lost the replayed tie by a similar score. Liverpool therefore feature in the only two FA Cup semi-finals to have been abandoned [see also April 15th].

1909	Middlesbrough	H	League Division 1	1–2
1920	Manchester City	A	League Division 1	1–2
1926	West Bromwich Albion	A	League Division 1	3–0
1937	Manchester United	H	League Division 1	2–0
1948	Grimsby Town	A	League Division 1	2–0
1959	Barnsley	H	League Division 2	3–2
1964	Tottenham Hotspur	A	League Division 1	3–1
1965	Chelsea	N	FA Cup semi-final	2–0
1967	Arsenal	H	League Division 1	0–0
1971	Everton	Old Trafford		
			FA Cup semi-final	2–1

A capacity crowd of 63,000 paid £75,000 receipts to watch the two Merseyside rivals fight for a place at Wembley. Alan Ball gave Everton an early lead, Liverpool's equaliser came through Steve Heighway and this seemed to knock Everton out of their stride, and with Howard Kendall and Colin Harvey starting to fade Liverpool's midfield took over and Brian Hall struck the winner 15 minutes from time to win the game and set up a final clash with Arsenal.

1976	Burnley	H	League Division 1	2–0

1979	Borussia Moenchengladbach	H	Friendly	0–1
1982	Everton	A	League Division 1	3–1

MARCH 28TH

1866 Jimmy Ross was born in Edinburgh.

1894	Northwich Victoria	A	League Division 2	3–2
1896	Crewe Alexandra	A	League Division 2	7–0
1903	Sheffield Wednesday	H	League Division 1	2–4
1908	Bury	A	League Division 1	1–3
1910	Sunderland	A	League Division 1	1–2
1914	Aston Villa	White Hart Lane FA Cup semi-final		2–0

Jimmy Nichol scored both goals that took Liverpool through to their first ever Cup final.

1921	Tottenham Hotspur	A	League Division 1	0–1
1925	Leeds United	A	League Division 1	1–4
1931	Portsmouth	H	League Division 1	3–1
1932	Huddersfield Town	H	League Division 1	0–3
1936	Derby County	A	League Division 1	2–2
1953	Charlton Athletic	H	League Division 1	1–2

Eric Anderson made his senior debut.

1959	Lincoln City	A	League Division 2	1–2
1962	Rotherham United	H	League Division 2	4–1
1964	Leicester City	A	League Division 1	2–0
1967	Arsenal	A	League Division 1	1–1
1970	West Ham United	A	League Division 1	0–1
1972	Stoke City	H	League Division 1	2–1
1981	Arsenal	A	League Division 1	0–1

Steve Heighway played his last game in a Liverpool shirt. His eleven years at the club were at the height of its success for which he was an important member. He very rarely missed a game, making a total of 444 appearances in all and scoring 76 goals. He won two European Cup winners' medals, two UEFA Cup winners' medals, one FA Cup winners' and four Championship medals. He also earned 32 caps for Eire whilst at the club.

1984	Everton	Wembley League Cup final replay		1–0

Graeme Souness scored the all-important goal to win the trophy. Liverpool become the first side to win one of the three major English competitions four seasons in a row with a 1–0 victory over local rivals Everton in the Milk Cup. This follows 1981's victory over West Ham United (2–1 in a replay), 1982's 3–1 against Spurs and last season's 2–1 win over Manchester United. At the same time Liverpool become the first club to win the League Cup and its variants four times.

1987	Wimbledon	H	League Division 1	1–2
1992	Sheffield United	A	League Division 1	0–2
1998	Barnsley	A	Premier League	3–2

MARCH 29TH

1902	Aston Villa	A	League Division 1	1–0
1907	Everton	A	League Division 1	0–0
1913	Manchester United	H	League Division 1	0–2
1915	Newcastle United	H	League Division 1	2–2
1924	Tottenham Hotspur	H	League Division 1	1–0
1929	Cardiff City	H	League Division 1	2–0
1930	Leeds United	A	League Division 1	1–1
1932	Huddersfield Town	A	League Division 1	3–4
1937	Manchester City	A	League Division 1	1–5

Gordon Milne was born in Preston. He started his career with his local side before moving to Liverpool in 1963 for £16,000.

1947	Burnley	N	FA Cup semi-final	0–0
1950	Manchester City	A	League Division 1	2–1
1952	Bolton Wanderers	A	League Division 1	1–1
1958	Ipswich Town	H	League Division 2	3–1
1969	Queens Park Rangers	A	League Division 1	2–1
1971	Ipswich Town	H	League Division 1	2–1
1975	Birmingham City	H	League Division 1	1–0
1978	Borussia Moenchengladbach	A	European Cup semi-final 1st leg	1–2
1980	Tottenham Hotspur	A	League Division 1	0–2
1986	Sheffield Wednesday	A	League Division 1	0–0

For some reason Dalglish decided not to play himself which may have had something to do with his achievement earlier in the week, when he won his 100th cap for Scotland in the 3–0 victory over Romania. A dull game that brought little cheer for the near 38,000 crowd.

1989	Derby County	H	League Division 1	1–0
1994	Manchester United	A	Premier League	0–1

MARCH 30TH

1895	Sheffield Wednesday	H	League Division 1	4–2
1899	Sheffield United	Derby	FA Cup semi-final replay	0–1
1901	Newcastle United	H	League Division 1	3–0
1903	Sunderland	H	League Division 1	1–1
1907	Aston Villa	A	League Division 1	0–4
1912	Preston North End	A	League Division 1	1–2
1923	Sheffield United	H	League Division 1	2–1
1929	Bolton Wanderers	A	League Division 1	0–0
1934	Huddersfield Town	H	League Division 1	2–2
1935	Leicester City	A	League Division 1	1–3
1956	Doncaster Rovers	A	League Division 2	0–1
1957	Lincoln City	A	League Division 2	3–3
1959	Barnsley	A	League Division 2	2–0
1960	Aston Villa	A	League Division 2	4–4
1963	West Ham United	H	FA Cup 6th round	1–0
1964	Tottenham Hotspur	H	League Division 1	3–1

1968	West Bromwich Albion	A	FA Cup 6th round	0–0
1970	Wolves	A	League Division 1	1–0
1974	Leicester City	N	FA Cup semi-final	0–0
1976	Barcelona	A	UEFA Cup semi-final 1st leg	1–0

One of Liverpool's greatest ever performances in their European conquests as they scored the all important away goal through John Toshack in the 13th minute, to set up an intriguing home game a fortnight later.

| 1982 | Birmingham City | H | League Division 1 | 3–1 |
| 1991 | Queens Park Rangers | H | League Division 1 | 1–3 |

MARCH 31ST

1894	Grimsby Town	A	League Division 2	1–0
1898	Bury	H	League Division 1	2–2
1900	Wolves	A	League Division 1	1–0
1906	Everton	Villa Park FA Cup semi-final		0–2

With both Liverpool and Everton making steady progress in the FA Cup there was a hope that the two might meet in the final for the first time. Sadly, they were instead paired in the semi-final which did at least mean a day out for both sets of supporters when Villa Park was chosen as the venue. Whilst Liverpool stayed overnight in Tamworth. Everton's goalkeeper Billy Scott (the brother of Elisha Scott, who was later recommended to Liverpool by Billy!) was the busiest of the two custodians in the opening exchanges, but gradually Everton began to exert control and had a number of chances in the first half to take the lead. The second half followed much the same pattern, but the deadlock was finally broken when Abbott shot home a low drive from the edge of the area. A second from Harold Hardman, later to become a director of Manchester United, sealed the game for Everton and took them into the final to meet Newcastle United.

1923	Birmingham City	A	League Division 1	1–0
1928	Middlesbrough	H	League Division 1	1–1
1934	Derby County	H	League Division 1	4–2
1948	Derby County	A	League Division 1	4–0
1951	Huddersfield Town	H	League Division 1	1–4
1956	Bristol Rovers	H	League Division 2	2–1
1961	Bristol Rovers	H	League Division 2	3–0
1962	Luton Town	A	League Division 2	0–1
1969	Arsenal	H	League Division 1	1–1
1973	Tottenham Hotspur	H	League Division 1	1–1
1975	Stoke City	A	League Division 1	0–2
1979	Manchester United	Maine Road		
			FA Cup semi-final	2–2
1984	Watford	A	League Division 1	2–0
1985	Manchester United	H	League Division 1	0–1
1986	Manchester City	H	League Division 1	2–0

Kenny Dalglish picked himself and the spark returned to the team, reflected by the fact that Liverpool won ten corners to the opposition's none. Steve McMahon scored a goal in each half that took Liverpool back to the top of the table, for the first time in nearly two years on goal difference from Everton who still had a game in hand.

| 1990 | Southampton | H | League Division 1 | 3–2 |

1992	Notts County	H	League Division 1	4–0
1996	Aston Villa	Old Trafford		
			FA Cup semi-final	3–0

With the other semi-final having been played earlier in the day, both sides knew Manchester United lay in wait at Wembley, but at Old Trafford the 39,021 only had thoughts for the semi-final. Villa started well creating plenty of chances and giving the Liverpool defence little time to dwell on the ball. The difference between the two sides on the day, however, was to be found up front: Liverpool took virtually every one of the chances they created, Villa converted nothing. Liverpool now stood between Manchester United and a double 'Double'.

APRIL 1ST

1899	Bolton Wanderers	A	League Division 1	1–2
1902	Sheffield Wednesday	A	League Division 1	1–1
1904	Everton	A	League Division 1	2–5
1905	Bolton Wanderers	H	League Division 2	1–1
1907	Manchester United	H	League Division 1	0–1
1911	Manchester United	A	League Division 1	0–2
1914	Newcastle United	A	League Division 1	2–1
1922	Oldham Athletic	H	League Division 1	2–0
1929	Cardiff City	A	League Division 1	2–1
1933	Derby County	A	League Division 1	1–1

Brian Jackson was born in Surrey. After a bright start with Leyton Orient, Brian arrived at Anfield in November 1951 as part of a £6,500 deal that saw Donald Woan move in the opposite direction to the East End of London.

1939	Blackpool	A	League Division 1	1–1
1950	Charlton Athletic	H	League Division 1	1–0
1961	Sheffield United	A	League Division 2	1–1
1965	Nottingham Forest	A	League Division 1	2–2
1967	Tottenham Hotspur	A	League Division 1	1–2
1972	West Bromwich Albion	H	League Division 1	2–0
1978	Aston Villa	A	League Division 1	3–0
1980	Stoke City	H	League Division 1	1–0
1981	West Ham United	Villa Park League Cup final replay		2–1

Liverpool's first-ever victory in the finals of the League cup competition. Alan Hansen scored the winner with a dynamic finish to start a run that was to last nearly five years undefeated in the competition.

| 1989 | Norwich City | A | League Division 1 | 1–0 |
| 1991 | Southampton | A | League Division 1 | 0–1 |

APRIL 2ND

1898	Notts County	A	League Division 1	2–3
1904	Middlesbrough	A	League Division 1	0–1
1906	Bury	A	League Division 1	0–0
1910	Preston North End	A	League Division 1	0–2
1915	Manchester United	A	League Division 1	0–2

The significance of this result did not occur until a couple of days later when a letter appeared in the *Athletic News* asking the football authorities to look more closely into the game, which was said to have been the most dull in football history; the crowd were booing the players for their lack of effort throughout. The letter, most probably written by a disgruntled bookmaker (the bookies had taken a rush of bets on United, near the bottom of the First Division, upsetting the form book and beating Liverpool 2–0) did indeed alert the authorities, who questioned just about everyone connected with this match and then, over a year later, announced the result to have been fixed. Life suspensions from the game were handed to virtually every player who took part, although most were lifted immediately after the First World War in recognition of the service given by the players to the war effort. The one exception was Enoch West, who as well as losing a libel case against the *Athletic News* did not have his suspension lifted until 1945, when he was 62 – a suspension of over 30 years. The result of this game was allowed to stand and had several repercussions when football resumed after the war: the two points United collected were enough to lift them above Chelsea in the League and out of a relegation spot. When the League was extended immediately after the war, Chelsea were allowed to keep their place in the First Division because the United v Liverpool match had been fixed. Spurs, who would have finished bottom regardless, were voted out in preference to Arsenal, who finished fifth in the Second Division, the only club, therefore, not to have earned their place in the First Division. One other participant in the United v Liverpool match was Billy Meredith, who was later to be embroiled in a similar match-rigging claim whilst playing for Manchester City.

1920	Oldham Athletic	A	League Division 1	1–1
1921	Blackburn Rovers	H	League Division 1	2–0
1923	Sheffield United	A	League Division 1	1–4
1924	Arsenal	H	League Division 1	0–0
1926	Bolton Wanderers	A	League Division 1	1–0
1927	Sunderland	H	League Division 1	1–2
1930	Arsenal	A	League Division 1	1–0
1932	Manchester City	A	League Division 1	1–0
1938	Huddersfield Town	A	League Division 1	2–1
1949	Portsmouth	A	League Division 1	2–3
1955	Luton Town	H	League Division 2	4–4
1956	Doncaster Rovers	H	League Division 2	1–2
1960	Lincoln City	H	League Division 2	1–3
1971	West Bromwich Albion	H	League Division 1	1–1
1977	Leeds United	H	League Division 1	3–1
1982	Notts County	H	League Division 1	1–0
1983	Sunderland	H	League Division 1	1–0
1988	Nottingham Forest	A	League Division 1	1–2
1994	Sheffield United	H	Premier League	1–2
1995	Bolton Wanderers	Wembley	League Cup final	2–1

Liverpool become the first club to have won the League Cup (and its various guises) five times with the 2–1 victory over Bolton Wanderers at Wembley. At the same time, Liverpool captain Ian Rush also won his fifth winners' medal in the competition, the most any individual player has won. Rush did not score on the day – both of the goals were brilliant strikes from Steve McManaman.

APRIL 3RD

1896	Manchester City	A	League Division 2	1–1
1897	Sheffield Wednesday	H	League Division 1	2–2

George Allan won his solitary cap for Scotland in the 2–1 win over England in London.

1899	Newcastle United	H	League Division 1	3–2

Bill Perkins made his debut in goal.

1909	Manchester City	A	League Division 1	0–4
1915	Aston Villa	A	League Division 1	2–6
1920	Derby County	H	League Division 1	0–3
1926	Birmingham City	H	League Division 1	2–2
1931	Manchester United	H	League Division 1	1–1
1934	Huddersfield Town	A	League Division 1	2–0
1937	Derby County	A	League Division 1	1–4
1948	Sunderland	H	League Division 1	0–0
1953	Cardiff City	H	League Division 1	2–1
1954	Sunderland	H	League Division 1	4–3
1965	Stoke City	H	League Division 1	3–2
1970	Crystal Palace	H	League Division 1	3–0
1972	Manchester United	A	League Division 1	3–0
1974	Leicester City	N	FA Cup semi-final replay	3–1
1976	Everton	H	League Division 1	1–0
1981	Stoke City	H	League Division 1	3–0
1985	Sunderland	A	League Division 1	3–0
1990	Wimbledon	H	League Division 1	2–1
1993	Blackburn Rovers	A	Premier League	1–4
1996	Newcastle United	H	Premier League	4–3

Witnessed by millions on TV, one of the most astonishing games the Premier League has ever seen. Kevin Keegan arrived with his Newcastle team knowing victory would push them closer to the title. In an end-to-end game as the match was well into injury time when Stan Collymore scored his second of the night to leave Keegan and Terry McDermott distraught on the touchline.

APRIL 4TH

1903	Grimsby Town	A	League Division 1	1–3
1908	Aston Villa	A	League Division 1	1–5
1914	Tottenham Hotspur	A	League Division 1	0–0
1925	Birmingham City	H	League Division 1	1–1
1931	Sheffield United	A	League Division 1	1–4
1936	Middlesbrough	H	League Division 1	2–2
1947	Preston North End	A	League Division 1	0–0
1953	Arsenal	A	League Division 1	3–5
1959	Derby County	H	League Division 2	3–0
1961	Bristol Rovers	A	League Division 2	3–4
1962	Roger Hunt won the first of his 34 caps for England in the 3–1 victory over Austria at Wembley.			
1964	Manchester United	H	League Division 1	3–0

| 1979 | Manchester United | Goodison Park | | |
| | | | FA Cup semi-final replay | 0–1 |

Emlyn Hughes played his last game in a Liverpool shirt. Known as 'Crazy Horse' for his tendency to foray deep from defence into the opposition half, he became Liverpool and England captain, playing 59 times for England whilst at Anfield picking up just about every honour the game has to offer, including four League Championship medals and winners' medals from the European Cup, UEFA Cup and FA Cup. The only domestic honour to elude him at Liverpool was the League Cup – he collected that when he was transferred to Wolverhampton Wanderers. He was Footballer of the Year in 1981 and, upon retirement, tried his hand briefly at management before moving into broadcasting and journalism.

1983	Manchester City	A	League Division 1	4–0
1984	Alan Kennedy gained international recognition for the first time in England's 1–0 victory over Northern Ireland at Wembley.			
1988	Manchester United	H	League Division 1	3–3
1989	Celtic	Dubai	Friendly	1–1
1994	Wimbledon	A	Premier League	1–1

APRIL 5TH

1902	Sheffield Wednesday	H	League Division 1	1–0
1912	Sunderland	H	League Division 1	2–1
1913	Aston Villa	A	League Division 1	3–1
1915	Blackburn Rovers	H	League Division 1	3–0
1924	Tottenham Hotspur	A	League Division 1	1–1
1926	Bolton Wanderers	H	League Division 1	2–2
1930	Sheffield Wednesday	H	League Division 1	1–3
1945	Tommy Smith was born in Liverpool. He joined the club straight from school in 1960.			
1947	Blackpool	H	League Division 1	2–3
1952	Stoke City	H	League Division 1	2–1
1958	Swansea Town	A	League Division 2	2–0
1969	Wolves	H	League Division 1	1–0

Roger Hunt scored the winning goal in the game, but the significant point in the game was it was to be the last in the Liverpool career of Gerry Byrne. Injury was to prove the downfall of this talented player who had been at the club for nearly 15 years. He played 329 games and his trophy cabinet boasts two Championship medals and one FA Cup winners' medal as well as the European Cup-Winners' Cup runners'-up medal he earned in 1966. He later joined the coaching staff at Anfield after his enforced retirement.

1975	Leeds United	A	League Division 1	2–0
1978	Everton	A	League Division 1	1–0
1980	Manchester United	A	League Division 1	1–2
1986	Southampton	White Hart Lane		
			FA Cup semi-final	2–0

Mark Wright suffered a broken leg and his loss seemed to hamper the Saints as they tried to cope without the linchpin of their defence. Peter Shilton kept them in the tie and the game was forced to go into extra time with Southampton not really making a worthwhile effort in the 90 minutes of open play. Extra time arrived and that man Rush, with two clinical strikes, took the Reds to Wembley for Kenny's first-ever visit. There they were to play Everton, their closest rivals in both geography, rivalry and in the

Championship. The double was on for one side of Merseyside. Kenny, of course, played down the possibility, saying he was only worried about the next game against Coventry. He learnt fast!

1987	Arsenal		Wembley Littlewoods Cup final	1–2

The Arsenal curse at Wembley struck again and this was even when Ian Rush scored. George Graham guided Arsenal to their first trophy under his management in what was to be the start of a very successful period for him, as we know only too well. Charlie Nicholas grabbed the headlines with two goals in a very close fought game. It was the first time in 144 matches that when Rush had scored Liverpool lost. Arsenal had now beaten Liverpool three times in each of their Wembley encounters.

1992	Portsmouth		Highbury FA Cup semi-final	1–1
1995	Southampton	H	Premier League	3–1

APRIL 6TH

1895	Nottingham Forest	A	League Division 1	0–3
1907	Derby County	H	League Division 1	2–0
1908	Blackburn Rovers	A	League Division 1	3–1
1912	Aston Villa	H	League Division 1	1–2
1926	Aston Villa	A	League Division 1	0–3
1928	Burnley	A	League Division 1	2–2
1929	Sheffield Wednesday	H	League Division 1	3–2
1931	Manchester United	A	League Division 1	1–4
1932	Chelsea	H	League Division 1	2–1
1935	Derby County	H	League Division 1	1–3
1938	Birmingham City	H	League Division 1	3–2
1949	Wolves	H	League Division 1	0–0
1953	Cardiff City	A	League Division 1	0–4
1957	Swansea Town	H	League Division 2	2–0
1960	Derby County	H	League Division 2	4–1

A game of two halves. After going into the break 0–1 down, it is fair to assume that Bill Shankly was none too pleased with his team's performance in the opening 45 minutes. Four goals in a 16-minute spell changed things round in the second half.

1965	West Bromwich Albion	H	League Division 1	0–3
1966	Sheffield Wednesday	H	League Division 1	1–0
1968	Manchester United	A	League Division 1	2–1
1971	Newcastle United	H	League Division 1	1–1
1974	Queens Park Rangers	H	League Division 1	2–1
1976	Leicester City	H	League Division 1	1–0
1977	FC Zurich	A	European Cup semi-final 1st leg	3–1

Liverpool set up a chance of reaching their first European Cup final with this superb performance in Switzerland. Two goals from Phil Neal and one from Steve Heighway secured the victory.

1985	Leicester City	A	League Division 1	1–0
1996	Coventry	A	Premier League	0–1
1997	Coventry City	H	Premier League	1–2

APRIL 7TH

1894	Burslem P.Vale	A	League Division 2	2–2
1900	Burnley	H	League Division 1	0–1

1900 Alex Raisbeck made his international debut for Scotland in the 4–1 victory over England in Glasgow. He won a total of eight caps in his career.

1906 Billy Dunlop made his only appearance for Scotland in the 2–1 win over England in Glasgow.

1923	Birmingham City	H	League Division 1	0–0
1928	Huddersfield Town	A	League Division 1	4–2
1934	West Bromwich Albion	A	League Division 1	2–2
1939	Birmingham City	H	League Division 1	4–0
1947	Preston North End	H	League Division 1	3–0
1950	Burnley	A	League Division 1	2–0
1951	Arsenal	A	League Division 1	2–1
1954	Manchester City	A	League Division 1	2–0
1956	Fulham	A	League Division 2	1–3
1958	Stoke City	H	League Division 2	3–0
1962	Middlesbrough	H	League Division 2	1–1
1967	Newcastle United	H	League Division 1	3–1
1969	Stoke City	A	League Division 1	0–0

Brian Hall made his debut when he came on as a substitute.

1973	Birmingham City	A	League Division 1	1–2
1979	Arsenal	H	League Division 1	3–0
1982	Manchester United	A	League Division 1	1–0
1984	West Ham United	H	League Division 1	6–0

APRIL 8TH

1899	Derby County	H	League Division 1	4–0
1901	Notts County	H	League Division 1	1–0
1905	Burslem Port Vale	H	League Division 2	8–1
1911	Oldham Athletic	H	League Division 1	1–0
1912	Bradford City	A	League Division 1	2–0

Elisha Scott made his debut.

1922	Oldham Athletic	A	League Division 1	0–4
1933	Blackpool	H	League Division 1	4–3
1939	Derby County	H	League Division 1	2–1
1950	Newcastle United	A	League Division 1	1–5
1955	Port Vale	A	League Division 2	3–4
1959	Middlesbrough	H	League Division 2	1–2
1961	Charlton Athletic	H	League Division 2	2–1
1963	Everton	H	League Division 1	0–0
1968	West Bromwich Albion	H	FA Cup 6th round replay	1–1
1970	All-Star XI	H	Friendly	8–8
1972	Coventry City	H	League Division 1	3–1
1974	Sheffield United	A	League Division 1	0–1
1978	Leicester City	H	League Division 1	3–2
1980	Derby County	H	League Division 1	3–0

1981	Bayern Munich	H	European Cup semi-final 1st leg	0–0
1989	Sheffield Wednesday	H	League Division 1	5–1
1990	Crystal Palace	N	FA Cup semi-final	3–4
1992	Wimbledon	H	League Division 1	2–3
1996	West Ham	H	Premier League	2–0

APRIL 9TH

1900	Bury	H	League Division 1	2–0
1906	Newcastle United	H	League Division 1	3–0
1909	Everton	A	League Division 1	0–5
1910	Notts County	H	League Division 1	2–1
1921	Derby County	A	League Division 1	0–0
1927	West Bromwich Albion	A	League Division 1	1–0
1932	Arsenal	H	League Division 1	2–1
1938	Blackpool	H	League Division 1	4–2
1949	Manchester City	H	League Division 1	0–1
1955	Nottingham Forest	A	League Division 2	1–3
1960	Leyton Orient	A	League Division 2	0–2
1965	Tottenham Hotspur	A	League Division 1	0–3
1966	Northampton Town	A	League Division 1	0–0

1975 Robbie Fowler was born in Liverpool.

1977	Manchester City	H	League Division 1	2–1
1983	Swansea Town	H	League Division 1	3–0
1988	Nottingham Forest	Hillsborough		
			FA Cup semi-final	2–1
1991	Coventry City	H	League Division 1	1–1
1994	Ipswich Town	H	Premier League	1–0
1995	Leeds United	H	Premier League	0–1

Mark Kennedy made his debut for the club after his surprise £2 million transfer from Millwall just before the March transfer deadline day.

APRIL 10TH

1897	Preston North End	H	League Division 1	0–0
1903	Everton	H	League Division 1	0–0
1909	Sheffield Wednesday	H	League Division 1	1–2
1914	Derby County	H	League Division 1	1–0

1920 Ephraim Longsworth made his debut for England in the thrilling 5–4 victory over Scotland in Sheffield. He won five caps in total.

1925	West Ham United	H	League Division 1	2–0
1926	Bury	A	League Division 1	1–0
1929	Huddersfield Town	A	League Division 1	3–1

1930 Tommy Younger was born in Edinburgh.

1936	Blackburn Rovers	H	League Division 1	4–1
1937	Wolves	H	League Division 1	1–0
1939	Birmingham City	A	League Division 1	0–0

1942 Ian Callaghan was born in Liverpool.

| 1948 | Blackburn Rovers | A | League Division 1 | 2–1 |

1950	Burnley	H	League Division 1	0–1
1954	Arsenal	A	League Division 1	0–3

This game will be remembered for two reasons. Joe Mercer broke his leg and was never to recover and therefore ended his career. But for Liverpool the defeat meant that they were relegated for the first time in 50 years.

| 1965 | Ian St John played his last game for Scotland in the 2–2 draw with England at Wembley scoring one of the goals. He played 21 times in all for his country scoring on nine occasions. |

1971	Stoke City	A	League Division 1	1–0
1973	Tottenham Hotspur	H	UEFA Cup semi-final 1st leg	1–0

Liverpool and Spurs had already met each other four times this season twice in the League and twice in the League Cup. Whilst Liverpool had won the League battles on points (winning at White Hart Lane 2–1 and drawing 1–1 at Anfield), Spurs had proven they are more of a cup team than a consistent league team with a 1–1 draw at Anfield and a 3–1 replay win at White Hart Lane. There was little therefore that one club did not know about the other; two tense and tight matches were expected in the UEFA Cup semi-finals. The first leg was undoubtedly tight, the only goal being little more than a freak as a Spurs clearance cannoned off Alec Lindsay's shin and careered into the net. It was possibly the only way Pat Jennings was going to be beaten all evening and much the same could be said for the custodian of the Liverpool goal Ray Clemence. Liverpool did most of the attacking and tried ever harder for the cushion of a second goal but could not break the Spurs defence that was high in numbers.

1976	Aston Villa	A	League Division 1	0–0
1979	Wolves	A	League Division 1	1–0
1982	Manchester City	A	League Division 1	5–0
1985	Panathinaikos	H	European Cup semi-final 1st leg	4–0
1993	Oldham Athletic	H	Premier League	1–0
1997	Paris St Germain	A	European Cup-Winners' Cup semi-final 1st leg	0–3
1998	Manchester United	A	Premier League	1–1

APRIL 11TH

| 1895 | John Bamber was born in St Helens. |

1898	Sheffield Wednesday	H	League Division 1	4–0
1903	Aston Villa	H	League Division 1	2–1

The game that effectively cost Villa the League title in 1902–03. A 2–1 defeat at Anfield was followed by five straight wins but Villa still finished the season two points behind Sheffield Wednesday at the top of the table. Had Villa won by the same score, they would have lifted the title on goal average. Goddard and Raybould scored the Liverpool goals.

1908	Newcastle United	A	League Division 1	1–3
1914	Aston Villa	H	League Division 1	0–1
1925	West Bromwich Albion	A	League Division 1	0–0
1931	Sunderland	H	League Division 1	2–4
1936	Preston North End	A	League Division 1	1–3
1952	Manchester City	A	League Division 1	2–1
1953	Derby County	H	League Division 1	1–1
1955	Port Vale	H	League Division 2	1–1
1959	Bristol Rovers	A	League Division 2	0–3

1966	Sunderland	A	League Division 1	2–2
1972	England XI	H	Friendly	8–6
1977	Stoke City	A	League Division 1	0–0
1981	Nottingham Forest	A	League Division 1	0–0
1984	Dinamo Bucharest	H	European Cup semi-final 1st leg	1–0
1987	Norwich City	A	League Division 1	1–2
1989	Millwall	A	League Division 1	2–1
1990	Charlton Athletic	A	League Division 1	4–0
1991	Tottenham Hotspur	H	League Division 1	2–0
1992	Aston Villa	A	League Division 1	0–1

APRIL 12TH

1895	Preston North End	A	League Division 1	2–2
1898	Derby County	A	League Division 1	1–3
1902	Nottingham Forest	A	League Division 1	1–1
1909	Sunderland	H	League Division 1	3–0
1913	Sunderland	H	League Division 1	2–5
1915	Sheffield United	H	League Division 1	2–1
1924	Middlesbrough	H	League Division 1	3–1
1930	Burnley	A	League Division 1	1–4
1947	Burnley	N	FA Cup semi-final replay	0–1
1952	Manchester United	A	League Division 1	0–4
1958	Sheffield United	H	League Division 2	1–0
1963	Tottenham Hotspur	H	League Division 1	5–2
1965	Everton	A	League Division 1	1–2
1968	Sheffield United	H	League Division 1	1–2
1969	Leicester City	A	League Division 1	2–1
1971	Chelsea	A	League Division 1	0–1
1974	Manchester City	A	League Division 1	1–1
1975	Carlisle United	H	League Division 1	2–0
1978	Borussia Moenchengladbach	H	European Cup semi-final 2nd leg	3–0
1980	Arsenal	N	FA Cup semi-final	0–0
1983	Coventry City	A	League Division 1	0–0
1986	Coventry City	H	League Division 1	5–0

Liverpool had six remaining games and victory in all of them, no mean task, was sure to bring them the title. Coventry languishing in the bottom three of the table were desperate in morale and performance. A hat-trick by Ronnie Whelan, one from Rush and Molby inflicted the defeat masterminded by the absolutely brilliant Dalglish. Bruce Grobbelaar had another quiet afternoon with only one effort for him to deal with, which he did.

1993	Manchester City	A	Premier League	1–1
1995	Arsenal	A	Premier League	1–0

APRIL 13TH

1901	Manchester City	H	League Division 1	3–1
1906	Everton	H	League Division 1	1–1
1907	Bristol City	H	League Division 1	2–4

| 1912 | Newcastle United | A | League Division 1 | 1–1 |
| 1914 | Bradford City | A | League Division 1 | 0–1 |

Arthur Goddard played his last game for the club. Captain for many years of his 12 at the club he played 415 in total with the highlight the 1906 Championship win.

1925	West Ham United	A	League Division 1	1–0
1929	Derby County	A	League Division 1	5–2
1935	Aston Villa	A	League Division 1	2–4
1936	Blackburn Rovers	H	League Division 1	4–1
1957	Sheffield United	A	League Division 2	0–3
1963	Manchester United	H	League Division 1	1–0
1968	Sunderland	H	League Division 1	2–1
1974	Ipswich Town	A	League Division 1	1–1
1982	Stoke City	H	League Division 1	2–0
1985	Manchester United	N	FA Cup semi-final	2–2
1988	Nottingham Forest	H	League Division 1	5–0
1991	Leeds United	A	League Division 1	5–4
1992	Portsmouth	N	FA Cup semi-final replay	0–0
1997	Sunderland	A	Premier League	2–1
1998	Crystal Palace	H	Premier League	2–1

APRIL 14TH

1894	Burslem Port Vale	H	League Division 2	2–1
1900	Preston North End	A	League Division 1	3–1
1902	Derby County	H	League Division 1	0–2
1906	Wolves	A	League Division 1	2–0
1911	Arsenal	A	League Division 1	0–0
1922	Burnley	A	League Division 1	1–1
1923	Huddersfield Town	A	League Division 1	0–0
1928	Newcastle United	H	League Division 1	0–0
1933	Huddersfield Town	H	League Division 1	2–2
1934	Arsenal	H	League Division 1	2–3
1951	Burnley	H	League Division 1	1–0
1952	Manchester City	H	League Division 1	1–2
1956	Port Vale	H	League Division 2	4–1
1959	Sheffield Wednesday	A	League Division 2	0–1
1964	Burnley	A	League Division 1	3–0
1966	Celtic	A	European Cup-Winners' Cup semi-final 1st leg	0–1

A packed Parkhead witnessed a tight game, as you would expect in a semi-final of a major European Cup competition. The home crowd went delirious when Bobby Lennox gave Celtic the lead, which they were to hold on to for the remainder of the game.

1971	Leeds United	H	European Fairs Cup semi-final 1st leg	0–1
1973	West Bromwich Albion	H	League Division 1	1–0
1976	Barcelona	H	UEFA Cup semi-final 2nd leg	1–1
1979	Manchester United	H	League Division 1	2–0
1981	Manchester United	H	League Division 1	0–1
1984	Stoke City	A	League Division 1	0–2

1987	Danish Select XI	H	Friendly	0–0
1990	Nottingham Forest	H	League Division 1	2–2
1995	Manchester City	A	Premier League	1–2

APRIL 15TH

1893	Southport	A	Lancashire League	1–1
1905	Bristol City	A	League Division 2	1–0
1911	Bury	H	League Division 1	2–0
1914	Manchester United	H	League Division 1	1–2
1922	Cardiff City	H	League Division 1	5–1
1927	Cardiff City	H	League Division 1	5–0
1931	Birmingham City	H	League Division 1	0–0
1933	Sunderland	A	League Division 1	0–0
1938	Middlesbrough	A	League Division 1	1–1
1939	Grimsby Town	A	League Division 1	1–2
1949	Huddersfield Town	H	League Division 1	0–1
1950	Fulham	H	League Division 1	1–1
1961	Norwich City	A	League Division 2	1–2
1963	Tottenham Hotspur	A	League Division 1	2–7
1968	Sheffield United	A	League Division 1	1–1
1970	Sunderland	A	League Division 1	1–0
1972	West Ham United	A	League Division 1	2–0
1978	Bristol City	A	League Division 1	1–1
1989	Nottingham Forest	N	FA Cup semi-final (abandoned)	0–0

This was by far the blackest day in British sporting history, as nearly a hundred Liverpool fans lost their lives at Hillsborough, in an incident that occurred shortly after the start of the FA Cup semi-final. Considerable congestion outside the Leppings Lane Stand (where Liverpool fans were trying to gain entry) led the police to order the opening of the gates. A roar from those already inside the ground indicated that the teams had come out onto the pitch and a surge began toward the central area of the terracing. In the corridors leading to the central area and at the front of the terracing, where the fans were fenced in, hundreds were trapped, 94 people were crushed to death and two others died later from the injuries they sustained. With six minutes of the match elapsed, referee Ray Lewis took the teams off the pitch and ultimately abandoned the game. The obvious effect on the club, its fans, the city and the whole country can never be measured, but nine years on the families of the victims are still trying to gain justice for what happened on that terrible day. The authorities, and the police in particular, will still not own up to their own errors of judgement. Whilst fences have been removed from football grounds as a result of the tragedy, it is of little or no consolation for what happened on that day and until the families get true justice, the fight will go on to find out what happened and who was responsible.

APRIL 16TH

1898	Aston Villa	H	League Division 1	4–0
1904	Bury	H	League Division 1	3–0
1904	Gordon Hodgson was born in Johannesburg, South Africa.			

1906	Bolton Wanderers	A	League Division 1	2–3
1910	Newcastle United	A	League Division 1	3–1
1921	Derby County	H	League Division 1	1–1
1927	Bury	H	League Division 1	2–2
1932	Birmingham City	A	League Division 1	1–3
1938	Derby County	A	League Division 1	1–4
1949	Middlesbrough	A	League Division 1	1–0
1954	Middlesbrough	A	League Division 1	1–0
1955	Leeds United	H	League Division 2	2–2
1960	Bristol Rovers	H	League Division 2	4–0

A young man by the name of Ian Callaghan replaced the legendary Billy Liddell in the No 7 shirt and he made such an impression in the game the rest of the players applauded him off the park. He went on to play just a few more games for the club – 842 to be precise.

1965	Chelsea	A	League Division 1	0–4
1966	Stoke City	H	League Division 1	2–0
1974	Manchester City	H	League Division 1	4–0
1977	Arsenal	H	League Division 1	2–0
1979	Aston Villa	A	League Division 1	1–3

This was the only time Liverpool conceded more than one goal in a game during the season.

1980	Arsenal	N	FA Cup semi-final replay	1–1
1983	Southampton	A	League Division 1	2–3
1986	Luton Town	A	League Division 1	1–0

A visit to Kenilworth Road and the plastic pitch had proved difficult for most teams during the season with only two coming away with wins. This match was never going to be easy, yet in the first half Liverpool contained and even gained the upper hand in a very enjoyable game. They eventually took the lead through Craig Johnston, who had not scored since 7 December. This ultimately proved to be the decisive goal but there was more to the game than just the single strike. Liverpool defended in the second half under an onslaught from the home side, but the Reds had a resolve about them that looked like they were determined to hold on to the lead they had fought so hard for.

1989   Prime Minister Margaret Thatcher announced a public inquiry into the Hillsborough disaster to be chaired by Lord Justice Taylor. Liverpool donated £100,000 and the Football Association £250,000 towards a fund for victims' families. The 14-ton master bell of the Anglican Cathedral in Liverpool was rung 94 times.

1991   Graeme Souness resigned as manager of Rangers in order to take over at Liverpool, his former club. David Murray, Rangers' chairman commented 'He's making the biggest mistake of his life,' which, given the way his managerial career panned out at Anfield, may well have been right.

| 1994 | Newcastle United | H | Premier League | 0–2 |
| 1996 | Everton | A | Premier League | 1–1 |

A 40,120 crowd at Goodison Park produced record receipts of £450,000.

APRIL 17TH

1894   John McNab was born in Lanarkshire.

1907	Middlesbrough	H	League Division 1	2–4
1908	Everton	H	League Division 1	0–0
1909	Bury	H	League Division 1	2–2

Billy Dunlop made his last-ever appearance for the club. The left back who joined in 1895 was a great servant, playing in over 350 games for Liverpool. On the same day Benjamin Dabbs was born. Dabbs signed for Liverpool in the summer of 1932.

1911	Arsenal	H	League Division 1	1–1
1915	Bradford	H	League Division 1	2–1
1920	West Bromwich Albion	H	League Division 1	0–0
1922	Burnley	H	League Division 1	2–1
1926	Blackburn Rovers	H	League Division 1	2–2
1929	Portsmouth	H	League Division 1	0–0
1937	Sunderland	A	League Division 1	2–4
1948	Manchester City	H	League Division 1	1–1
1954	Cardiff City	H	League Division 1	0–1
1965	Burnley	H	League Division 1	1–1
1971	Tottenham Hotspur	H	League Division 1	0–0
1973	Coventry City	A	League Division 1	2–1
1976	Stoke City	H	League Division 1	5–3
1982	West Bromwich Albion	H	League Division 1	1–0
1985	Manchester United	N	FA Cup semi-final replay	1–2
1993	Coventry City	H	Premier League	4–0
1995	Leicester City	H	Premier League	2–0

APRIL 18TH

1903	Nottingham Forest	A	League Division 1	0–1
1908	Middlesbrough	H	League Division 1	0–1
1914	Middlesbrough	A	League Division 1	0–4
1923	Bolton Wanderers	A	League Division 1	1–1
1924	Chelsea	A	League Division 1	1–2
1925	Tottenham Hotspur	H	League Division 1	1–0
1927	Cardiff City	H	League Division 1	0–2
1930	Newcastle United	A	League Division 1	1–3
1931	Arsenal	A	League Division 1	1–3
1933	Huddersfield Town	A	League Division 1	1–3
1936	Brentford	H	League Division 1	0–0
1938	Middlesbrough	H	League Division 1	1–1

1940 John Morrissey born in Liverpool. A product of Liverpool's youth scheme he made 36 appearances in three seasons at Anfield before moving across Stanley Park for a cut-price fee of £10,000 in 1962. He was a key member of the side that won the League title in 1963 and 1970, but after this latter success found his place in the side under threat and moved to Oldham Athletic in 1972. Six months later he was forced to retire through injury.

1949	Huddersfield Town	A	League Division 1	4–0
1953	Blackpool	A	League Division 1	1–3
1959	Ipswich Town	H	League Division 2	3–1
1960	Rotherham United	H	League Division 2	3–0

1963	Nottingham Forest	H	League Division 1	0–2
1964	Arsenal	H	League Division 1	5–0

This was to be the last victory of the season that brought Liverpool their sixth League Championship. Just two years after Bill Shankly guided them out of Division Two Liverpool were back on top. Peter Thompson scored two of the goals, with Hunt who was to score 31 in total for the season, St John and Alf Arrowsmith getting the others in a very one-sided game.

1968	West Bromwich Albion	N	FA Cup 6th round 2nd replay	1–2
1970	Chelsea	A	League Division 1	1–2
1978	Ipswich Town	H	League Division 1	2–2
1981	Leeds United	A	League Division 1	0–0
1984	Leicester City	A	League Division 1	3–3
1987	Nottingham Forest	H	League Division 1	3–0
1990	Arsenal	A	League Division 1	1–1
1992	Leeds United	H	League Division 1	0–0
1998	Coventry City	A	Premier League	1–1

APRIL 19TH

1902	Bury	H	League Division 1	1–0
1913	Bolton Wanderers	H	League Division 1	5–0
1924	Middlesbrough	A	League Division 1	1–1
1930	Sunderland	H	League Division 1	0–6
1935	Stoke City	H	League Division 1	5–0
1947	Sunderland	H	League Division 1	1–0
1952	Tottenham Hotspur	H	League Division 1	1–1
1954	Middlesbrough	H	League Division 1	4–1
1957	Bristol Rovers	H	League Division 2	4–1
1958	West Ham United	A	League Division 2	1–1
1960	Rotherham United	A	League Division 2	2–2
1965	Chelsea	H	League Division 1	2–0
1966	Celtic	H	European Cup-Winners' Cup semi-final 2nd leg	2–0

Another one of those marvellous European nights in Liverpool's history. Trailing 0–1 from the first leg five days earlier, Liverpool attacked from the moment the referee blew the first whistle. Celtic miraculously held on in the first 45 minutes to go in level at half-time. In the second half kicking towards the Kop, which on occasions seemed like they could suck the ball in, Liverpool continued the barrage of shots on Ronnie Simpson's goal. In the 60th minute Tommy Smith stepped up to take a free kick and drilled a thunderbolt into the back of the net to bring the scores level on aggregate. The noise from the Kop was loud as it could get and Liverpool continued to press. It erupted when Geoff Strong, who had been injured earlier, headed home. Liverpool were on the verge of their first European final. However, there was nearly a twist in the tail as Celtic had a goal disallowed in the last minute for offside. Celtic fans were aggrieved and hurled missiles on the pitch and after a short delay the game restarted briefly before the final whistle went. The final was to be a disappointment for Liverpool as they lost. Celtic, on the other hand, only had to wait 12 months for their moment of glory.

1969	Ipswich Town	H	League Division 1	4–0

1971	Manchester United	A	League Division 1	2–0
1975	Middlesbrough	A	League Division 1	0–1
1976	Manchester City	A	League Division 1	3–0
1980	Arsenal	H	League Division 1	1–1
1982	Glentoran	A	Friendly	1–1
1986	West Bromwich Albion	A	League Division 1	2–1

Sometimes the result is more important than the performance and this was one of those occasions, however, this was still a disciplined performance and goals by Rush and Dalglish in each half secured the victory that put them closer to the title.

1991 UEFA announced the additional ban imposed on Liverpool as a result of the Heysel tragedy had been lifted – they are free to enter European competition should they qualify.

1997	Manchester United	H	Premier League	1–3

APRIL 20TH

1895	Preston North End	H	League Division 1	2–5

1898 George 'Dod' Allan was signed back from Celtic where he had been on loan for a season for a small fee of £50 as a goodwill gesture.

1899	Bury	H	League Division 1	1–0
1901	Bury	A	League Division 1	0–0

1902 Ernie Blenkinsop was born in Yorkshire. Ernie started his career with local side Cudworth United Methodists before being sold to Hull City for the princely sum of £100 in October 1921. He moved on to Sheffield Wednesday where he enjoyed real success and was part of the two successive Championship winning teams of 1929 and 1930 in addition to the Division 2 Championship winners' medal he won four years earlier in 1926. The left back moved to Liverpool in March 1934 for a fee in the region of £5,000.

1907	Notts County	A	League Division 1	0–2
1908	Chelsea	A	League Division 1	2–0
1910	Nottingham Forest	H	League Division 1	7–3
1912	Sheffield United	H	League Division 1	2–0
1929	Sunderland	H	League Division 1	5–2

Henry Race scored a hat-trick.

1935	Chelsea	H	League Division 1	6–0
1953	Manchester United	A	League Division 1	1–3
1957	Nottingham Forest	H	League Division 2	3–1
1963	Fulham	A	League Division 1	0–0
1968	West Ham United	A	League Division 1	0–1
1970	Bristol Rovers	A	Friendly	1–1
1974	Everton	H	League Division 1	0–0
1977	FC Zurich	H	European Cup semi-final 2nd leg	3–0

After the impressive performance in the first leg, Liverpool made no mistake in getting to their first European Cup final. Two goals from Jimmy Case and one from Keegan sealed the very easy 6–1 aggregate victory. Next stop Rome!

1985	Newcastle United	H	League Division 1	3–1
1987	Manchester United	A	League Division 1	0–1
1988	Norwich City	A	League Division 1	0–0

| 1991 | Norwich City | H | League Division 1 | 3–0 |
| 1992 | Arsenal | A | League Division 1 | 0–4 |

APRIL 21ST

1900	Nottingham Forest	H	League Division 1	1–0
1902	Grimsby Town	H	League Division 1	2–2
1905	Doncaster Rovers	H	League Division 2	1–0
1906	Sheffield United	H	League Division 1	3–1

Victory meant Liverpool were the first team in history to win the Division Two title and win the Division Championship the following year. This was the second League title the club had won.

| 1923 | Huddersfield Town | H | League Division 1 | 1–1 |

Despite a stuttering in the previous few games Liverpool still had a very good chance of retaining the Championship they won 12 months earlier. Huddersfield arrived at Anfield with Herbert Chapman in charge and put up a sterling defensive performance and even took the lead. In the second half Liverpool pressed and got the equaliser that the crowd had been eagerly awaiting when Harry Chambers scored. The results from around the country soon filtered through and when it was known that Sunderland had beaten Burnley, Liverpool had claimed their fourth League title.

1928	Birmingham City	A	League Division 1	0–2
1930	Newcastle United	H	League Division 1	0–0
1934	Sheffield Wednesday	A	League Division 1	2–1
1948	Everton	H	League Division 1	4–0
1951	Chelsea	A	League Division 1	0–1
1956	Rotherham United	A	League Division 2	1–0
1962	Southampton	H	League Division 2	2–0
1973	Newcastle United	A	League Division 1	1–2
1976	Tranmere Rovers	A	Friendly	5–6
1979	Bristol City	H	League Division 1	1–0
1984	West Bromwich Albion	H	League Division 1	3–0
1990	Chelsea	H	League Division 1	4–1
1993	Leeds United	H	Premier League	2–0

APRIL 22ND

1899	Blackburn Rovers	H	League Division 1	2–0
1901	Sheffield United	A	League Division 1	2–0
1905	Manchester United	H	League Division 2	4–0
1922	Cardiff City	A	League Division 1	0–2
1933	Birmingham City	H	League Division 1	1–0
1935	Stoke City	A	League Division 1	1–1
1939	Sunderland	H	League Division 1	1–1
1950	Portsmouth	A	League Division 1	1–2
1957	Bristol Rovers	A	League Division 2	0–0
1959	Scunthorpe United	H	League Division 2	3–0
1961	Stoke City	H	League Division 2	3–0
1964	Birmingham City	A	League Division 1	1–3
1967	West Bromwich Albion	H	League Division 1	0–1

1969	Coventry City	A	League Division 1	0–0
1972	Ipswich Town	H	League Division 1	2–0
1978	Norwich City	H	League Division 1	3–0
1981	Bayern Munich	A	European Cup semi-final 2nd leg	1–1

1989 Every League match in the country kicked off at 3:06 p.m., the time the Liverpool v Nottingham Forest FA Cup semi-final was abandoned. As a further mark of respect to the dead of Hillsborough, a minute's silence was held at every game played in the country.

1992	Nottingham Forest	A	League Division 1	1–1

APRIL 23RD

1904	Blackburn Rovers	A	League Division 1	3–2
1910	Middlesbrough	A	League Division 1	2–2
1921	Bolton Wanderers	A	League Division 1	0–1
1927	Birmingham City	A	League Division 1	0–3
1932	Portsmouth	H	League Division 1	1–3
1938	Bolton Wanderers	H	League Division 1	2–1
1949	Newcastle United	H	League Division 1	1–1
1955	Middlesbrough	A	League Division 2	2–1
1960	Ipswich Town	A	League Division 2	1–0
1962	Stoke City	H	League Division 2	2–1
1966	Burnley	A	League Division 1	0–2
1973	Leeds United	H	League Division 1	2–0

Liverpool claimed their eighth League Championship after this victory over their old rivals Leeds. Goals from Kevin Keegan and Peter Cormack ensured the title was on its way back to Anfield after seven years away. It was also the first part of a unique Double the club were to achieve combined with their first European trophy: the UEFA Cup.

1977	Everton	Maine Road		
			FA Cup semi-final	2–2
1980	Stoke City	A	League Division 1	2–0
1983	Norwich City	H	League Division 1	0–2
1988	Tottenham Hotspur	H	League Division 1	1–0
1991	Crystal Palace	H	League Division 1	3–0
1994	West Ham United	A	Premier League	2–1

APRIL 24TH

1915	Oldham Athletic	A	League Division 1	2–0
1920	West Bromwich Albion	A	League Division 1	1–1
1926	Cardiff City	A	League Division 1	2–2
1937	Huddersfield Town	H	League Division 1	1–1
1948	Aston Villa	A	League Division 1	1–2
1954	Blackpool	A	League Division 1	0–3
1962	Stoke City	A	League Division 2	0–0
1965	Manchester United	A	League Division 1	0–3
1971	Nottingham Forest	A	League Division 1	1–0
1974	Arsenal	H	League Division 1	0–1
1979	Southampton	A	League Division 1	1–1

1982	Southampton	A	League Division 1	3–2
1985	Panathinaikos	A	European Cup semi-final 2nd leg	1–0

Mark Lawrenson scored the winning goal but the Greeks were never going to be able to overturn their 0–4 deficit from the first game at Anfield a couple of weeks earlier.

| 1997 | Paris St Germain | H | European Cup-Winners' Cup semi-final 2nd leg | 2–0 |

APRIL 25TH

1903	Bury	H	League Division 1	2–0
1914	Burnley	Crystal Palace		
			FA Cup final	0–1

The club's first major final and it ended in disappointment. Over 72,000 crowded into the Crystal Palace, which had hosted the previous 18 finals, though this was to be the last. King George V, the first monarch to attend a football Cup final, presented the trophy to Burnley at the end of the game and even though Liverpool lost they put up a brave performance.

1925	Bolton Wanderers	A	League Division 1	0–2
1928	Leicester City	H	League Division 1	1–1
1936	Sheffield Wednesday	A	League Division 1	0–0
1951	Aston Villa	H	League Division 1	0–0
1953	Chelsea	H	League Division 1	2–0
1959	Swansea Town	A	League Division 2	3–3
1964	West Bromwich Albion	A	League Division 1	2–2
1973	Tottenham Hotspur	A	UEFA Cup semi-final 2nd leg	1–2

A match that was a credit to English football, Liverpool's goal was enough to ensure they progressed to the final by virtue of the away goal counting double. And doubles were the order of the day at Anfield – this win kept them on target for placing the UEFA Cup alongside the League championship trophy in the Anfield boardroom. Spurs really needed to cancel out Liverpool's 1–0 lead from the first leg relatively early to have a realistic chance of keeping their hold on the UEFA Cup. Then Liverpool would have been forced out into the open themselves but were too experienced to let Spurs gain the initiative and they had the match under control virtually from the first whistle. Mike England had drifted upfield when an Emlyn Hughes clearance sailed over his head, Kevin Keegan latched onto the ball and sent a low cross into the goalmouth where Steve Heighway was waiting to side foot home. That left Spurs once again chasing two goals to win, they managed only one, again through Martin Peters, in the 71st minute. Spurs fans had cheered both teams onto the pitch before the start and cheered Liverpool off at the end knowing the far-superior team had won.

| 1978 | Arsenal | H | League Division 1 | 1–0 |

Tommy Smith made his last appearance for the club. The midfield hard man had been at the club for nearly 18 years in total and was one of the most popular players ever to wear the red shirt. Whilst there were many great moments in his career the one that will possibly be remembered most was his goal in the European Cup final in Rome 1977 when he climbed to head home a corner for the second goal. His playing record consisted of 632 games with 48 goals scored makes him the sixth in the all time appearance table for the club. Apart from his European Cup winners' medal he also won two UEFA, four Championship and two FA Cup winners' medals.

| 1981 | Tottenham Hotspur | A | League Division 1 | 1–1 |

| 1984 | Dinamo Bucharest | A | European Cup semi-final 2nd leg | 2–1 |
| 1987 | Everton | H | League Division 1 | 3–1 |

The top two in the League clashed at Anfield, with Liverpool in greater need of the points if they were to catch their rivals. Everton arrived having won their previous seven games, whilst Liverpool were beginning to falter in their title challenge. Despite this, a crowd of 44,827 expected as full-blooded a Merseyside derby as of right, and they were not to be disappointed. Liverpool took the lead after just nine minutes, ex-Everton player Steve McMahon latching onto an Ian Rush pass to fire past Neville Southall. Everton were level soon after Kevin Sheedy curled home the free kick from 25 yards. Rush restored Liverpool's lead right on the stroke of half-time and forced Southall into a number of saves in the second period, finally scoring some six minutes from time with a delicate chip.

| 1998 | Chelsea | A | Premier League | 1–4 |

APRIL 26TH

1902	Blackburn Rovers	A	League Division 1	1–1
1924	Notts County	H	League Division 1	1–0
1947	Aston Villa	A	League Division 1	2–1
1952	Preston North End	A	League Division 1	0–4
1955	West Ham United	A	League Division 2	3–0
1958	Barnsley	H	League Division 2	1–1
1965	Wolves	A	League Division 1	3–1

John Sealey became only the second player in the club's history to score on his only appearance in a Liverpool shirt.

| 1971 | Manchester City | A | League Division 1 | 2–2 |

Ron Yeats ended his ten-year spell at the club. The towering centre half that captained the team for several of those seasons played 450 times. He only missed six games during the two championship seasons of 1964 and 1966. A true Liverpool great. He was later to become player manager at Tranmere Rovers.

1975	Queens Park Rangers	H	League Division 1	3–1
1980	Crystal Palace	A	League Division 1	0–0
1986	Birmingham City	H	League Division 1	5–0

Relegation-threatened Birmingham came to Anfield and put up a resolute performance in the first half despite going behind to an Ian Rush goal after 25 minutes courtesy of his knee. Gary Gillespie who was sensationally picked by Dalglish instead of Lawrenson justified his place with a second half hat-trick, the last being a penalty after the Kop had screamed for him to take it, Molby who had already scored from the spot didn't object either. Everton could only manage a draw at Nottingham Forest which meant that Liverpool were now two points ahead of their rivals who had a game in hand, but faced two potentially difficult away games to finish off the season at Chelsea and Leicester.

| 1992 | Manchester United | H | League Division 1 | 2–0 |

APRIL 27TH

1892	Daniel Shone was born in Cheshire.			
1901	Nottingham Forest	H	League Division 1	2–0
1903	Wolves	A	League Division 1	2–0

1904	Bobby Done was born in Runcorn. After starring for his local side the full-back who could play on either side of the defence signed for Liverpool in April 1926.			
1907	Sheffield United	H	League Division 1	2–2
1908	Bury	H	League Division 1	2–1
1912	Oldham Athletic	A	League Division 1	1–0
1914	Sheffield United	H	League Division 1	2–1
1929	Blackburn Rovers	A	League Division 1	1–2
1935	Tottenham Hotspur	A	League Division 1	1–5
1957	West Ham United	H	League Division 2	1–0
1963	Leicester City	N	FA Cup semi-final	0–1
1968	Fulham	H	League Division 1	4–1
1974	West Ham United	A	League Division 1	2–2
1977	Everton	Maine Road		
		FA Cup semi-final replay		3–0

Liverpool took the initiative straight from the kick-off. Having been seen as the villain of the piece in the first match, referee Clive Thomas did little to further enamour himself to the Everton fans by awarding a penalty to Liverpool after adjudging Mike Pejic had pushed David Johnson which he clearly did unless you had blue and white glasses on, Phil Neal put Liverpool ahead from the spot. Everton were themselves denied a penalty, Clemence allegedly catching Duncan McKenzie with a raised foot but all they got was an indirect free-kick which was subsequently cleared. A goal by Jimmy Case drained the fight out of Everton and it was no surprise when Ray Kennedy added a third to finish the game and their rivals.

1985	Ipswich Town	A	League Division 1	0–0
1991	Arsenal	A	Friendly	3–1
1996	Middlesbrough	H	Premier League	1–0

APRIL 28TH

1894	Newton Heath	Ewood Park		
		Test Match		2–0

Once again Newton Heath finished bottom of the First Division. This time the Test Match system pitched them against Liverpool, who had topped the Second Division without losing a single game who didn't look likely to lose this one either, scoring through McLean and McQueen by half-time and holding on to their lead without ever being really troubled. Thus, when League football resumed in September, Liverpool would take their place among the elite in the First Division and Newton Heath was condemned to the Second Division. This proves if you wish hard enough . . .

1900	Glossop	A	League Division 1	2–1
1923	Stoke City	A	League Division 1	0–0
1928	Tottenham Hotspur	H	League Division 1	2–0
1956	Bristol Rovers	A	League Division 2	2–1
1962	Plymouth Argyle	A	League Division 2	3–2
1967	Sheffield United	A	League Division 1	1–0
1969	Leeds United	H	League Division 1	0–0
1971	Leeds United	A	European Fairs Cup semi-final 2nd leg	0–0
1973	Leicester City	H	League Division 1	0–0
1974	Dominic Matteo was born in Dumfries.			

| 1976 | FC Bruges | H | UEFA Cup final 1st leg | 3–2 |

The Belgians came to Anfield as underdogs but quickly silenced the crowd with two early goals. Bob Paisley surprised everyone by replacing Toshack with Jimmy Case at half-time and it proved a masterstroke. Shortly after the interval Liverpool had grabbed the lead through Kennedy, Case and a Keegan penalty but despite further pressure couldn't grab another one.

1979	Nottingham Forest	A	League Division 1	0–0
1980	Arsenal	N	FA Cup semi-final 2nd replay	1–1
1984	Ipswich Town	H	League Division 1	2–2
1990	Queens Park Rangers	H	League Division 1	2–1

After the disappointment of the previous season Liverpool made no mistake when trying to hold on to the lead and claim their eighteenth League Championship. When news came through that Norwich had scored, ironically a last-minute equaliser, against Aston Villa it meant that the title was safe. This is the last time to date the club has won the title yet still remain with six victories more in total than any other club.

APRIL 29TH

| 1899 | Aston Villa | A | League Division 1 | 0–5 |

In one of the closest of League battles for years, Villa and Liverpool were locked together at the top of the table for much of the season. The final game of the campaign saw Liverpool visit Villa Park, with the two side's level on 43 points. Liverpool's away form was impressive, with seven victories recorded on their travels, but Villa had yet to lose at home during the campaign and had already netted 53 goals in front of their own supporters. A crowd of over 41,000 packed into Villa Park to see the head to head, including a fair contingent from Merseyside, but it was they who were to go home empty handed as goals from John Devey (two), Fred Wheldon (two) and Jim Crabtree gave Villa a 5–0 win and the title for the fourth time in their history. It was not to be for Liverpool, for another couple of seasons anyway.

| 1901 | West Bromwich Albion | A | League Division 1 | 1–0 |

John Walker scored the most historic goal in the club's history. His effort meant that the club had won the First Division Championship for the very first time, but as we know there were many more to follow.

1905	Burnley	H	League Division 2	3–0
1911	Aston Villa	H	League Division 1	3–1
1922	West Bromwich Albion	H	League Division 1	1–2
1925	Cardiff City	H	League Division 1	1–2
1933	West Bromwich Albion	A	League Division 1	1–2
1950	Arsenal		Wembley FA Cup final	0–2

This was the club's second appearance in the final of the great competition and their first at Wembley and once again they returned home without the trophy. Bob Paisley who has won everything in football except the FA Cup was unlucky to be left out of the team, but on the day Arsenal thoroughly deserved their win with two goals from Reg Lewis. Joe Mercer collected the trophy for the Gunners, which was rather ironic as he had been training at Anfield quite regularly before the final but in the few days leading up to the game had to train at the other end of the pitch to the Liverpool lads.

| 1961 | Sunderland | A | League Division 2 | 1–1 |
| 1963 | Sheffield Wednesday | H | League Division 1 | 0–2 |

1964	Stoke City	A	League Division 1	1–3
1968	Tottenham Hotspur	H	League Division 1	1–1
1975	Don Revie Select	H	Friendly	6–2
1978	West Ham United	A	League Division 1	2–0
1992	Oldham Athletic	A	Friendly	2–2
1995	Norwich City	A	Premier League	2–1

APRIL 30TH

| 1909 | Newcastle United | A | League Division 1 | 1–0 |

Ronnie Orr scored his 20th league goal of the season. Alex Raisbeck played his last game for the club. In his eleven years at the club this inspirational leader had played 340 times scoring on 21 occasions. He won two Championship medals and a Division 2 winners' medal. It was also the last game for Jack Cox. The flying winger who had been an ever present virtually for the previous decade had played in 380 games scoring on 80 occasions. He was a key member of the 1901 and 1906 Championship winning teams.

1910	Aston Villa	H	League Division 1	2–0
1921	Bolton Wanderers	H	League Division 1	2–3
1927	Tottenham Hotspur	H	League Division 1	1–0
1932	Derby County	A	League Division 1	2–1
1938	Arsenal	A	League Division 1	0–1
1949	Burnley	A	League Division 1	2–0

Alun Evans was born in Bewdley. After shinning as a schoolboy in the Midlands, Alun signed for Wolverhampton Wanderers in 1966. He showed great promise in the early stages of his professional career and joined Liverpool in September 1968 for £100,000 which at the time was a record for a teenager.

1951	Brighton & Hove Albion	A	Friendly	1–1
1955	Birmingham City	H	League Division 2	2–2
1960	Sunderland	H	League Division 2	3–0
1962	Charlton Athletic	H	League Division 2	2–1
1966	Chelsea	H	League Division 1	2–1

Liverpool needed a draw to ensure they won their seventh League Championship. Chelsea applauded the Liverpool team on to the pitch as if they had already consigned themselves to losing on the day. But, the Londoner's put on a very spirited performance before Roger Hunt scored the winner to seal the title.

1973	Chelsea	H	Friendly	4–2
1977	Ipswich Town	H	League Division 1	2–1
1983	Tottenham Hotspur	A	League Division 1	0–2
1986	Leicester City	A	League Division 1	2–0

Liverpool started slowly but slowly turned the screw on Leicester who had to win to have any chance of survival in the top flight. They went behind to Ian Rush's 31st goal of the season, after he was set up by the master Kenny Dalglish. Ten minutes later it was over bar the shouting when Ronnie Whelan scored with an elegant chip to make it 2–0. Hansen marshalled the troops in the second half and Liverpool held on to the lead. News came through that Everton had been beaten at Oxford which meant the title was now in the club's own hands, with victory away to Chelsea in the next game meaning the title would be won and King Kenny's first year in charge would end on the highest possible note, not to forget that they were also in the Cup final.

1988	Chelsea	A	League Division 1	1–1
1989	Celtic	A	Friendly	4–1
1994	Norwich City	H	Premier League	0–1

MAY 1ST

1920	Sunderland	A	League Division 1	1–0
1926	Sheffield United	H	League Division 1	2–2
1937	Chelsea	H	League Division 1	1–1
1948	Wolves	H	League Division 1	2–1
1957	Bristol Rovers	H	League Division 2	2–1
1965	Leeds United	Wembley	FA Cup final	2–1

After 72 years of trying and in their third final appearance Liverpool at last won the coveted trophy although it wasn't easy. With two of the best defensive teams in the country there was never going to be a goal glut and for the first time in 18 years the final went into extra time after the first 90 minutes failed to provide a goal. This was with Liverpool playing with Gerry Byrne who it later transpired broke his collarbone in the first few minutes. Roger Hunt gave Liverpool the lead before Billy Bremner equalised shortly afterwards to make things level again. Then with five minutes remaining Ian St John scored with a header to ensure victory. Ron Yeats climbed the thirty-nine steps to receive the trophy from Her Majesty the Queen to become the first Liverpool player to do so.

| 1971 | Southampton | H | League Division 1 | 1–0 |

Bill Shankly paid £35,000 to bring Kevin Keegan to Liverpool from Scunthorpe.

1972	Derby County	A	League Division 1	0–1
1978	Manchester City	H	League Division 1	4–0
1979	Bolton Wanderers	A	League Division 1	4–1
1980	Arsenal	Coventry	FA Cup semi-final 3rd replay	0–1

Ian Rush was signed from Chester City for £300,000

1982	Nottingham Forest	H	League Division 1	2–0
1990	Derby County	H	League Division 1	1–0
1993	Norwich City	A	Premier League	0–1
1996	Arsenal	A	Premier League	0–0

MAY 2ND

1921	Arsenal	A	League Division 1	0–0
1925	Huddersfield Town	A	League Division 1	1–1
1931	West Ham United	H	League Division 1	2–0
1934	Manchester City	H	League Division 1	3–2

One of the finest players in the history of the club, Elisha Scott, played his last game in goal for the club. The great man who had been at Anfield for over two decades played 467 times. He won two Championship medals in 1922 and 1923 as well as playing nearly 30 times for his country whilst at the club.

1936	Stoke City	A	League Division 1	1–2
1952	Portsmouth	A	Friendly	0–2
1955	Rotherham United	A	League Division 2	1–6
1956	Lincoln City	A	League Division 2	0–2

1963	Leyton Orient	A	League Division 1	1–2
1975	Rosenborg BK	A	Friendly	0–2
1981	Sunderland	H	League Division 1	0–1
1983	Nottingham Forest	A	League Division 1	0–1
1987	Coventry City	A	League Division 1	0–1
1988	Southampton	H	League Division 1	1–1
1992	Sheffield Wednesday	A	League Division 1	0–0
1995	Wimbledon	A	Premier League	0–0
1998	West Ham United	H	Premier League	5–0

MAY 3RD

1881 Joe Hewitt was born in Chester. Joe was associated virtually all his life with the club. His playing career between 1904 and 1910 earned him 164 appearances with a very commendable 69 goals to his name. He was an instrumental part of the Championship-winning team in 1906. He later joined the coaching staff and moved on to various other positions within the club. He died in November 1971.

| 1924 | Notts County | A | League Division 1 | 2–1 |

1926 Kenneth 'Doug' Rudham was born in Johannesburg. He moved to England and Liverpool in 1954.

| 1930 | Blackburn Rovers | A | League Division 1 | 0–1 |

Tom Bromilow's last game for the club. In the 11 years after his first appearance he had played in 374 games scoring 11 goals. Tom gained successive championship medals in 1922 and 1923.

| 1947 | Manchester United | H | League Division 1 | 1–0 |

After one of the worst winters on record had decimated the League programme, fixtures were still being completed by mid-June! A single goal by Bert Stubbins was enough to give Liverpool the upper hand, but was not to be crowned Champions until the 14th June when Stoke's surprising defeat by Sheffield United helped Liverpool win the Championship.

1950	Huddersfield Town	H	League Division 1	2–3
1957	Brighton & Hove Albion	A	Friendly	2–0
1961	Stoke City	A	League Division 2	1–3
1967	Leeds United	A	League Division 1	1–2
1977	Manchester United	H	League Division 1	1–0
1980	Aston Villa	H	League Division 1	4–1

This victory ensured that the glory trail continued as Liverpool gained their twelfth League Championship (fourth in five years).

| 1982 | Tottenham Hotspur | A | League Division 1 | 2–2 |
| 1986 | Chelsea | A | League Division 1 | 1–0 |

It was fitting that Kenny Dalglish scored the goal that was to clinch the title for a record-breaking 16th time in the club's history (which at the time was twice as many as the next in the list Arsenal and Everton). It was also incredibly their 11th victory out of the last 12 games which is a worthy statistic of any team that wins the Championship. In his first year in charge after Heysel it was an incredible achievement by not only the manager, who after Joe Fagan became the second manager ever to win the League in their first season in charge, but the whole squad staff etc. It was also the first leg of the Double that the club achieved. Reigning champions Everton finished runners-up after their win against West Ham.

| 1989 | Everton | A | League Division 1 | 0–0 |

Liverpool and Everton were due to meet in the FA Cup final at the end of the season, but the League meeting at Goodison was not seen as a trial run, for it was Liverpool's first competitive game since the Hillsborough disaster. Manager Colin Harvey pointed out in his programme notes 'Football people round the country have always marvelled at the way Everton and Liverpool supporters could gather together as both friends and rivals at derby matches. This was a special quality in happy times, and in the last two and a half weeks it has been a great strength in tragedy. The crowd of 45,994 hushed before the game in memory of the dead and then the two teams cancelled themselves out in a 0–0 draw; the cup final clash would be a rather more entertaining affair.

| 1997 | Tottenham Hotspur | H | Premier League | 2–1 |

MAY 4TH

| 1929 | Manchester City | H | League Division 1 | 1–1 |

Louis Bimpson was born in Rainford. Louis started his career for local team Burscough before joing Liverpool in the January of 1953.

1935	Sunderland	H	League Division 1	2–2
1949	Derby County	A	League Division 1	0–3
1962	Swansea Town	A	League Division 2	2–4
1965	Inter Milan	H	European Cup semi-final 1st leg	3–1

One of the greatest games ever seen at Anfield according to Bill Shankly. Three days after beating Leeds to win the FA Cup for the first time in 73 years Liverpool were up against a very strong Inter Milan team. Shankly started the psychology by having the injured Gerry Byrne and Gordon Milne parading the Cup whilst the Milan players were warming up. The noise and the atmosphere – the gates had been locked some two hours before kick off with a further 30,000 locked outside, produced near deafening noise. The ploy worked and the Italians were clearly affected by the crowd as Liverpool went ahead after just three minutes through Roger Hunt. The euphoria was short-lived as Milan soon responded after Yeats failed to clear from Piero who went on and scored. Ian Callaghan soon restored the lead after good work from Hunt. Milan pressed in the second half and could have snatched an equaliser but Liverpool held firm and with just 15 minutes to go grabbed a third when Ian St John pounced on a loose ball in the area. Liverpool were just 90 minutes from appearing in their first European Cup final.

| 1968 | Leeds United | A | League Division 1 | 2–1 |
| 1974 | Newcastle United | Wembley FA Cup final | | 3–0 |

This was Liverpool's fifth appearance in the final against a Newcastle team making a record eleventh. It was to be the most one-sided in many a year. Newcastle striker Malcolm McDonald had spent the previous four weeks, saying how easy it would be for him and his team-mates to score. This proved to be a very embarrassing boast as he hardly had a decent effort in the game (something that occurred to him on another visit in a Cup final with Arsenal). Even though the first half ended without a goal, Liverpool were slowly gaining control. The second half proved too much for Newcastle as Liverpool ran riot with Keegan pulling all the strings. Keegan opened the scoring before Heighway added another on 75 minutes. From then on it was only going to be a question of how many Liverpool scored. Lindsay had an effort ruled out before the icing-on-the-cake goal from Keegan who scored with a couple of minutes left after there had been what seemed like two dozen passes without a Newcastle player getting near the ball. Wild celebrations followed. However, Shankly seemed to be taking everything in his stride – little did anyone know this was to be his swan song.

| 1976 | Wolves | A | League Division 1 | 3–1 |

In 1976 Liverpool arrived at Molineux needing to either draw by a low score or win to claim their ninth League Championship. Things didn't get off to a good start when Steve Kindon opened the scoring for the home side. From that moment Wolves tried to defend the lead which proved to be the wrong tactic as Liverpool poured forward at every opportunity. Kevin Keegan eventually got the equaliser before second half goals from Toshack and Kennedy sealed the Championship. This was the start of the Bob Paisley's list of honours and his first as a manager.

1978	Nottingham Forest	H	League Division 1	0–0
1985	Chelsea	H	League Division 1	4–3
1987	Watford	H	League Division 1	1–1
1991	Chelsea	A	League Division 1	2–4

MAY 5TH

| 1923 | Stoke City | H | League Division 1 | 1–0 |
| 1928 | Manchester United | A | League Division 1 | 1–6 |

Ephraim Longworth at the age of 40 made his last appearance for Liverpool. The versatile defender who could play on either side of the defence made 370 first team appearances for the club. He won two Division 1 Championships in 1922 and 1923 as well as a runners-up medal in the Cup final defeat in 1914. He also had the honour of becoming the first Liverpool player to captain England in an international. A true Anfield legend.

| 1936 | Bert Slater was born in Musselburgh. He arrived from Falkirk in a part-exchange deal with Tommy Younger in 1959. |

1951	Tottenham Hotspur	A	League Division 1	1–3
1966	Borussia Dortmund	Hampden Park		
		European Cup-Winners' Cup final	1–2

Liverpool's first-ever European final and the club's only appearance in the final of this competition. After winning the Championship this was or should have been the icing on the cake. Appalling weather conditions hit Glasgow on the day of the tie and only 41,000 turned up to see the game, and it turned out to be one of those days. The Germans went ahead, but in the second half Liverpool started to get a grip of the game and eventually equalised through Hunt. He quickly turned from saint to sinner when in the dying moments he missed from a couple of yards with the goal at his mercy. Extra time took its toll and the Germans grabbed the winner.

1979	Southampton	H	League Division 1	2–0
1981	Middlesbrough	A	League Division 1	2–1
1984	Birmingham City	A	League Division 1	0–0
1990	Coventry City	A	League Division 1	6–1
1993	Oldham Athletic	A	Premier League	2–3
1996	Manchester City	A	Premier League	2–2

MAY 6TH

| 1922 | West Bromwich Albion | A | League Division 1 | 4–1 |

Just a week earlier West Brom visited Anfield and left with both points preventing Liverpool claiming their third League Championship. No mistake was made this time as Liverpool ran out comfortable winners to clinch the title, in the end by six points from their nearest rivals Tottenham.

1933	Sheffield Wednesday	H	League Division 1	4–1
1939	Manchester United	A	League Division 1	0–2

1953 Graeme Souness was born. Graeme started his career with Spurs where he made only one appearance for the north London team before moving to Middlesbrough for £30,000 in January 1973. Five years later his value increased tenfold when Liverpool paid £352,000, a Football League record at the time, for his services.

1967	Tottenham Hotspur	H	League Division 1	0–0

1969 Jim Magilton was born in Belfast.

1975	Plymouth Argyle	A	Friendly	4–3
1980	Middlesbrough	A	League Division 1	0–1
1985	Coventry City	A	League Division 1	2–0
1986	Norwich City	H	Screen Sport Super Cup semi-final 2nd Leg	3–1
1991	Nottingham Forest	A	League Division 1	1–2
1995	Aston Villa	A	Premier League	0–2
1997	Wimbledon	A	Premier League	1–2

The start of Michael Owen's career. Michael came on as a 57th minute substitute and took just 13 minutes to make his mark and score. He is now the youngest ever player to score for the club.

1998	Arsenal	H	Premier League	4–0

MAY 7TH

1921	Arsenal	H	League Division 1	3–0
1927	West Ham United	A	League Division 1	3–3

Gordon Hodgson saved the day with a last-minute equaliser.

1932	Bolton Wanderers	A	League Division 1	1–8

Apparently the fourth goal was offside. Not a lot can be said of this dismal effort.

1938	Stoke City	A	League Division 1	0–2
1949	Preston North End	H	League Division 1	0–2
1952	Essen Select	A	Friendly	2–2
1977	Queens Park Rangers	A	League Division 1	1–1
1981	Swansea City	A	Friendly	6–7
1983	Aston Villa	H	League Division 1	1–1
1984	Coventry City	H	League Division 1	5–0

Ian Rush scored four goals to take his tally to 31 in the League for the season.

1988	Sheffield Wednesday	A	League Division 1	5–1
1989	Nottingham Forest	Old Trafford		
		FA Cup semi-final		3–1
1994	Aston Villa	A	Premier League	1–2

MAY 8TH

1963	Birmingham City	H	League Division 1	5–1

Tommy Smith made his debut for the club.

On the same day Gordon Milne made his debut for England in the 1–1 draw with Brazil at Wembley. He was to go on and play another 13 times for England. As a consequence for the honour of playing for his country, the game against Birmingham was the only one he missed all season.

| 1964 | Boston Metros | Everett | Friendly | 8–1 |
| 1971 | Arsenal | Wembley | FA Cup final | 1–2 |

Liverpool's fourth appearance in the Cup final and they lost for the third time to the newly crowned champions, Arsenal, who became only the fourth team this century to complete the 'Double'. On an energy-sapping hot afternoon both teams fought hard and gave nothing away and like the last final Liverpool played against Leeds in 1965, the match went into extra time. Almost immediately Liverpool went ahead through Steve Heighway who splendidly found a gap at the near post left by Bob Wilson to send the vastly outnumbered Liverpool fans into rapturous applause and song. The enjoyment didn't last long when Arsenal equalised through Eddie Kelly (even though George Graham claims he touched it and TV evidence doesn't prove conclusively who really scored). Into the second half and Arsenal gained the initiative and scored the winner from Charlie George who celebrated in a now-famous style. It was a young Liverpool team that fought hard but their time was to come even though it was not to be on this occasion.

1972	Arsenal	A	League Division 1	0–0
1974	Tottenham Hotspur	A	League Division 1	1–1
1979	Aston Villa	H	League Division 1	3–0
1982	Birmingham City	A	League Division 1	1–0
1993	Tottenham Hotspur	H	Premier League	6–2

MAY 9TH

| 1951 | Saarbrucken | H | Friendly | 1–1 |
| 1967 | Coventry City | A | Friendly | 1–2 |

1968 Neil Ruddock was born in Wandsworth. The rugged centre half started his career with Millwall where after only three games he was sold to Tottenham for £50,000. He then moved back to Millwall then was later sold back to Tottenham via Southampton where he had a short spell. It was in his second spell at Tottenham that Neil started to flourish as a top-quality defender and moved to Liverpool in the July of 1993.

| 1973 | Borussia Moenchengladbach | H | UEFA Cup final 1st leg (abandoned) | 0–0 |

For the second time in 10 years a European game had been abandoned as the tie had to be called off due to torrential rain bordering on Monsoon conditions hit Liverpool. The game was scheduled to go ahead subject to a pitch inspection the following evening.

1987	Chelsea	A	League Division 1	3–3
1988	Luton Town	H	League Division 1	1–1
1992	Sunderland	Wembley	FA Cup final	2–0

Ronnie Moran had the honour of leading the team out at Wembley as Graeme Souness sat on the bench with his doctor beside him following his recent heart troubles. He was to have no worries during the afternoon, as Sunderland put up a poor performance in this extremely one-sided final. Ian Rush and Michael Thomas scored the goals that brought the club its fifth FA Cup victory in ten attempts. For the first time since the FA Cup began in 1872, the losers were sent up to collect their medals first. This break in tradition obviously confused the FA officials within the Royal Box, for the losers, Sunderland, were given the medals destined for the winners, Liverpool, and vice versa. The mistake did not come to light until all the players were back on the pitch ready for their respective laps of honour and effected a swap. It was to be the only trophy Souness won whilst in charge.

| 1994 | Shelbourne | A | Friendly | 5–0 |

MAY 10TH

| 1922 | Huddersfield Town | Old Trafford | | |
| | | | Charity Shield | 0–1 |

20,000 spectators witnessed Liverpool's first appearance in the Charity Shield.

1947	Charlton Athletic	A	League Division 1	3–1
1964	New York All-Stars	A	Friendly	7–1
1966	Nottingham Forest	A	League Division 1	1–1
1973	Borussia	H	UEFA Cup final 1st leg	3–0
	Moenchengladbach			

After the pitch got the go-ahead Liverpool finally got to play their first UEFA cup final. Shankly had decided that the Germans looked suspect in the air so for the rescheduled match he called in Toshack in place of Hall. Liverpool played the long-ball game and he was rewarded when Toshack flicked on the ball for Keegan to grab the first. Lloyd and Keegan scored again to give the Kop something to sing about and it looked like a mere formality for the second leg two weeks later.

| 1977 | Coventry City | A | League Division 1 | 0–0 |
| 1978 | FC Bruges | Wembley European Cup final | | 1–0 |

One year on and Kenny Dalglish finally laid the ghost of Kevin Keegan to rest, after having a great first year as Keegan's replacement. Kenny had already notched 29 goals but had nothing to show for a marathon season that spanned nearly 60 games. Liverpool had already lost the League Cup to Forest and was to finish runners-up in the League title race but still had the chance of glory in the defence of the European Cup. With nearly the whole of the 100,000 capacity being Liverpool supporters it was like the biggest home game the club had ever played in. Bruges, obviously intimidated by the huge support, decided they were going to spoil the evening and defend which they did for most of the game. It was fitting however that Kenny Dalglish scored the all-important goal, after receiving a through ball from Souness to notch his 30th and most important goal of the season. Bruges still had no intention of attacking and got their just rewards: losers' medals, as Liverpool became the first British team to win successive European Cups.

| 1983 | England XI | H | Friendly | 0–2 |
| 1986 | Everton | Wembley FA Cup final | | 3–1 |

Liverpool's seventh appearance in an FA Cup final. All kinds of records were broken in this the 135th Merseyside derby and first-ever FA Cup final meeting of the two giants of football. Liverpool became only third team this century following Spurs and Arsenal to achieve the League and Cup 'Double'. Dalglish became the first-ever player-manager to achieve the feat in his 800th club appearance (including Celtic) and they won it without a single Englishman, not that that had any real significance but something that often appears in football quizzes years later. Ian Rush, who not surprisingly won the man of the match award, scored his 29th and 30th goals of the season (this was Rush's 120th game in which he had scored for Liverpool, and each time he had scored they had never been beaten) and one for Craig Johnston. The inevitable reply came from Gary Lineker – his 40th of the season – who took the congratulations on a marvellous occasion. Whilst the club have won many trophies over the years and completed various combinations of trophy victories many will argue that this completed one of the most remarkable in the club's distinguished history.

1989	Nottingham Forest	H	League Division 1	1–0
1995	West Ham United	A	Premier League	0–3
1998	Derby County	A	Premier League	0–1

MAY 11TH

1958	Real Sociedad	A	Friendly	1–0
1963	Sheffield United	A	League Division 1	0–0
1968	Nottingham Forest	H	League Division 1	6–1
1979	Middlesbrough	A	League Division 1	1–0
1981	Everton	A	Friendly	2–2
1982	Arsenal	A	League Division 1	1–1
1985	Aston Villa	H	League Division 1	2–1
1987	Israel	Tel Aviv	Friendly	0–3
1993	Wrexham	A	Friendly	2–2
1996	Manchester United	Wembley	FA Cup final	0–1

The club's eleventh FA Cup final and possibly one of their most inept. Even though it took a very good goal to decide it, Liverpool never really got going and the score reflected the game. It was to be Ian Rush's last appearance for the club. He achieved many great things in his career including five Championships in 1982, 1983, 1984, 1986 and 1990; three FA Cup winners' medals in 1986, 1989 and 1992; four League Cup winners' medals in 1981, 1982, 1983 and 1984; plus one European Cup winners' medal in 1984. Although renowned for his goalscoring prowess he was a fantastic team player. He finished with a record of 228 goals in 469 League games, 39 goals in 59 FA Cup games, 48 goals in 78 League Cup games and 20 goals in 37 European games, giving him a grand total of 335 goals in 643 appearances. He is the club's highest-ever goalscorer and his status as an Anfield legend will endure.

| 1997 | Sheffield Wednesday | A | Premier League | 1–1 |

MAY 12TH

| 1946 | New York All-Stars | A | Friendly | 3–1 |
| 1965 | Inter Milan | A | European Cup semi-final 2nd leg | 0–3 |

A hostile crowd got behind the home team and with the help of some very dodgy refereeing on the night helped Inter pull back the deficit that Liverpool had gained in the first leg. Apart from the disappointment of losing out on a place in the final it was also the end of the playing career of Ronnie Moran, 13 years after he made his debut. He played a total of 379 games scoring on 16 occasions. The left back was a key member of the 1964 Championship winning team, which was to be the only winners' medal he won as a player. He was however to go and help later managers at the club in their success as part of the staff.

| 1969 | Manchester City | A | League Division 1 | 0–1 |

1971	Chris Lawler won his first cap for England and managed to score as well in the 5–0 drubbing of Malta at Wembley in a European Championship qualifier. He won four caps in total.			
1978	Bolton Wanderers	A	Friendly	5–5
1981	Phil Neal won his 50th cap for England in the 1–0 defeat by Brazil at Wembley.			
1984	Notts County	A	League Division 1	0–0

MAY 13TH

1921	Bill Jones was born in Derbyshire.			
1963	Bolton Wanderers	A	League Division 1	0–1
1964	Catholic Youth XI	St Louis	Friendly	1–1
1967	Blackpool	H	League Division 1	1–3

Gordon Milne played his last game for the club after seven years in the first team. Milne who arrived in 1960 from Preston played 277 games scoring 19 times. He was an integral part of the 1964 (he played in every game) and 1966 Championship-winning teams.

1974	Celtic	H	Friendly	1–4
1989	Wimbledon	A	League Division 1	2–1
1997	Sunderland	A	Friendly	0–1

MAY 14TH

1940	Tommy Lawrence was born in Ayrshire.			
1950	William Jones made his debut for England in the 5–3 win over Portugal at Kenilworth Road.			
1951	AIK Stockholm	A	Friendly	7–0
1952	FK Austria Wien	A	Friendly	0–2
1953	Irish Internationals	Easter Road	Friendly	4–0
1961	VTI Tabor	A	Friendly	2–2
1962	Bohemians	A	Friendly	1–0
1977	West Ham United	H	League Division 1	0–0

The gates were locked nearly two hours before the game as Liverpool tried to successfully defend their League title and win their tenth overall. A draw was what was needed and West Ham couldn't find a way through the defence. Whilst not one of the greatest seasons in terms of away form, the team hadn't lost since January and in all 13 different players had scored showing the all-round strength the club had.

1980	RSC Anderlecht	H	Friendly	6–1
1983	Watford	A	League Division 1	1–2
1985	Southampton	A	League Division 1	1–1
1988	Wimbledon	Wembley	FA Cup final	0–1

This was the club's eighth FA Cup final appearance. Wimbledon's Dave Beasant became the first goalkeeper to save a penalty in an FA Cup final when he turned John Aldridge's spot-kick around the post. Spurred on by this, Wimbledon held on to the only goal of the game through Lawrie Sanchez to beat the 4–1 on favourites Liverpool and win the cup. Beasant, Wimbledon's captain, thus became the first goalkeeper to lead a side up the Wembley steps. It was the last game that Craig Johnston was to play for the club. He became disillusioned with the game and decided to go back to Australia and become a journalist. The lively winger played nearly 340 games for the club scoring 39 goals.

| 1995 | Blackburn Rovers | H | Premier League | 2–1 |

1946	Baltimore All-Stars	A	Friendly	9–0
1958	CA Osasuna	A	Friendly	3–1
1961	Brno	A	Friendly	2–1
1968	Stoke City	A	League Division 1	1–2
1982	Tottenham Hotspur	H	League Division 1	3–1

An emotional return to Anfield for Ray Clemence as he kept goal for Spurs. His former team-mates took no pity on him as they scored three second half goals to continue the impressive run that was to take them to their 13th title.

| 1984 | Norwich City | H | League Division 1 | 1–1 |

1931 Jimmy McDougal played the first of his two games for Scotland in the 0–5 thrashing by Austria in Vienna.

1948	New York All–Stars	A	Friendly	5–1
1956	SCO Angers	A	Friendly	0–0
1962	Limerick	A	Friendly	5–3
1977	Bristol City	A	League Division 1	1–2
1983	Israel	Tel Aviv	Friendly	3–4
1988	England XI	H	Friendly	3–2
1989	Queens Park Rangers	H	League Division 1	2–0
1995	UCD	A	Friendly	3–1

1947	Brentford	A	League Division 1	1–1
1953	American Select	New York	Friendly	4–1
1964	Monterrey	Chicago	Friendly	3–0

Peter Thompson made his debut for England in the 4–3 victory over Portugal in Lisbon.

| 1969 | Newcastle United | A | League Division 1 | 1–1 |
| 1979 | Leeds United | A | League Division 1 | 3–0 |

Liverpool had already secured their eleventh title and their third in four years, by the time Leeds arrived at Anfield. However this team was by far the best defensively any other Championship-winning team could ever boast. By not conceding a goal in the final game it meant that Liverpool had only conceded 16 all season, a record that stands today and unlikely ever to be bettered.

1984	Newcastle United	A	Friendly	2–2
1985	Watford	H	League Division 1	4–3
1991	Arsenal	Singapore	Friendly	1–1

1863 Matthew McQueen was born in Harthill, Scotland.

| 1951 | Malmo FF | A | Friendly | 4–1 |
| 1952 | Bristol City Augsburg | A | Friendly | 4–1 |

1954   Jimmy Case was born in Liverpool.

1963   Aston Villa   A   League Division 1   0–2
        Alan A'Court made his final appearance for the club after 13 years service. He played
        in 382 games and scored 63 goals. He won a Division 2 Championship medal in 1962.

1982   Middlesbrough   A   League Division 1   0–0

MAY 19TH

1946   American Select   New York Friendly   5–0

1971   Larry Lloyd and Tommy Smith both made their international debuts for England in the
        0–0 draw with Wales at Wembley.

1976   FC Bruges   A   UEFA Cup final 2nd leg   1–1
        With the narrowest of margins from the first leg and knowing the Belgians had two
        away goals this was never going to be an easy night and it became even more difficult
        when Bruges scored from a penalty, which meant Liverpool now had to score. The
        despair lasted barely five minutes when Keegan scored with a lovely curling shot to
        level things on the night. The second half started with the Belgians running out of ideas
        and the defence held on to claim the trophy. Like three years earlier Liverpool had won
        the Championship and a European trophy in the same year.

1979   Alan Hansen made his debut for Scotland in the 0–3 defeat by Wales in Cardiff. One
        of the modern game's biggest mysteries is how this great talent was only chosen to play
        for his country on 26 occasions in total.

1981   Manchester City   H   League Division 1   1–0

1982   Bury Select XI   A   Friendly   8–7

MAY 20TH

1948   Baltimore All –Stars   A   Friendly   9–2
1953   New England XI   Fall River Friendly   4–0
1958   Elche CF   A   Friendly   0–1
1985   West Ham United   A   League Division 1   3–0
1989   Everton   Wembley FA Cup final   3–2
        Liverpool had a chance to erase the memory of the previous year's defeat at the hands
        of Wimbledon in their ninth FA Cup final appearance. However this was no normal
        occasion. With the events of Hillsborough firmly in everyone's mind it seemed fitting
        that the opposition on the day was Everton. Segregation in and outside the ground was
        nowhere to be seen and not needed as fans mingled happily. After a moving rendition of
        'You'll Never Walk Alone' and a minute's silence the game was under way and
        Liverpool got off to the best possible start when Aldridge slotted home (quickly erasing
        his nightmare from the previous year). In the second half Everton brought on Stuart
        McCall and he scored a dramatic last-minute equaliser to force the game into extra time.
        Ian Rush was brought into the game as a replacement for Aldridge and it didn't take him
        long to get in the action when he scored with a stinging right-foot shot that left Southall
        helpless. This made Rush the highest goalscorer in Merseyside derbies taking him past
        Dixie Dean's record. Everton refused to lie down and substitute McCall equalised yet
        again. However, Ian Rush sealed a magnificent day with a winner with a great header
        from a Barnes cross, and the second half of extra time produced no goals. In one of the
        most traumatic seasons in the club's history Liverpool had now set up the chance to
        become the first team to do a double 'Double' only Arsenal hadn't read the script.

MAY 21ST

| 1961 | TJ Tatran Presov | A | Friendly | 1–1 |
| 1977 | Manchester United | Wembley | FA Cup final | 1–2 |

This was the club's sixth Cup final appearance and their third in six years though it was not to prove a good day out. A week after winning the title, and the prospect of winning the domestic 'Double' and the European Cup final still to come it was no surprise that Liverpool were to dominate the game. Jimmy Case scored a fantastic goal though it was not enough as United scored a couple of lucky goals through Pearson and the winner from Greenhoff after Case's great equaliser. The despair of missing out on the Double was there to see, but it was all forgotten a few days later.

1980   Ian Rush came on as substitute for Wales to make his international debut in the 0–1 defeat by Scotland at Hampden Park.

MAY 22ND

1946	New England XI	A	Friendly	3–2
1951	IFK Norrkoping	A	Friendly	1–0
1952	Madrid Select	A	Friendly	1–3
1967	Tranmere Rovers	A	Friendly	3–1
1968	FC Porto	A	Friendly	0–1
1969	Real Mallorca	A	Friendly	2–1

1974   Alec Lindsay made his debut for England in the 2–2 draw with Argentina at Wembley. He was to go on and win another three more caps in a too brief international career.

1984	Israel	Tel Aviv	Friendly	4–1
1994	Aston Villa	Johannesburg		
			Friendly	2–1

MAY 23RD

1948	Philadelphia XI	A	Friendly	5–2
1956	RCF Contors	Besancon	Friendly	8–1
1973	Borussia Moenchengladbach	A	UEFA Cup final 2nd leg	0–2

More adverse weather conditions threatened the game but it went ahead. The Germans scored two goals in the first half and the danger signs were there. But Liverpool showed their resilience and carried on and held out for a shutout in the second half to claim the trophy. They became the first team to win the League and a European trophy in the same season.

| 1985 | Everton | A | League Division 1 | 0–1 |
| 1989 | West Ham United | H | League Division 1 | 5–1 |

MAY 24TH

| 1947 | Arsenal | A | League Division 1 | 2–1 |

The penultimate game of the season saw Liverpool travel to London and pull off a fantastic victory thanks to goals from Bob Priday and Jack Balmer. This result set up the final game of the season a week later in the title showdown with Wolves.

1951	Goteborg Select	A	Friendly	5–3
1953	IFC Nurnberg	New York	Friendly	4–3
1956	Rouen	A	Friendly	6–2

| 1961 | Banik Most | A | Friendly | 4–1 |
| 1964 | Hamburger Sv | New York | Friendly | 0–2 |

MAY 25TH

1958	Cd Hospitalet	A	Friendly	1–2
1971	AGF Aarhus	A	Friendly	2–3
1977	Borussia Moenchengladbach	Rome	European Cup final	3–1

The first appearance in the final of the biggest club competition in the world for Liverpool and what a night. The disappointment of losing to Manchester United four days earlier in the FA Cup final was soon a thing in the distant past as Liverpool won the European Cup in glorious style in Rome in front of nearly 30,000 of their own supporters who travelled from Merseyside. John Toshack who had been injured was declared fit but wasn't to be risked by Paisley so his place went to Ian Callaghan. Terry McDermott opened the scoring on the half-hour after some great work from Heighway. The Germans got back at Liverpool straight away and just after half-time they equalised through a fantastic strike from Danish international Alan Simonsen, Clemence had no chance. Liverpool hardly got out of their half as the Germans pushed forward relentlessly but fortunately could not find their way through the defence superbly marshalled by Hughes. In the 65th minute Liverpool won a corner and as the ball was floated in a red shirt appeared and headed the ball in. It was Tommy Smith of all people (he had said he was going to retire after the game, so it was fairytale stuff) and he wheeled away with the biggest toothless grin ever seen. Kevin Keegan was taking control up front and it came as no surprise when he was tripped in the area with seven minutes to go. Phil Neal made no mistake from the spot and they held on and were crowned Champions with Emlyn having the honour of picking up the great trophy for the first time. However, whilst it was a piece of history it was also the end of two great careers at Anfield. The curtain finally fell on Ian Callaghan's long and illustrious career. His total of 843 appearances and 69 goals is a club record and may never be beaten. Among his medals during his 21 years at Anfield include five Division 1 Championships, one Division 2 Championship, two FA Cup winners' medals, one European Cup winners' medal and two UEFA Cup winners' medals. He surprisingly only gained four international caps for England. Kevin Keegan, by far the biggest star in Britain at the time, wanted a new challenge and wanted to try his luck abroad and to the dismay of the fans and the club this proved to be his last-ever game for the club. He played 321 games scoring exactly 100 goals in his six years at Anfield winning three Championships, two UEFA Cup winners' medals, one FA Cup winners' medal, in addition to the medal from this game. Hamburg stepped in and signed him for £500,000 and he helped the club to the German title in 1979 and the final of the European Cup the following season. He returned to England with Southampton in 1980 and then in 1982 moved on to Newcastle United, leading them from the front to promotion to the First Division in 1983–84 and then announcing his retirement from the game. In 1992 he was lured back to Newcastle as manager and took them to the First Division title in 1992–93. He won 63 caps for England, was Footballer of the Year in 1976 and European Footballer of the Year in 1978 and 1979.

MAY 26TH

| 1909 | Sir Matt Busby was born. After a brief spell with some local teams Busby joined |

Manchester City in 1928 where he appeared in two successive FA Cup finals winning once, before moving to Liverpool in March 1936 for a fee in the region of £8000. He later enjoyed a reasonably successful time as manager for a club in Manchester.

1946	Philadelphia XI	A	Friendly	12–0

Tommy Smith decided that after the victory the previous day he still had something left to offer and decided not to retire after all and stay on for another season.

1978	Al Nasr	A	Friendly	5–0
1980	Bahrain XI	A	Friendly	2–1
1989	Arsenal	H	League Division 1	0–2

For excitement and tension at its climax, this game may never be surpassed. What should have been one of the greatest nights in the club's history, however, turned out to be one of the saddest. With the FA Cup already in the trophy room, Liverpool could have afforded a defeat – so long as it was by only a single goal. They would still have been able to claim the title and the Double in what was undoubtedly the most traumatic season the club had ever played in following the events of Hillsborough. Arsenal took the lead in the second half when Alan Smith was adjudged to have headed in an indirect free-kick, although TV evidence does not clearly support this. Liverpool still held on, even though Arsenal were the better team on the night, until injury time when all but the 3,000-strong travelling away fans screamed for the final whistle. Three passes starting from Lukic ended up with Michael Thomas bursting through to poke the ball past Bruce Grobbelaar. The very last kick of the season had deprived Liverpool of a great moment in history.

1994	Cape Town Spurs	A	Friendly	3–0

MAY 27TH

1953	Montreal All-Stars	A	Friendly	10–0
1956	AS Saint-Etienne	Vichy	Friendly	1–1
1958	Perpignan	A	Friendly	4–0
1964	MSV Duisburg	Detroit	Friendly	4–1

Roger Hunt scored four goals for England against the USA in New York. England won the game by the narrow margin of 10–0.

1971	IFK Lulea	A	Friendly	5–0
1976	Hercules CF	A	Friendly	1–3
1977	Bobby Charlton XI	H	Friendly	9–9
1981	Real Madrid	Paris	European Cup final	1–0

Liverpool's third appearance in the European Cup final and they were desperate to make it three wins out of three. The game as expected was a close-fought one with both teams not prepared to give any ground. It wasn't until the 80th minute that Liverpool scored what was to be the winner through a brilliant solo effort from Alan Kennedy. In the dying moments Liverpool pressed even further and held on comfortably to win the trophy, enabling Bob Paisley to become the first manager to win the European Cup three times. What nobody realised was at the time it was to be goalkeeper Ray Clemence's last game in goal for the club before his shock move to Spurs a few weeks later [see June 24th].

1998	Michael Owen created history when he became the youngest-ever player to score for England in a full international, against Morocco in Casablanca.

MAY 28TH

1909 Tom Gardner born in Huyton. He began his career with Liverpool, making his debut in 1930 but was transferred to Grimsby after only four games. A year later he joined Hull City and in February 1934 moved on again and joined Aston Villa. His performances during the rest of the season earned him the first of two caps for England. He remained with the club until 1938 when he joined Burnley where he finished his career in 1946. During the war he guested for a number of clubs including Blackpool and he died in 1970.

| 1948 | New England XI | A | Friendly | 6–0 |
| 1950 | RSC Anderlecht | A | Friendly | 1–1 |

1976 Peter Thompson scored the winner for England in the 3–2 victory over Italy in an exhibition game in New York.

| 1979 | Israel | Tel Aviv | Friendly | 3–3 |

MAY 29TH

1951	Malmo FF	A	Friendly	1–2
1964	MSV Duisburg	Chicago	Friendly	0–0
1968	LLD Las Palmas	A	Friendly	1–1
1975	Benidorm	A	Friendly	2–1
1980	Al Nasr	A	Friendly	8–0
1985	Juventus	Brussels	European Cup final	0–1

This was the worst night in the club's history (at the time); not because the club had failed to win a trophy for the first time in nine years, but because of the tragic events off the pitch. Before the game started Liverpool and Juventus fans, who appeared to be in the same section of the crowd, began fighting. With innocent bystanders trying to get out of the way, a small wall at the front of the terracing gave way and hundreds of people were crushed beneath it, with 39 losing their lives – the majority of whom were Italians. After a lengthy delay, during which the reality of the preceding events became apparent, it was decided to go ahead with the match, although by now it had lost its significance. There were obvious repercussions, not only for Liverpool but also for the whole of English football when UEFA banned the country's clubs from participating in European competitions. It was also the end of Joe Fagan's reign as manager. One of Liverpool's great servants, he followed Bob Paisley, and while he was only in charge for two years he achieved what no other manager before him could do – winning three trophies in one season.

1991 Ian Rush won his 50th cap for Wales in the 0–0 draw with Poland in Radam.

1994 Iwisa Kaizer Chiefs   Johannesburg
                            Friendly   0–0

MAY 30TH

1902 George Livingston was signed from Celtic a week after he appeared in the Scottish Cup final where he was on the losing side in the 0–1 defeat by Hibernian.

1948	American Select	New York	Friendly	9–2
1956	Toulouse	A	Friendly	1–3
1984	AS Roma	Rome	European Cup final	1–1

This was Liverpool's fourth appearance in the final of the European Cup and they had won all of them. They were also bidding to become the first English team to win three

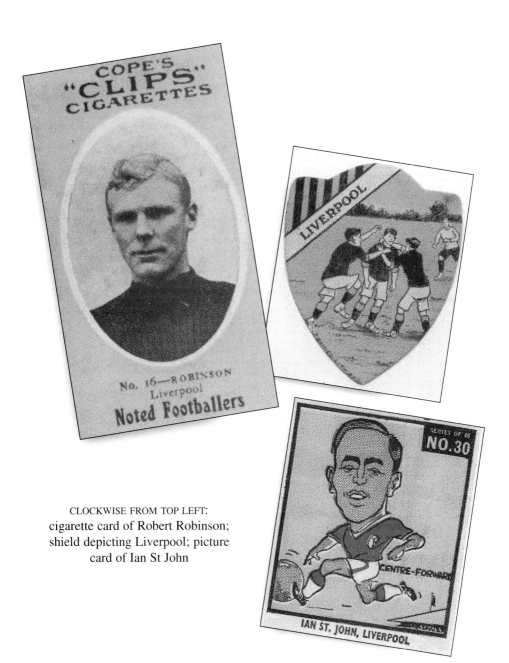

CLOCKWISE FROM TOP LEFT:
cigarette card of Robert Robinson;
shield depicting Liverpool; picture
card of Ian St John

CLOCKWISE FROM TOP LEFT:
cigarette cards depicting
Liverpool, Don McKinlay, Alun
Evans and Billy Liddell

CLOCKWISE FROM TOP LEFT: Mobil badge; picture card of Alan A'Court; cigarette card of Alex Raisbeck

The 1946–47 championship-winning side

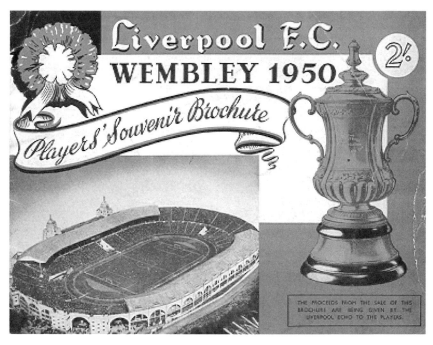

Players' brochure for the 1950 FA Cup final between Liverpool and Arsenal, which Arsenal won 2–0

Ticket stub from the 1965 FA Cup final between
Liverpool and Leeds at Wembley. Liverpool
won 2–1 after extra time

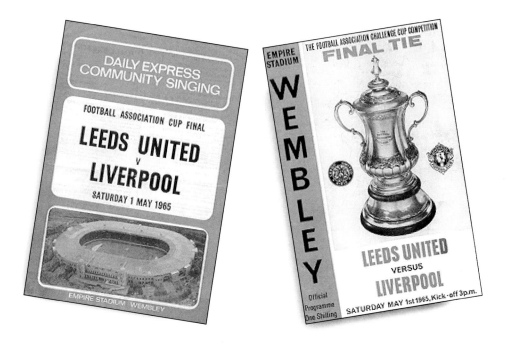

The songsheet and progamme for the same match

Programme from the 1971 FA
Cup final between Arsenal
and Liverpool, which Arsenal
won 2–1 after extra time to
complete the double

Programme from the 1974 FA
Cup final between Liverpool
and Newcastle, which
Liverpool won 3–0

Programme from the 1977
European Cup final between
Liverpool and Borussia
Moenchengladbach, which
Liverpool won 3–1

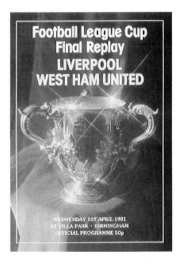

Programme from the 1981
League Cup final replay
against West Ham, which
Liverpool won 2–1

Programme from the 1981
League Cup final at Wembley

Programme from the 1983
Milk Cup final between
Liverpool and Manchester
United, which Liverpool won
2–1

Programme from the 1984
Milk Cup final between
Liverpool and Everton, which
finished goalless at Wembley

Programme from the 1984
Milk Cup final replay, which
Liverpool won 1–0 thanks to
Graeme Souness's goal

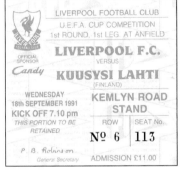

TOP: Ticket stub from the UEFA Cup clash with Strasbourg, October 1997

ABOVE LEFT: Ticket stub from the UEFA Cup tie with Genoa

ABOVE RIGHT: Ticket stub from the UEFA Cup clash with Kuusysi Lahti

LEFT: Programme from the UEFA Cup clash with Spartak Alania

major trophies in a season having already won the League and League Cup. This time unlike in 1978 against Bruges at Wembley, it was their opponents who really did have home advantage. Phil Neal put the Reds in the lead with a somewhat dubious goal but nobody cared – they were in front and held on until just before half-time when they let in a soft goal from Pruzzo. Roma came out with all guns blazing but could not break down the defence and the game went into extra time. Ian Rush had a half chance but couldn't quite squeeze the ball in and the game moved on to penalties. Steve Nicol took the first penalty but unfortunately for him ballooned it over the bar. His despair was not to last for long as Italian international Conti copied Nicol and did the same with his kick. Neal, Souness and Rush all scored with their kicks as did two of the Italians when, as Graziani stepped up to take his kick, Bruce decided to start clowning about in goal, pretending he had wobbly legs and jumping all over the place, this act of sportsmanship did the trick as Graziani promptly missed the target. All that was left for Liverpool to claim their fourth European Cup victory was for Alan Kennedy to score, which is what he did with ease. On a sour side to the evening was the behaviour of the Italian fans. Countless stories of innocent Liverpool fans being attacked seemed to go unnoticed by the authorities and UEFA when an official complaint was made. If that behaviour had happened in England the repercussions would have been much different. Captain Graeme Souness played in what was to be his last game for the club, as he moved to Sampdoria in the summer for £650,000. He scored 56 goals in 352 appearances for the club and his roll of honour includes: five Championship medals, three League Cup winners' medals and three European Cup winners' medals. Often criticised for his tough play but a true winner in all senses. He was to later return to the club as manager after time in Italy and Scotland with Rangers.

1985   In the aftermath of the Heysel Stadium disaster, the Belgian FA announced an immediate ban on British clubs (they initially made no distinction between English and British) playing in the country. This was seen as the first step on the way to a European ban on English clubs competing in the three cups the following season, which affected Manchester United, Liverpool, Everton, Spurs, Norwich City and Southampton.

MAY 31ST

1874	John Walker was born in Coatbridge.			
1946	St Louis All-Stars	A	Friendly	5–1
1947	Wolves	A	League Division 1	2–1

This was a championship decider in itself. Both teams needed victory to have a chance of lifting the first Championship after the war. On a very hot afternoon Liverpool took the game to the home side and went ahead with goals by Jackie Balmer and Albert Stubbins. Liverpool obviously couldn't keep up the pressure in the second half and managed to keep Wolves at bay, conceding just one goal. The victory meant Liverpool had to hope that Stoke didn't win their final game on June 14th at Sheffield United in order to become champions.

1950	Saarbrucken	A	Friendly	1–4
1953	Toledo All-Stars	A	Friendly	10–3

JUNE 1ST

1948	St Louis All-Stars	A	Friendly	4–2
1971	Gif Sundsvall	A	Friendly	4–0

JUNE 2ND

1946 Chicago Maroons   A   Friendly   9–3

1957 Mark Lawrenson was born in Preston. Mark arrived at Anfield in a then club record deal of £900,000 from Brighton where he made his name as an elegant centre-half.

1964 Mark Walters was born in Birmingham. Mark started his career on the wing for Aston Villa in 1982 where he played over 200 games for the Midlanders. After five years he moved to Glasgow Rangers in a £500,000 deal. He won over the majority of the fans despite suffering some terrible racist abuse even by his own fans, and produced good enough form to win his only cap for England in the summer of 1991 against New Zealand. He joined Liverpool shortly after in a £1.25 million deal.

JUNE 3RD

1948 Montreal All-Stars   A   Friendly   4–2

1964 San Francisco XI   A   Friendly   14–0

1984 Tottenham Hotspur   Swaziland Friendly   5–2

1984 Jim Beglin made his debut in the Republic of Ireland's win over China in Sappurro.

JUNE 4TH

1905 David Davidson was born in Aberdeen.

1966 John Scales was born in Harrogate.

JUNE 5TH

1946 Ulster United   Toronto   Friendly   11–1

1963 Jimmy Melia scored one of the goals in England's crushing 8–1 victory over Switzerland in Zurich. It was his second and last cap for his country.

1971 Kevin Baron died aged 44. After his ten years' service to Liverpool Kevin moved down the Leagues and into non-League football with teams Wisbech, Bedford, Maldown where he had a brief spell as player-coach before retiring through injury.

1983 Bulova Hong Kong   A   Friendly   2–0

JUNE 6TH

1964 MSV Duisburg   Vancouver Friendly   1–1

JUNE 7TH

1953 Chicago All-Stars   A   Friendly   4–2

1938 Ian St John was born. He started with his local club before joining Liverpool in a then club record deal of £37,500 in May 1961.

1964 Paul Stewart born in Manchester. Signed by Blackpool in October 1981 Paul scored 56 goals in 201 appearances for the Seasiders before transferring to Manchester City for £200,000 in 1987. In a little over twelve months Paul found the net with regularity for City and was then signed by Terry Venables for Spurs then record fee of £1,700,000, joining at the same time as Paul Gascoigne. By the end of the 1991–92 season Paul's desire to return back to his native north had become too great and he was transferred to Liverpool for £2,300,000, subsequently appearing on loan for Crystal Palace and Wolves and later Sunderland.

JUNE 8TH

1993 Nigel Clough was signed for £2.275 million from Nottingham Forest.

JUNE 9TH

1946	Kearny Celtic	A	Friendly	3–1
1948	New York All-Stars	A	Friendly	5–2
1953	St Louis All-Stars	A	Friendly	5–1

1963 Tommy Lawrence won the first of his three caps for Scotland in the 0–1 defeat by the Republic of Ireland in Dublin.

1984	Tottenham Hotspur	Swaziland Friendly	1–1

JUNE 10TH

1964	Vancouver All-Stars	A	Friendly	2–0
1983	Thailand	Bangkok	Friendly	3–0

1994 Dean Saunders was cleared in the High Court of making a reckless challenge on Paul Elliott during a match between Liverpool and Chelsea. In addition to losing out on a claim for compensation after the tackle ended his career, Elliott was also facing a possible legal bill for £500,000. In his summing up Mr Justice Drake said that whilst he felt players should have the right to seek redress from the courts for career-wrecking injuries as a result of foul play, he was satisfied in this instance that Saunders had made an honest attempt to play the ball.

JUNE 11TH

1946	American Select	A	Friendly	10–1

1958 Tommy Younger played his last game for Scotland in the World Cup qualifier against Paraguay. He won 24 caps in total.

JUNE 12TH

1889 Tom Gracie was born in Glasgow.

JUNE 13TH

1910 Elections were held for the first time to fill the post of President of the Football League; John McKenna of Liverpool being duly elected.

1941 Tony Hateley born in Derby. First introduced to League football with Notts County he scored 77 goals in just 131 League appearances and was transferred to Aston Villa in August 1963 for £23,000. At Villa he showed he was capable of scoring goals at the highest level, netting 68 in 127 appearances before a £100,000 move to Chelsea in October 1966. At the end of the season, having helped them to the FA Cup final he was sold to Liverpool in a £100,000 move. After two seasons at Anfield where he scored 28 goals in 56 appearances he was sold to Coventry, remaining just less than a year before joining Birmingham City. After a second spell with Notts County he ended his career with Oldham Athletic. His son Mark also enjoyed a highly successful football career.

1953	Irish Internationals	Toronto Friendly	3–1

1955 Alan Hansen was born. Alan started his career with Partick Thistle before joining Liverpool in 1977 for £100,000 certainly one of the best acquisitions the club has ever made.

JUNE 14TH

1947 Sheffield United beat Stoke City 2–1 which meant that Liverpool had retained their top spot in the League to win their fifth Championship.

1953 BSC Young Boys   New York Friendly   1–1

JUNE 15TH

1948 Ulster Select   Toronto   Friendly   5–1

1950 Laurence Hughes made his international debut for England in the World Cup group game against Chile in Rio De Janeiro.

JUNE 16TH

1935 Barry Wilkinson was born in Bishop Auckland.

JUNE 17TH

1997 Bjorn Kvarme was signed on a free transfer from Rosenborg.

JUNE 18TH

1948 Djurgardens IF   New York Friendly   3–2

1971 Jason McAteer was born in Birkenhead.

JUNE 19TH

1996 Anfield witnessed one of the games of the tournament during Euro 96 when a last-minute goal earned the Czech Republic a 3–3 draw with Italy, which put the Italians out of the competition. Those present will remember the joyous scenes from the Czech players at the final whistle when they learnt that they had progressed to the next round.

JUNE 20TH

1948 Kearny Celtic   A   Friendly   8–0

1972 Alun Evans, the first teenager to change hands for £100,000 when Liverpool bought him in 1968, was now a 23-year-old 'veteran' when Aston Villa paid £72,000 for his services. He scored 33 goals in just over 100 games for Liverpool.

1985 UEFA announced that Liverpool were to be banned for three years from European competition, the ban to take effect whenever the ban on English clubs was lifted.

JUNE 21ST

1964 Dean Saunders born in Swansea. He joined the local club and made appearances on loan to Cardiff City before moving to Brighton and then Oxford United where he made his name as a regular goalscorer. He then joined Derby County, scoring 42 goals in 106 appearances before a £2.9 million move to Liverpool. After 42 appearances, during which time he scored 11 goals and won an FA Cup winners' medal he moved on to Aston Villa.

JUNE 22ND

1906 Shortly after completing their second championship victory, work on one of the most famous terraces in the world started. It started life as a tinder bank and when a local journalist Ernest Edwards, observed the construction he said it looked like a hill in South Africa called the Spion Kop, site of the famous battle during the Boer War. Many locals read the article in the *Liverpool Echo* and the name has stuck ever since though known as 'The Kop'.

1998 Michael Owen scored England's equalising goal in their World Cup match against Romania in Toulouse. He later hit a post that would have squared the match again but England lost 1–2. Glenn Hoddle for some reason decided that Owen didn't warrant a start from the beginning of the game, something that baffled every person in the country and the travelling fans in France.

JUNE 23RD

1997 Michael Owen scored England's only goal in the 1–0 victory over Mexico in Malaysia in the U–20 World championships.

JUNE 24TH

1967 Ray Clemence signed from Scunthorpe United. Began his career with Scunthorpe and after only fifty appearances was signed by Liverpool and eventually took over from Tommy Lawrence as Liverpool's first-choice keeper in the 1969/70 season. In the following eleven seasons he amassed over 650 appearances (he missed only six), winning five League titles, the FA Cup, three European Cups, two UEFA Cups, the League Cup and the European Super Cup. Undoubtedly one of the finest goalkeepers ever to have played for Liverpool. He also won 61 England caps, a figure that might have been considerably higher had it not been for the fact that he and Peter Shilton were often played in alternate matches by Ron Greenwood since there was little or nothing to choose between them. In 1981 he was transferred to Tottenham for £300,000 and made his debut at Wembley in the FA Charity Shield. By the end of the season he had picked up another FA Cup winners' medal and might have added a further UEFA Cup medal in 1984 but for injury which kept him on the bench as reserve goalkeeper. He returned to first-team action the following season and made another FA Cup final appearance in 1987 (his first in 1971 and his last in 1987 gives him the record for the longest time span for first and last Cup final appearances). Like his peers Jennings and Shilton he completed over 1,000 first-class first-team appearances and might have continued into his forties but for a serious knee injury in October 1987 which forced him to retire. Awarded the MBE for his services to football in 1987, he joined the coaching staff at Spurs and became assistant first-team coach in May 1992. The arrival of Ossie Ardiles and his own backroom staff hastened his departure and he became general manager of Barnet in 1994.

JUNE 25TH

1927 Goalkeeper Russell Crossley was born. Spotted playing for the Army, where he quickly built a reputation for being brave and daring, Crossley joined Liverpool in the summer of 1947.

1940 Right-back Tommy Cooper died in a motorcycle accident aged 36. Tommy was a regular for Liverpool after signing from Derby where he was captain, in December 1934 for £7,500. He made 160 appearances for the club and was an England internationalist winning 15 caps.

1973 Jamie Redknapp was born in Barton-on-Sea. Son of West Ham manager Harry, Jamie quickly impressed as a youngster at Bournemouth even though he played only a handful of games, before signing for the Reds in 1991.

JUNE 26TH

1966   Ian Callaghan won the first of his four international caps for England in the 3–0 victory over Finland in Helsinki. Roger Hunt scored one of the goals.

JUNE 27TH

1992   David James was signed from Watford in a £1 million deal. Despite wild speculation in the tabloid newspapers Bruce Grobbelaar was not retiring through injury.

JUNE 28TH

1994   Ronnie Whelan won his 50th cap for Republic of Ireland in the World Cup game against Norway in New York, in the same game Ray Houghton won his 61st cap.

JUNE 29TH

1890   Tom Miller was born in Motherwell. Played for several teams in Scotland before arriving at Anfield for £400 in February 1912.

1949   Harry Chambers died aged 53. The charismatic Chambers was a member of the Championship-winning teams of 1922 and 1923.

1990   Ronny Rosenthal was signed from Standard Liege for £1 million.

JUNE 30TH

1917   Harry Eastham was born in Blackpool. (Uncle of George, who rocked the Football world when he took on the transfer system in the sixties). He joined Liverpool in February 1936.

1998   Once again Michael Owen was the hero as he scored England's second goal in their World Cup second round game against Argentina in Saint Etienne. The goal was undoubtedly the goal of the tournament and it has catapulted Owen into superstar status, and will no doubt change his life forever. The game went into a penalty shoot-out, which Owen took one and scored and unfortunately Paul Ince, who had an outstanding tournament, missed one. Once again England were dealt a cruel hand, but serious questions must be asked as to why Michael Owen was not allowed to play from the beginning of England's group game against Romania.

JULY 1ST

1904   Joseph Gordon Gunson was born in Chester.

1986   Ian Rush was sold to Juventus in a £3.6 million deal that saw him loaned back to Liverpool.

JULY 2ND

1986   Barry Venison was signed from Sunderland for £250,000. He had skippered them in the 1985 League Cup final defeat by Norwich at the tender age of 20.

JULY 3RD

1995   Stan Collymore was signed for a British club record £8.5 million from Nottingham Forest. Stan started his career with Stafford Rangers before moving to Crystal Palace and then on to Southend where he made a name for himself scoring 15 goals in 30 games. Barry Fry, quick to realise his potential and possible value in the transfer market, hyped Stan up before reluctantly letting him join Nottingham Forest for £2 million in

July 1993. Stan continued to score regularly with some spectacular goals and joined Liverpool after netting 44 times in 75 games for Forest.

JULY 4TH

1886 Full-back Bob Crawford was born in Blythswood.

1963 Jan Molby was born in Kolding. The robust midfielder joined the club from Ajax in August 1984 after a brief spell with the Dutch giants.

1966 John Scales was born in Harrogate. After appearing on Leeds United's books as a youngster John later joined Bristol Rovers on a free transfer before moving on to Wimbledon where he helped them to that unforgettable day in the FA Cup final of 1988. He made over 250 appearances for the Dons before moving to Anfield in 1994.

JULY 5TH

1960 Gary Gillespie was born in Stirling.

JULY 6TH

1998 Liverpool announced that Michael Owen was to stay with them and would not be sold, even for the £30 million that was quoted in the tabloids.

JULY 7TH

1931 Alex South was born in Brighton. The much acclaimed centre half joined Liverpool in December 1954 for £5,000 but failed to make an impact at the top level. Just two years later he was transferred to Halifax for half the fee, where he stayed and played nearly 300 games for them.

JULY 8TH

1991 Mark Wright signed from Derby County for £2.2 million pounds. Some considered this a lot of money for a near 30-year-old but, when fit, he is a bargain.

JULY 9TH

1994 Roy Evans brought Danish goalkeeper Michael Stensgaard to the club as his first signing. Injury was to force the Danish keeper to retire two years later without him ever making a first-team appearance.

JULY 10TH

1988 There was a threat of a split in the Football League when ITV offered £33m over four years to screen League and Littlewoods Cup matches. The amount to be shared between ten clubs. The top five of these – Liverpool, Everton, Manchester United, Arsenal and Tottenham Hotspur – would have been guaranteed £600,000 a year plus £150,000 per game. The second five – Aston Villa, Newcastle United, Nottingham Forest, Sheffield Wednesday and West Ham United – were guaranteed £400,000 a year plus £150,000 per game. BBC and BSB were offering between £39m and £47m over four years to be divided between the Football League and the FA.

JULY 11TH

1932 Harold Taylor signed pro forms with the club. The left winger played in all positions along the front line and in his four years at the club played 71 times.

1958   Michael Robinson was born in Leicester. The highly rated centre forward who had combined transfer fees of approaching £2 million arrived at Anfield in the summer of 1983.

1974   One of the darkest days in the history of the club. A press conference had been called to reveal the transfer of Ray Kennedy from Arsenal for £200,000 to break the club record at the time for the striker. However the bombshell that followed stunned everyone that was present when John Smith announced that Shankly was to retire from League football. The great man had single-handedly transformed the club into greatness. Many books have been written about him so we cannot add anything that nobody doesn't already know. During his 15 years in charge, Liverpool returned to the First Division and won three League titles, one UEFA Cup, two FA Cups and reached the final of the European-Cup Winners' Cup. He did leave a squad that was to go on and achieve a lot more.

1978   Kevin Sheedy signed for £80,000 from Hereford United. Kevin was to spend four years at Anfield making only one full appearance before moving across Stanley Park to Everton for £100,000 where he was to find major success.

1871   Billy Dunlop was born in Kilmarnock. Played at local level before joining Liverpool in January 1895 for a fee in the region believed to be £35 guineas.

1991   Derby striker Dean Saunders turned down a chance to join Everton and Nottingham Forest in order to sign for Liverpool.

1920   Ray Minshull was born in Bolton. After playing in the Army he moved to Liverpool shortly after the war. Injuries forced him to be constantly out of the game for long periods and in his five years at the club only managed 28 appearances.

1989   Steve Harkness was signed from Carlisle United for £75,000. He had made 12 appearances for Carlisle.

1998   The club announced that they are to restructure at management level, and the club decided to break with tradition by appointing their first foreign coach in Frenchman Gerard Houllier. Houllier who was linked with the vacant Celtic manager's job for nearly eight weeks, agreed to join the club in a dual role with Roy Evans. The duties of each man were not disclosed but Evans was very happy to have someone in to help him. Only time will tell if the very bold move of Houllier's appointment is the right one. If he is half as successful as Arsene Wenger at Highbury, then it will be. He is vastly experienced and he has managed at the highest level, managing the French national team in 1993. With British football fast becoming a European based game, his knowledge hopefully will be invaluable.

1919   Albert Stubbins was born in Wallsend. He started out with his boyhood heroes Newcastle before moving to Liverpool in 1946 for £12,500.

1946   Peter Cormack was born in Edinburgh. After a brief spell with Hearts at the start to his career he moved to Hibernian where he made a name for himself before coming south to Nottingham Forest in March 1970 for £80,000. After a couple of unsuccessful years at Forest he was signed by Liverpool in the summer of 1972 for £110,000.

1997   IFK Goteborg   A   Friendly   0–1

1998   The first task of the new management team of Evans and Houllier was to appoint an assistant coach in Patric Beruges who was widely tipped to become the successor to Aime Jacquet, as French National coach.

JULY 18TH

1922   Ray Lambert was born in Bagillt, Flintshire. Ray made history when he joined Liverpool as a mere 13-year-old to become the youngest-ever player to be signed by a League club. The foresight by the club turned out be a good one as he stayed for another 24 years in total.

JULY 19TH

1926   Kevin Baron was born in Preston. Kevin joined Liverpool as an amateur in 1944 after a brief spell with his home-town club Preston North End, and turned professional in 1945.

JULY 20TH

1938   Roger Hunt born in Golborne. He signed for Liverpool in May 1959 and was a prolific goalscorer for the club, hitting 245 League goals in 401 appearances and remained their record League goalscorer until Ian Rush overtook him in 1992. Domestically he won an FA Cup winners' medal and two League titles, as well as 34 caps for England, scoring 18 goals. It was widely believed that he was the player most at risk if Alf Ramsey decided to bring back Jimmy Greaves for the 1966 World Cup final, but Hunt held his place (he had scored three of England's goals during the tournament) and picked up a winners' medal. He joined Bolton Wanderers in December 1969 and spent nearly two seasons with the Trotters, scoring a further 24 League goals. Upon retiring as a player he turned his back on football completely, going into the family haulage business.

1997   Brondby IF   A   Friendly   1–1

JULY 21ST

1969   Mike Marsh was born in Liverpool. Mike arrived on a free transfer from Kirby Town in August 1987.

JULY 22ND

1993   Neil Ruddock was bought from Tottenham for £2.5 million.

JULY 23RD

1987	Bayern Munich	A	Friendly	2–3
1991	Dundalk	A	Friendly	0–0
1993	K. Keegan All-Stars	Sheffield	Friendly	5–0
1997	Bristol City	A	Friendly	1–1

JULY 24TH

1870   Harry Storer was born in Derbyshire. Harry arrived at Anfield via Gainsborough, Loughborough and Arsenal in 1895.

1979   Liverpool signed a shirt sponsorship deal with Japanese electronics company Hitachi. The club was allowed to carry the company's logo on their shirts in non-televised matches only. This was the first such shirt sponsorship deal in British League football.

1987   Liverpool broke the transfer record again to buy classy Newcastle forward Peter Beardsley for £1.8 million. Peter had previously had two spells with Vancouver Whitecaps and had been on the books at Old Trafford who failed to recognise his outstanding potential and never really gave him a chance before he made his name with Newcastle.

1996   Crewe Alexandra   A   Friendly   1–0

JULY 25TH

1891   Don McKinlay was born in Glasgow.

1968   Linfield   A   Friendly   3–1

JULY 26TH

1928   John Wheeler was born in Liverpool. Played in the 1953 Cup final for Bolton and moved to Liverpool in 1956 for £10,000.

1969   Linfield   A   Friendly   2–1

1974   Bob Paisley was confirmed as manager of Liverpool in succession to Bill Shankly two weeks after the great man's retirement.

1987   Aalborg Chang   A   Friendly   4–0

1991   Bayer Leverkusen   A   Friendly   0–0

1992   AS Monaco   Paris   Friendly   1–2

1994   Bolton Wanderers   A   Friendly   1–4

1995   Birmingham City   A   Friendly   1–0

1997   Linfield   A   Friendly   2–1

JULY 27TH

1985   Burnley   A   Friendly   5–1

1992   Borussia Dortmund   Paris   Friendly   2–3

1996   FC Porto   H   Friendly   0–2

JULY 28TH

1945   Raf XI   Celle   Friendly   7–0

1951   Ray Kennedy was born.

1971   Wrexham   A   Friendly   1–0

1987   Bronshoj BK   Ringsted   Friendly   1–1

1991   IK Sirius   A   Friendly   0–0

1992   Ray Houghton was sold to Aston Villa for £900,000 after reportedly wanting to return home to his family in London. The much capped Republic of Ireland international had spent five very successful years at Liverpool playing nearly 200 games and scoring 37 goals. He won two Championship medals in 1988 and 1990, as well as the FA Cup in 1989 and 1992.

1993   Birmingham City   A   Friendly   1–1

| 1996 | Everton | A | Friendly | 0–0 |
| 1997 | Shelbourne/UCD | Dublin | Friendly | 6–0 |

JULY 29TH

1945	Army XI	Hannover	Friendly	3–3
1963	Jim Beglin was born in Waterford.			
1969	Blackpool	A	Friendly	0–0
1989	Dinamo Kiev	Wembley	Friendly	2–0
1992	Rosenborg BK	Oslo	Friendly	0–1
1994	Borussia Moenchengladbach	A	Friendly	1–0
1995	Ajax	A	Friendly	0–5

JULY 30TH

1968	Tranmere Rovers	A	Friendly	3–0
1980	Dundalk	Dublin	Friendly	2–0
1985	Crewe Alexandra	A	Friendly	2–2
1986	Danish Select XI	Holbaek	Friendly	1–1
1989	Arsenal	Wembley	Friendly	0–1
1991	Ludvika FK	A	Friendly	3–2
1995	AC Fiorentina	Monchengladbach	Friendly	1–1

JULY 31ST

1970	League Of Ireland	Dublin	Friendly	2–1
1971	Blackburn Rovers	A	Friendly	1–0
1992	Tromso Il	A	Friendly	2–1
1993	Tranmere Rovers	A	Friendly	4–3
1994	Bayern Munich	Fulda	Friendly	0–2
1997	Norway XI	Oslo	Friendly	3–1

AUGUST 1ST

1970	David James was born in Welwyn Garden City, Herts. David earned his reputation playing for Watford, he starred in the Youth cup win of 1989 and earned a regular place in the England U-21 side winning 10 caps. He made just over 90 appearances for the 'Hornets' before joining Liverpool in the June of 1992.			
1979	Borussia Moenchengladbach	A	Friendly	4–2
1980	RSC Anderlecht	A	Friendly	3–4
1986	IS Halmia	A	Friendly	3–0
1987	Vejle BK	Spjald	Friendly	3–0
1989	Malmo FF	A	Friendly	2–1
1991	Rosenborg BK	Oslo	Friendly	3–2

AUGUST 2ND

| 1958 | Edinburgh Select | Tynecastle | Friendly | 2–2 |
| 1968 | Hull City | A | Friendly | 5–3 |

1969	Feyenoord	A	Friendly	1–1
1972	VFL Bochum	A	Friendly	2–0
1975	FC Utrecht	A	Friendly	2–0
1978	Bass League XI	Dublin	Friendly	3–1
1985	Oldham Athletic	A	Friendly	0–1
1990	AC Fiorentina	Massa	Friendly	0–0
1993	Raufoss Il	A	Friendly	7–2
1995	Norway XI	Oslo	Friendly	0–3
1996	Linfield	A	Friendly	2–2

AUGUST 3RD

1971	Hamburger SV	A	Friendly	4–4
1977	Hamburger SV	A	Friendly	2–3
1979	Feyenoord	Gelsenkirchen		
			Friendly	2–2
1980	Hvidovre IF	A	Friendly	3–1
1983	Manchester United	Belfast	Friendly	3–4
1987	Karlstad BK	A	Friendly	3–0
1988	Bryne IL	A	Friendly	5–0
1989	Vasalunds IF	A	Friendly	1–1
1994	Norway XI	Oslo	Friendly	1–3

AUGUST 4TH

1951	Edinburgh Select	A	Friendly	2–1

1957 John Wark was born in Glasgow. Wark was a star in the Ipswich team that won the FA Cup in 1978 and the UEFA cup in 1981 under Bobby Robson. He moved to Anfield in January 1988 for £450,000.

1967	IFC Koln	A	Friendly	0–1
1970	Preston North End	A	Friendly	5–0
1976	Feyenoord	A	Friendly	0–2
1981	Scunthorpe United	A	Friendly	2–1
1984	Borussia Dortmund	A	Friendly	1–0
1986	Swedish Select XI	Orebro	Friendly	3–1
1991	IF Elfsborg	A	Friendly	2–1
1992	Tranmere Rovers	A	Friendly	7–1
1993	Rosenborg BK	Oslo	Friendly	1–0
1996	Dundalk	A	Friendly	1–0
1997	Crewe Alexandra	A	Friendly	3–1

AUGUST 5TH

1948 Ray Clemence born in Skegness. Started his career with Scunthorpe United in August 1965 before moving to Anfield in June 1967.

1972	FC Utrecht	A	Friendly	1–0
1975	Borussia Dortmund	A	Friendly	2–0
1977	Ajax	A	Friendly	1–2
1979	Benfica	Gelsenkirchen		
			Friendly	1–1

1980	VFB Stuttgart	A	Friendly	2–3
1983	Hamburger SV	Rotterdam		
			Friendly	0–0
1985	Brighton & Hove Albion	A	Friendly	4–1
1988	Sunnmore XI	Alesund	Friendly	4–1
1989	Halmstads BK	A	Friendly	1–0
1990	Lillestrom SK	A	Friendly	3–0
1994	Hamburger SV	A	Friendly	1–3

AUGUST 6TH

1880	Ronald Orr was born in Ayrshire. Joined Liverpool after a distinguished career with Newcastle United where he helped them to two Division 1 Championships in 1905 and 1907 sandwiched between a Cup final defeat by Everton in 1906.			
1974	FC Kaiserslautern	A	Friendly	3–1
1978	FC Basel	A	Friendly	6–0
1984	RSC Charleroi	A	Friendly	6–0
1986	Kolding IF	A	Friendly	1–1
1987	Valerengens IF	A	Friendly	4–1
1996	Millwall	A	Friendly	0–0

AUGUST 7TH

1970	Middlesbrough	A	Friendly	1–3
1971	Leicester City	A	Charity Shield	0–1
1976	Roda JC Kerkrade	A	Friendly	1–1
1977	Barcelona	Amsterdam		
			Friendly	1–0
1979	Fbu Select	Odense	Friendly	5–2
1983	Feyenoord	A	Friendly	3–3
1985	Charlton Athletic	A	Friendly	2–1
1989	HJK Helsinki	A	Friendly	0–0
1993	Burnley	A	Friendly	4–0
1994	Hertha BSC	A	Friendly	3–0
1995	Yeovil Town XI	A	Friendly	7–1

AUGUST 8TH

1967	Hamburger SV	A	Friendly	2–2
1975	Roda Jc Kerkrade	A	Friendly	1–1
1978	Bayern Munich	A	Friendly	1–1
1981	FC Zurich	A	Friendly	3–0
1982	Portsmouth	A	Friendly	3–0
1984	BSC Young Boys	A	Friendly	1–0
1986	Hamburger SV	A	Friendly	0–1
1988	Tromso IL	A	Friendly	2–2
1990	Stockholm Alliance	Stockholm		
			Friendly	1–0
1992	Leeds United	Wembley	Charity Shield	3–4

AUGUST 9TH

1969	Chelsea	H	League Division 1	4–1
1980	West Ham United	Wembley	Charity Shield	1–0
1987	Celtic	A	Friendly	1–0
1993	Newcastle United	H	Friendly	1–0
1996	PSV Eindhoven	H	Friendly	2–3
1997	Wimbledon	A	Premier League	1–1

AUGUST 10TH

1968	Manchester City	H	League Division 1	2–1
1974	Leeds United	Wembley	Charity Shield	1–1

The FA Charity Shield moved to its new home of Wembley. Ray Kennedy made his debut for the club. The two teams are involved in almost continuous brawling that exploded, with Kevin Keegan and Billy Bremner swapping punches and subsequently getting sent off by referee Bob Matthewson. As they were leaving the field, both players removed their shirts and threw them down on the ground [see August 28th]. The game itself ended 1–1 and was settled by penalties; Ian Callaghan took Liverpool's decisive spot kick to win the trophy 6–5.

1976	Twente Enschede	A	Friendly	0–2

Kenny Dalglish was bought from Celtic for £440,000, a British transfer record at the time. Dalglish, a winner of 4 Championships, 4 Scottish Cups and a League Cup winners' medals, made over 320 appearances for the club, scoring 170 goals.

1982	Servette Geneva	A	Friendly	0–0
1983	WAC Casablanca	A	Friendly	3–0
1984	Grasshopper	Bern	Friendly	1–0
1985	Bristol City	A	Friendly	3–3
1990	Landskrona Bois	A	Friendly	6–3
1994	Wrexham	A	Friendly	3–1
1995	Celtic	A	Friendly	0–0

AUGUST 11TH

1960	Nantes	A	Friendly	2–0
1978	FK Austria Wien	A	Friendly	1–0
1979	Arsenal	Wembley	Charity Shield	3–1
1981	Servette Geneva	A	Friendly	1–2
1992	Leeds United	A	Friendly	4–1

AUGUST 12TH

1967	Hannover 96	A	Friendly	4–1
1969	Manchester City	H	League Division 1	3–2
1972	Manchester City	H	League Division 1	2–0
1974	Celtic	A	Friendly	1–1
1983	Atletico Madrid	La Linea	Friendly	1–2
1984	KR Reykjavik	A	Friendly	2–2
1985	Everton	A	Friendly	2–3
1986	Real Sociedad	A	Friendly	0–0
1988	Atletico Madrid	La Coruna	Friendly	1–5

1989	Arsenal	Wembley	Charity Shield	1–0
1990	HJK Helsinki	A	Friendly	2–0
1991	Tranmere Rovers	A	Friendly	0–1
1995	Shelbourne	A	Friendly	1–0
1996	Burnley	A	Friendly	4–0

AUGUST 13TH

1966   Everton   A   Charity Shield   1–0

Whilst Everton and Liverpool had met many times in the League and occasionally in the cup and could point to a vast number of trophy wins between them, they had never met in the FA Charity Shield prior to this match. A crowd of 63,329 packed into Goodison Park for the first clash between the two Merseyside rivals and was treated to something special right at the very start. The two teams came out on to the pitch side by side, headed by Ray Wilson and Roger Hunt. Both had been members of the England side that had won the World Cup, and each had a hand on the gleaming Jules Rimet Trophy. Behind them came captains Brian Labone and Ron Yeats, and they were carrying the FA Cup and League trophy respectively. Three of the greatest prizes on offer in the game on show at the same time. The game itself was one way with Liverpool always in the ascendancy. Roger Hunt opened the scoring with what turned out to be the only goal of the match after nine minutes. Liverpool should have scored more, Everton didn't look as though they could score any, and the shield found its way to Anfield.

1977   Manchester United   Wembley   Charity Shield   0–0

Kenny Dalglish made his debut after his record signing from Celtic. Although there were no goals and each side got to retain the Shield for six months, the most controversial incident occurred when Emlyn Hughes appeared to have pulled David McCreery down inside the penalty area. Although the linesman waved to indicate a penalty, the referee thought he was too far away from the incident to be certain it had been a penalty. It proved to be the right decision as TV evidence proved later on.

1981   Neuchatel Xamax   A   Friendly   0–0

AUGUST 14TH

1965   Manchester United   A   Charity Shield   2–2

A crowd of 48,502 saw two evenly matched sides produce a thrilling curtain raiser to the new season. Goals from George Best and Herd were cancelled out by those from Ron Yeats and Stevenson and each side retained the Shield for six months.

1968	Southampton	A	League Division 1	0–2
1971	Nottingham Forest	H	League Division 1	3–1
1973	Hertha BSC	A	Friendly	1–1
1976	Southampton	Wembley	Charity Shield	1–0
1978	Celtic	A	Friendly	3–2
1982	Real Betis	Marbella	Friendly	2–0
1983	Dinamo Bucuresti	La Linea	Friendly	3–2
1988	Real Sociedad	La Coruna	Friendly	4–0
1993	Sheffield Wednesday	H	Premier League	2–0

Nigel Clough scored on his debut shortly after he had signed for the club in a £2.275 million deal. Neil Ruddock also made his debut. Both players had impressed and it looked like money being well spent by manager Souness.

1995	Linfield	A	Friendly	1–0

AUGUST 15TH

1905 Tommy Reid was born in Motherwell. He joined Liverpool via Clydebank for £1000 in April 1926.

1964	West Ham United	H	Charity Shield	2–2
1970	Burnley	A	League Division 1	2–1
1972	Manchester United	H	League Division 1	2–0
1982	CD Malaga	Marbella	Friendly	1–1
1987	Arsenal	A	League Division 1	2–1

Peter Beardsley made his debut after his record-breaking transfer in the summer. John Barnes also made his debut. It was rather ironic that John helped mastermind the victory on the left wing after Arsenal couldn't agree terms with John a few months earlier when trying to sign him from Watford.

1990	Real Sociedad	H	Friendly	3–1
1994	Dundalk	A	Friendly	2–1

1996 Patrik Berger was signed from Borussia Dortmund for £3,25 million.

AUGUST 16TH

1964 Barry Venison was born in County Durham.

1969	Tottenham Hotspur	A	League Division 1	2–0
1975	Queens Park Rangers	A	League Division 1	0–2
1980	Crystal Palace	H	League Division 1	3–0
1986	Everton	Wembley	Charity Shield	1–1

Liverpool's double success of 1985–86, both trophies being won at the expense of Everton, meant a FA Charity Shield date with their closest rivals at Wembley and a chance to inflict another victory. By now Wembley's capacity was down to just over 88,000, an insufficient figure given that Liverpool and Everton had struggled to accommodate all those who wished to see the game when there were 100,000 tickets available (even if not all the tickets were originally intended for sale on Merseyside). Heath gave Everton the lead with just ten minutes remaining in the match, but Liverpool fought back to equalise two minutes from time through who else but Ian Rush. As a result both sides would share the Shield for six months each.

1992	Nottingham Forest	A	Premier League	0–1
1997	Leicester City	H	Premier League	1–2

AUGUST 17TH

1964	Reykjavik	A	European Cup 1st round 1st leg	5–0
1968	Arsenal	A	League Division 1	1–1
1970	Blackpool	A	League Division 1	0–0
1971	Wolves	H	League Division 1	3–2
1973	Rsc Anderlecht	A	Friendly	0–0
1974	Luton Town	A	League Division 1	2–1

| 1985 | Arsenal | H | League Division 1 | 2–0 |

Liverpool kicked off the season with the whole of the football world watching, as it was the first game played after the May European Cup final in Brussels against Juventus, at the Heysel Stadium, in which 39 fans tragically lost their lives. Most so-called experts thought the end of the Liverpool dynasty was near and that no club could bounce back from such adversity but history tells a completely different story. Kenny Dalglish was appointed player-manger within 24 hours of that horrific night and whilst there was no questioning his status as a world-class player, no one knew how he could cope with both jobs. Arsenal arrived at Anfield with Don Howe in charge and it was quite obvious that the Gunners came for a draw. Liverpool inspired by Alan Hansen, now captain, dominated from the kick-off and the only surprise was that they led 1–0 at half-time thanks to a Ronnie Whelan effort. The second half continued in much the same fashion with Steve Nicol adding a second. Liverpool had showed that they meant business with a fluent and entertaining style that set the tone for the whole of the season.

| 1991 | Oldham Athletic | H | League Division 1 | 2–1 |
| 1996 | Middlesbrough | A | Premier League | 3–3 |

AUGUST 18TH

| 1931 | Dick White was born in Scunthorpe. He joined Liverpool from Scunthorpe in 1955. |

| 1935 | Jimmy Harrower was born. The promising youngster who joined Hibernian after a bright career at Schoolboy level, joined Liverpool in 1958 for £11,000. |

1951	Portsmouth	H	League Division 1	0–2
1956	Huddersfield Town	H	League Division 2	2–3
1962	Blackpool	H	League Division 1	1–2
1979	League Of Ireland	Dublin	Friendly	2–0
1984	Everton	Wembley	Charity Shield	0–1
1986	Irish Internationals	Cork	Friendly	2–1
1990	Manchester United	Wembley	Charity Shield	1–1
1993	Queens Park Rangers	A	Premier League	3–1

AUGUST 19TH

1950	Wolves	A	League Division 1	0–2
1953	Portsmouth	H	League Division 1	3–1
1961	Bristol Rovers	A	League Division 2	2–0
1967	Manchester City	A	League Division 1	0–0
1972	Crystal Palace	A	League Division 1	1–1
1975	West Ham United	H	League Division 1	2–2
1978	Queens Park Rangers	H	League Division 1	2–1
1980	Coventry City	A	League Division 1	0–0
1981	Atletico Madrid	A	Friendly	1–2
1987	Irish Olympic XI	Dublin	Friendly	5–0
1989	Manchester City	H	League Division 1	3–1
1992	Sheffield United	H	Premier League	2–1
1995	Sheffield Wednesday	H	Premier League	1–0
1996	Arsenal	H	Premier League	2–0

AUGUST 20TH

1895	Richard Forshaw was born in Preston.			
1940	Kevin Lewis was born in Cheshire.			
1949	Sunderland	H	League Division 1	4–2
1955	Nottingham Forest	A	League Division 2	3–1
1960	Leeds United	H	League Division 2	2–0

1961 Steve McMahon was born in Liverpool. He started his soccer life as an apprentice with Everton before moving on to Aston Villa in 1983 for £350,000. He joined the playing staff at Anfield in September 1985 for a similar fee.

1966	Leicester City	H	League Division 1	3–2

The Liverpool B team for the match against Southport included one K. Dalglish in its line-up. Dalglish was on a two-week trial from Celtic with a view to a permanent transfer. Dalglish failed to impress, with the result that he would subsequently cost Liverpool a hefty fee a few year's later.

1968	Stoke City	H	League Division 1	2–1
1969	Manchester City	A	League Division 1	2–0
1974	Wolves	A	League Division 1	0–0
1977	Middlesbrough	A	League Division 1	1–1

How ironic that eleven years to the day that Kenny Dalglish played a trial game for the club he made his League debut for them after his record-breaking transfer from Celtic. He scored after three minutes!

1983	Manchester United	Wembley Charity Shield	0–2

This was the first time in many a year that the FA Cup holders had beaten the League champions in the FA Charity Shield, but two goals from Bryan Robson were enough to give Manchester United victory. It was Liverpool's first defeat in the Charity Shield since losing 1–0 to Leicester in 1971.

1984	Home Farm	A	Friendly	3–0
1988	Wimbledon	Wembley Charity Shield		2–0
1994	Crystal Palace	A	Premier League	6–1

AUGUST 21ST

1947	Preston North End	H	League Division 1	3–1
1948	Aston Villa	A	League Division 1	1–2
1951	Burnley	A	League Division 1	0–0
1954	Doncaster Rovers	H	League Division 1	3–2

Tony Rowley scored a hat-trick on his debut for the club.

1965	Leicester City	A	League Division 1	3–1
1971	Newcastle United	A	League Division 1	2–3
1976	Norwich City	H	League Division 1	1–0
1979	Bolton Wanderers	H	League Division 1	0–0
1982	Tottenham Hotspur	Wembley Charity Shield		1–0
1985	Aston Villa	A	League Division 1	2–2

After the fantastic display against Arsenal in the opening game of the season Liverpool travelled to Villa Park to play a very young Aston Villa side. Villa started the game very brightly and it was a deserved lead they had when Gary Shaw put them ahead after just seven minutes. Ian Rush –who else – grabbed the equaliser with a fantastic header in the 38th minute, for his 11th goal in his last nine games against the Midlanders. After the break Liverpool slowly regained control until Mark Walters scored in the 75th minute. The lead was only short-lived as the Danish international grabbed an 84th-minute equaliser to bring the game level again for the second time. The excitement did not there, Ian Rush was pushed in the area with just two minutes to go and stepped up to take the penalty, only for him to see it brilliantly saved by Nigel Spink and the chance of victory gone.

1991	Manchester City	A	League Division 1	1–2

Steve McManaman scored his first goal for the club.

1995	Leeds United	A	Premier League	0–1

AUGUST 22ND

1953	Manchester United	H	League Division 1	4–4
1959	Cardiff City	A	League Division 2	2–3
1962	Manchester City	A	League Division 1	2–2
1964	Arsenal	H	League Division 1	3–2

The BBC launched *Match of the Day* with this being the main featured game. The viewing figures for the BBC2 programme were 75,000, only slightly up on the attendance figure at Anfield.

1967	Arsenal	H	League Division 1	2–0
1970	Huddersfield Town	H	League Division 1	4–0
1978	Ipswich Town	A	League Division 1	3–0
1981	Home Farm	A	Friendly	5–0
1993	Swindon Town	A	Premier League	5–0

AUGUST 23RD

1875 George Allan was born in west Lothian, Scotland. George joined Liverpool from Leith Athletic where he scored almost a goal a game. After spending two seasons at Anfield he moved on loan to Glasgow to play for his beloved Celtic with Liverpool keeping his registration. He scored 16 goals in 19 games for Celtic helping them to their 4th League Championship in 1898 before returning to Anfield in 1898.

1950	Manchester United	H	League Division 1	2–1
1952	Preston North End	A	League Division 1	1–1
1954	Plymouth Argyle	A	League Division 1	0–1
1956	Notts County	A	League Division 2	1–1
1958	Grimsby Town	H	League Division 2	3–3
1961	Sunderland	H	League Division 2	3–0
1969	Burnley	H	League Division 1	3–3
1972	Chelsea	A	League Division 1	2–1
1975	Tottenham Hotspur	H	League Division 1	3–2
1977	Newcastle United	H	League Division 1	2–0
1980	Leicester City	A	League Division 1	0–2
1986	Newcastle United	A	League Division 1	2–0
1987	Atletico Madrid	A	Friendly	1–0
1989	Aston Villa	A	League Division 1	1–1
1992	Arsenal	H	Premier League	0–2
1997	Blackburn Rovers	A	Premier League	1–1

AUGUST 24TH

1873 Thomas Harry Bradshaw was born in Liverpool. Harry started his career with Northwich Victoria before moving to Liverpool in October 1893.

1894 Elisha Scott was born in Belfast. He joined the club in 1912 where he was to stay for 22 years and build his legendary career.

1955	Sheffield Wednesday	H	League Division 2	0–3
1957	Bristol Rovers	A	League Division 2	2–1
1960	Southampton	A	League Division 2	1–4
1963	Blackburn Rovers	A	League Division 1	2–1

Peter Thompson made his league debut for the club. This outstanding player was to miss only six games in the next nine years.

1966	Manchester City	A	League Division 1	1–2

1967 Michael Thomas was born in Lambeth.

1968	Sunderland	H	League Division 1	4–1
1971	Crystal Palace	A	League Division 1	1–0
1974	Leicester City	H	League Division 1	2–1
1981	Crusaders	A	Friendly	5–0

1984 Danish international Jan Molby signed from Ajax for £575,000.

1985	Newcastle United	A	League Division 1	0–1

Newcastle, who themselves were still reeling from the sudden departure of Jack Charlton as their manager in the week before the season started, were determined to try and make a bright start for their caretaker manager Willie McFaul and they never let their fans down either. The game didn't start too brightly for the Reds when Kenny Dalglish, who selected himself in place of Paul Walsh, limped off in the first half hour with a badly cut knee to be replaced by Craig Johnston. It didn't really matter because on the day Newcastle were first to every ball and Liverpool only managed one shot on target by Steve Nicol. The second half went very much the same way and George Reilly scored what was to be the winner from an easy header, supplied by the fantastic Peter Beardsley who had dominated the game from the first whistle.

1991	Luton Town	A	League Division 1	0–0
1996	Sunderland	H	Premier League	0–0

AUGUST 25TH

1923	West Bromwich Albion	A	League Division 1	0–2
1928	Bury	H	League Division 1	3–0

Liverpool opened the new Kop which had been redesigned with a huge roof erected to accommodate 30,000. Alongside the Kop sat the mast of the Great Eastern, one of the first iron ships, which had been rescued from the breakers yard. The Kop, after the Spion Kop hill in South Africa where more than 300 local soldiers lost their lives in a battle during the Boer War, was named by Ernest Jones in 1906.

1934	Blackburn Rovers	H	League Division 1	2–0
1948	Sheffield United	H	League Division 1	3–3
1951	Chelsea	A	League Division 1	3–1
1956	Bury	A	League Division 2	2–0
1965	Sheffield United	H	League Division 1	0–1
1970	Crystal Palace	H	League Division 1	1–1

1973	Stoke City	H	League Division 1	1–0
1976	West Bromwich Albion	A	League Division 1	1–0
1979	West Bromwich Albion	H	League Division 1	3–1
1984	Norwich City	A	League Division 1	3–3

Jan Molby made his debut for the club after his move from Ajax.

1986	Manchester City	H	League Division 1	0–0
1990	Sheffield United	A	League Division 1	3–1
1992	Ipswich Town	A	Premier League	2–2
1993	Tottenham Hotspur	H	Premier League	1–2

AUGUST 26TH

| 1922 | Arsenal | A | League Division 1 | 5–2 |
| 1933 | Wolves | A | League Division 1 | 2–3 |

Sam English made his debut for the club shortly after his £8,000 move from Glasgow Rangers. Sam, who was a Championship winner and Scottish Cup winner with Rangers as well as top scorer in Scotland with over 50 goals in season 1931–32 will always be remembered as the player who was involved in the tragic accident with Celtic goalkeeper John Thompson who lost his life after a collision with English in an Old Firm game. Even though he was not to blame it had a deep effect on his career and he decided to move south, although it is safe to say he never reached the heights of his potential after that tragic day on 5 September 1931.

1950	Sunderland	H	League Division 1	4–0
1953	Newcastle United	H	League Division 1	2–2
1959	Bristol Rovers	H	League Division 2	4–2
1961	Leeds United	H	League Division 2	5–0

Roger Hunt scored his first hat-trick of the season.

1962	Blackburn Rovers	A	League Division 1	0–1
1964	Leeds United	A	League Division 1	2–4
1967	Newcastle United	H	League Division 1	6–0
1972	West Ham United	H	League Division 1	3–2
1975	Leeds United	A	League Division 1	3–0
1978	Manchester City	A	League Division 1	4–1
1985	Ipswich Town	H	League Division 1	5–0

After experiencing many emotions in the opening three games of the season, Dalglish who was to miss the next four games, had called for an improved all-round performance from his team, and unfortunately for Ipswich they felt the backlash as Liverpool were rampant from the kick-off. After 25 minutes Liverpool lead 3–0 thanks to Steve Nicol and two goals from Ian Rush and it could quite easily have been five. Not sitting back on their lead Liverpool continued to attack in the second half in an even more relentless fashion and added a couple of more goals through Molby and substitute Craig Johnston. It was a truly remarkable performance and after four games played Liverpool had earned seven points and were in 4th position in the table five points behind leaders Manchester United.

| 1989 | Luton Town | A | League Division 1 | 0–0 |
| 1995 | Tottenham Hotspur | A | Premier League | 3–1 |

AUGUST 27TH

1921	Sunderland	A	League Division 1	0–3
1927	Sheffield United	A	League Division 1	1–1
1932	Wolves	H	League Division 1	5–1
1938	Chelsea	H	League Division 1	2–1
1947	Manchester United	A	League Division 1	0–2
1949	Everton	A	League Division 1	0–0
1952	Sheffield Wednesday	H	League Division 1	1–0
1955	Hull City	H	League Division 2	3–0
1960	Middlesbrough	A	League Division 2	1–1
1966	Everton	A	League Division 1	1–3
1968	Everton	A	League Division 1	0–0
1969	Crystal Palace	A	League Division 1	3–1

1971 Steve Harkness was born in Carlisle.

1974	Wolves	H	League Division 1	2–0
1977	West Bromwich Albion	H	League Division 1	3–0
1980	Bradford City	A	League Cup 2nd round 1st leg	0–1
1983	Wolves	A	League Division 1	1–1
1984	West Ham United	H	League Division 1	3–0
1988	Charlton Athletic	A	League Division 1	3–0
1991	Queens Park Rangers	H	League Division 1	1–0

Steve Harkness made his debut on his 20th birthday.

AUGUST 28TH

1920	Manchester City	H	League Division 1	4–2
1926	Manchester United	H	League Division 1	4–2

John Evans was born in Essex. John started his career with Charlton Athletic where he stayed for three years before being brought to Anfield for £12,500 in December 1953.

1937 Chelsea   A   League Division 1   1–6

Ted Hartson made his debut for Liverpool after his summer transfer from Mansfield Town where he scored an amazing 81 goals in just 70 appearances. He managed just five games for the Reds but kept up his impressive goal ratio with three goals before the War interrupted his career.

1947 Emlyn Hughes born in Barrow. He joined Blackpool in September 1964 and after barely 27 appearances was signed by Liverpool for £65,000 in March 1967.

1948	Sunderland	H	League Division 1	4–0
1954	Derby County	A	League Division 1	2–3
1957	Huddersfield Town	H	League Division 2	1–1
1963	Nottingham Forest	H	League Division 1	1–2
1967	Arsenal	A	League Division 1	0–2
1971	Leicester City	H	League Division 1	3–2
1973	Coventry City	A	League Division 1	0–1

1974 For both their actions that led to their sending off and their reactions as they left the field, Kevin Keegan of Liverpool and Billy Bremner of Leeds were both fined £500 and banned from the game until the end of September by the FA. The charge, bringing the game into disrepute, relates to the FA Charity Shield on August 10th. Leeds chairman Manny Cussins said after the punishment had been announced: 'It is a colossal fine –

and all because they took off their shirts. It was a show of temper in the heat of the moment.'

1976	Birmingham City	A	League Division 1	1–2
1978	Sheffield United	A	League Cup 2nd round	0–1
1982	West Bromwich Albion	H	League Division 1	2–0
1990	Nottingham Forest	H	League Division 1	2–0
1993	Leeds United	H	Premier League	2–0
1994	Arsenal	H	Premier League	3–0

Robbie Fowler of Liverpool netted the fastest hat-trick in the Premier Division with three goals in four minutes 33 seconds. The remaining 85 minutes didn't produce much else except three points!

| 1997 | Leeds United | H | Premier League | 2–0 |

AUGUST 29TH

1923	Birmingham City	H	League Division 1	6–2
1925	Leicester City	A	League Division 1	1–3
1931	Newcastle United	A	League Division 1	1–0
1932	Sheffield United	A	League Division 1	2–6
1934	Manchester City	A	League Division 1	1–3
1936	Stoke City	H	League Division 1	2–1

1938   Gerry Byrne was born in Liverpool. A purely one-club man for Gerry who joined the professional ranks straight from school, where he was to stay for his entire career.

1951	Burnley	H	League Division 1	3–1
1953	Bolton Wanderers	A	League Division 1	0–2
1956	Notts County	H	League Division 2	3–3
1959	Hull City	H	League Division 2	5–3
1962	Manchester City	H	League Division 1	4–1
1964	Blackburn Rovers	A	League Division 1	2–3
1970	West Bromwich Albion	A	League Division 1	1–1
1979	Tranmere Rovers	A	League Cup 2nd round	0–0
1981	Wolves	A	League Division 1	0–1

Bruce Grobbelaar made his debut after being bought as a replacement for Ray Clemence who had moved to Spurs. Bruce was not to miss a game for the next five years. Mark Lawrenson also made his debut after his record-breaking move a few days earlier from Brighton and Hove Albion.

1987	Coventry City	A	League Division 1	4–1
1988	Nottingham Forest	H	Mercantile Credit Trophy	4–1
1992	Leeds United	A	Premier League	2–2

AUGUST 30TH

| 1919 | Bradford City | A | League Division 1 | 3–1 |

Harry Chambers scored on his debut for the club.

1922	Sunderland	A	League Division 1	0–1
1924	Aston Villa	H	League Division 1	2–4
1926	Aston Villa	A	League Division 1	1–1
1930	Blackburn Rovers	H	League Division 1	2–1
1933	Stoke City	H	League Division 1	1–1

1947	Stoke City	A	League Division 1	2–0
1948	Sheffield United	A	League Division 1	2–1
1950	Manchester United	A	League Division 1	0–1
1952	Stoke City	H	League Division 1	3–2
1958	Sunderland	A	League Division 2	1–2
1961	Sunderland	A	League Division 2	4–1

1961 Roger Hunt scored another two goals, which meant he had scored seven goals in just three games. It was to set the tone for the season as he finished with 41 goals in 41 games.

1966	Manchester City	H	League Division 1	3–2
1969	Sheffield Wednesday	A	League Division 1	1–1
1972	Leicester City	A	League Division 1	2–3
1975	Leicester City	A	League Division 1	1–1
1977	Chelsea	H	League Cup 2nd round	2–0
1980	Norwich City	H	League Division 1	4–1
1986	Arsenal	H	League Division 1	2–1
1989	Real Madrid	A	Friendly	0–2

1994 Don Hutchinson was sold to West Ham for £1.5 million after four years at the club. He had made 49 appearances scoring on 10 occasions.

1995	QPR	H	Premier League	1–0

AUGUST 31ST

1909 The dispute between the Football Association and the Players Union had grown over the previous few weeks to such an extent there was now a real threat that the Football League season, due to start the following day would have to be postponed. Whilst it was Manchester United's players who had been the most resolute throughout the dispute, support for their actions had grown and players from Newcastle, Sunderland, Middlesbrough, Liverpool and Everton had soon joined with their Manchester counterparts. This forced the FA to the bargaining table and an agreement was hammered out at the eleventh hour; the players had the right to join the Union and the FA would recognise it, only if the Union in turn dropped plans to affiliate with the General Federation of Trade Unions.

1921	Manchester City	H	League Division 1	3–2
1927	Bury	H	League Division 1	5–1
1929	Middlesbrough	A	League Division 1	0–5
1935	Chelsea	A	League Division 1	2–2
1946	Sheffield United	A	League Division 1	1–0

1946 Despite playing for the previous six years during the war it wasn't until this game that Billy Liddell played his first official game for the club.

1948	Stoke City	H	League Division 1	1–1

1954 Alan Kennedy was born in Sunderland. Alan started his career with Newcastle where he had six very steady years, and was unlucky to have lost in both his visits to Wembley in the 1974 FA Cup final and the 1976 League Cup final. He moved to Liverpool in the August of 1978 for £330,000.

1955	Sheffield Wednesday	A	League Division 2	1–1
1957	Cardiff City	H	League Division 2	3–0
1960	Southampton	H	League Division 2	0–1

Fifteen years to the day after making his official debut for the club Billy Liddell played his last game. If it wasn't for the War years he might have gone on and broken all sorts of club records but still ended up with an impressive record of 229 goals in 537 appearances. His outstanding ability deserved more than his one medal he won in 1946/47 season for the Division 1 Championship.

1963	Blackpool	H	League Division 1	1–2
1968	Leeds United	A	League Division 1	0–1
1974	Chelsea	A	League Division 1	3–0
1976	West Bromwich Albion	H	League Cup 2nd round	1–1
1982	Birmingham City	A	League Division 1	0–0

Steve Nicol started his long and distinguished career with the club with his first appearance.

| 1983 | Norwich City | A | League Division 1 | 1–0 |
| 1985 | West Ham United | A | League Division 1 | 2–2 |

This game will not be remembered in history as one of the club's finest performances, however, it will be remembered as a point gained rather than anything else. Bruce Grobbelaar had one of those eccentric days, and both West Ham goals scored by Frank McAvennie could have been prevented, but that was Bruce's style and fortunately they only occurred every now and again. Johnston and Whelan with two very similar efforts both headed goals earned the point against a West Ham team that proved very hard to beat during the season at Upton Park, winning 17 out of their 21 games.

1991	Everton	H	League Division 1	3–1
1994	Southampton	A	Premier League	2–0
1996	Norway XI	Oslo	Friendly	1–1

SEPTEMBER 1ST

| 1892 | Rotherham Town | H | Friendly | 7–1 |

The first-ever game for the newly formed team and a convincing victory to start with.

1894	Blackburn Rovers	A	League Division 1	1–1
1896	Sheffield Wednesday	A	League Division 2	2–1
1900	Blackburn Rovers	H	League Division 1	3–0
1904	Burton United	H	League Division 2	2–0
1906	Stoke City	H	League Division 1	1–0
1908	Aston Villa	H	League Division 1	3–2
1913	Derby County	A	League Division 1	1–1
1919	Arsenal	H	League Division 1	2–3
1920	West Bromwich Albion	A	League Division 1	1–1
1923	West Bromwich Albion	H	League Division 1	0–0
1928	Aston Villa	A	League Division 1	1–3
1930	West Ham United	A	League Division 1	0–7
1934	Arsenal	A	League Division 1	1–8
1937	Portsmouth	H	League Division 1	3–2
1951	Huddersfield Town	H	League Division 1	2–1
1954	Plymouth Argyle	H	League Division 2	3–3
1956	Grimsby Town	H	League Division 2	3–2
1959	Bristol Rovers	A	League Division 2	0–1
1962	Sheffield United	H	League Division 1	2–0

1965	Sheffield United	A	League Division 1	0–0
1971	Manchester City	A	League Division 1	0–1
1973	Leicester City	A	League Division 1	1–1
1979	Southampton	A	League Division 1	2–3
1981	Middlesbrough	H	League Division 1	1–1
1984	Queens Park Rangers	H	League Division 1	1–1

1989 John Aldridge was sold to Spanish club Real Sociedad after nearly two and a half years at Liverpool. The prolific goalscorer played 101 games scoring 61 times. After a short time in Spain John returned to England to play for Tranmere Rovers where he later went on to the position of Player–Manager. Still scoring goals, John passed Jimmy Greaves' record of 468 career goals.

| 1990 | Aston Villa | H | League Division 1 | 2–1 |
| 1992 | Southampton | H | Premier League | 1–1 |

Mark Wright scored his first ever goal against the club where he made his name at.

| 1993 | Coventry City | A | Premier League | 0–1 |

SEPTEMBER 2ND

| 1893 | Middlesbrough | A | League Division 2 | 2–0 |

After spending just one year in the Lancashire League the club were duly elected to the Football League and this was the first fixture that they played. The honour of the first ever goal recorded for the club in the Football League went to Malcolm McVean.

1899	Stoke City	A	League Division 1	2–2
1901	Small Heath	A	League Division 1	0–0
1905	Arsenal	A	League Division 1	1–3
1907	Nottingham Forest	A	League Division 1	3–1
1911	Arsenal	A	League Division 1	2–2
1914	Bolton Wanderers	H	League Division 1	4–3
1922	Arsenal	A	League Division 1	0–1
1925	Notts County	H	League Division 1	2–0
1931	Bolton Wanderers	H	League Division 1	2–2
1933	Sheffield United	H	League Division 1	3–2
1936	Portsmouth	A	League Division 1	2–6
1950	Aston Villa	A	League Division 1	1–1
1953	Newcastle United	A	League Division 1	0–4
1961	Norwich City	A	League Division 2	2–1
1964	Leeds United	H	League Division 1	2–1
1967	West Bromwich Albion	A	League Division 1	2–0
1972	Derby County	A	League Division 1	1–2
1978	Tottenham Hotspur	H	League Division 1	7–0

Spurs parading their World Cup stars Ossie Ardilles and Ricky Villa left Anfield totally humiliated and thankful that they never conceded double figures. One of the most comprehensive performances in modern times at Anfield.

| 1980 | Bradford City | H | League Cup 2nd round 2nd leg | 4–0 |

1994 John Scales was bought from Wimbledon for £3.5 million.

SEPTEMBER 3RD

| 1892 | Higher Walton | H | Lancashire League | 8–0 |

The first-ever competitive game for the club. Whilst it was as comprehensive a victory imaginable there was only an estimated crowd of 200, however, news soon reached other parts of the city and the crowds started to rise dramatically.

1894	Burnley	A	League Division 1	3–3
1898	Sheffield Wednesday	H	League Division 1	4–0

After playing in blue and white quartered shirts for the previous five years Liverpool changed to a new strip of all red which was worn for the first time. Alex Raisbeck made his debut after signing for the club from Hibernian. He was to prove as influential over the next 11 years at the club and ranks as one of the all-time greats of Liverpool.

1904	Glossop	H	League Division 2	2–2
1910	Bradford City	H	League Division 1	1–2
1921	Sunderland	H	League Division 1	2–1
1927	Aston Villa	H	League Division 1	0–0
1932	Newcastle United	A	League Division 1	3–4

1937 Tom Leishman was born in Stirling. Joined Liverpool from St.Mirren, where he won a Scottish Cup winners' medal, in November 1959 for a fee in the region of £10,000.

1938	Preston North End	A	League Division 1	0–1
1947	Manchester United	H	League Division 1	2–2
1949	Arsenal	A	League Division 1	2–1
1952	Sheffield Wednesday	A	League Division 1	2–0
1955	Blackburn Rovers	A	League Division 2	3–3
1956	West Ham United	A	League Division 2	1–1
1958	Brighton & Hove Albion	H	League Division 2	5–0
1960	Brighton & Hove Albion	H	League Division 2	2–0
1962	West Ham United	A	League Division 1	0–1
1963	Nottingham Forest	A	League Division 1	0–0
1966	West Ham United	A	League Division 1	1–1
1969	Watford	A	League Cup 2nd round	2–1
1977	Birmingham City	A	League Division 1	1–0
1983	Nottingham Forest	H	League Division 1	1–0
1985	Nottingham Forest	H	League Division 1	2–0

Nottingham Forest arrived at Anfield and played their familiar counter-attacking game, and proved very hard to break down. It was always going to be something special that beat them and Ronnie Whelan provided two pieces of magic. The first came 10 minutes into the second half with a shot from all of 35 yards that left Forest keeper Hans Segers groping in thin air as the ball hit the net. Whilst the first was spectacular his second was equally brilliant, curling the ball in the corner, just like he did in the 2–1 victory over Manchester United in the 1983 League Cup final.

1986	Leicester City	A	League Division 1	1–2
1988	Manchester United	H	League Division 1	1–0

SEPTEMBER 4TH

1897	Stoke City	A	League Division 1	2–2
1909	Chelsea	A	League Division 1	1–2
1911	Bolton Wanderers	A	League Division 1	1–2
1912	Oldham Athletic	H	League Division 1	2–0

Centre-half Bob Ferguson made his debut after his much publicised move from Third Lanark.

1920	Manchester City	A	League Division 1	2–3
1926	Derby County	A	League Division 1	1–2
1929	Huddersfield Town	H	League Division 1	3–0
1930	Roy Saunders was born in Salford. He joined the professional ranks at Anfield in 1948.			
1933	Stoke City	A	League Division 1	1–1
1935	Manchester City	H	League Division 1	0–2
1937	Charlton Athletic	H	League Division 1	1–2
1946	Middlesbrough	H	League Division 1	0–1
1948	Wolves	A	League Division 1	0–0
1954	West Ham United	H	League Division 2	1–2
1957	Huddersfield Town	A	League Division 2	1–2
1965	Blackpool	A	League Division 1	3–2
1968	Sheffield United	H	League Cup 2nd round	4–0
1971	Tottenham Hotspur	A	League Division 1	0–2
1973	Derby County	H	League Division 1	2–0
1976	Coventry City	H	League Division 1	3–1
1979	Tranmere Rovers	H	League Cup 2nd round replay	4–0
1982	Arsenal	A	League Division 1	2–0
1984	Luton Town	A	League Division 1	2–1
1996	Coventry City	A	Premier League	1–0

SEPTEMBER 5TH

| 1896 | Blackburn Rovers | A | League Division 1 | 0–1 |

Referee C.E. Sutcliffe disallowed six goals, a record, in this First Division match. Only one goal was deemed allowable and Rovers scored it!

1903	Nottingham Forest	A	League Division 1	1–2
1908	Chelsea	H	League Division 1	2–1
1914	Notts County	H	League Division 1	1–1
1923	Birmingham City	A	League Division 1	1–2
1925	West Ham United	H	League Division 1	0–0
1928	Sheffield United	H	League Division 1	1–2
1931	Aston Villa	H	League Division 1	2–0
1934	Manchester City	H	League Division 1	2–1
1936	Charlton Athletic	A	League Division 1	1–1
1951	Arsenal	A	League Division 1	0–0
1953	Preston North End	H	League Division 1	1–5
1959	Sheffield United	A	League Division 2	1–2
1964	Blackpool	H	League Division 1	2–2
1966	Blackpool	A	League Division 1	2–1
1967	Nottingham Forest	A	League Division 1	1–0
1970	Manchester United	H	League Division 1	1–1
1972	Carlisle United	A	League Cup 2nd round	1–1
1981	Arsenal	H	League Division 1	2–0
1987	West Ham United	A	League Division 1	1–1
1992	Chelsea	H	Premier League	2–1

Paul Elliott of Chelsea was carried off the field after a challenge by Dean Saunders. Although not apparent at the time, the injury was of such severity that Elliott's career ended and it precipated civil court action brought by Elliott against Saunders

SEPTEMBER 6TH

1892	Kenny Campbell was born in Glasgow. After an initial period in Scotland at the beginning of his career with Glencairn and Cambuslang Rovers, the likeable goalkeeper moved to Liverpool in May 1911.			
1902	Blackburn Rovers	H	League Division 1	5–2
1909	Bolton Wanderers	A	League Division 1	2–1
1913	Blackburn Rovers	A	League Division 1	2–6
1919	Bradford City	H	League Division 1	2–1
1920	West Bromwich Albion	H	League Division 1	0–0
1922	Sunderland	H	League Division 1	5–1
1924	Arsenal	A	League Division 1	0–2
1930	Middlesbrough	A	League Division 1	3–3
1947	Burnley	H	League Division 1	1–1
1950	Tottenham Hotspur	H	League Division 1	2–1
1952	Manchester City	A	League Division 1	2–0
1954	Bristol Rovers	A	League Division 2	0–3
1958	Middlesbrough	A	League Division 2	1–2
1965	West Ham United	A	League Division 1	5–1
1969	Coventry City	H	League Division 1	2–1
1975	Sheffield United	H	League Division 1	1–0
1976	West Bromwich Albion	A	League Cup 2nd round replay	0–1
1980	Birmingham City	A	League Division 1	1–1
1983	Southampton	H	League Division 1	1–1
1985	Steve McMahon was signed from Aston Villa for £350,000.			
1986	West Ham United	A	League Division 1	5–2
1995	Jason McAteer was signed from Bolton Wanderers from £4.5 million.			
1996	John Barnes made his 79th and final appearance for England in the 0–0 draw with Colombia at Wembley. Often the target, unfairly, from abuse by his own so-called supporters at Wembley, Barnes was a good servant to his country, scoring on 11 occasions, including that famous one against Brazil in 1984. As one international career ended another began when Jamie Redknapp won his first cap in the same game.			

SEPTEMBER 7TH

1895	Notts County	A	League Division 2	3–2
1896	Bolton Wanderers	H	League Division 1	0–2
1901	Stoke City	A	League Division 1	0–1
1907	Manchester United	A	League Division 1	0–4
1912	Arsenal	H	League Division 1	3–0
1921	Manchester City	A	League Division 1	1–1
1929	Everton	H	League Division 1	0–3
1932	Sheffield United	H	League Division 1	2–2
1935	Everton	H	League Division 1	6–0

A crowd of 48,000 were at Anfield for the opening derby of the season, in what was to be one the most one-sided derby matches ever. Fred Howe opened the scoring on a quarter of an hour with a glancing header, Gordon Hodgson's snap shot made it two before half an hour had passed and Hodgson added a third five minutes later. Shortly before half-time Howe made it four to Liverpool, although in fairness to Everton they had suffered two bad injuries to Dixie Dean and Williams. Liverpool eased off the pedal in the second half, but the strain of having to battle with only nine fully fit players finally told in the final four minutes as Howe netted twice to take his tally to four for the game and complete a great derby win.

1938	Manchester United	H	League Division 1	1–0
1946	Chelsea	H	League Division 1	7–4

Billy Liddell scored his first official goal for the club after seven minutes in a game where Bob Paisley made his senior debut for the club.

1949	Manchester United	H	League Division 1	1–1
1953	Wolves	A	League Division 1	1–2
1955	Bristol Rovers	H	League Division 2	0–0
1957	Fulham	A	League Division 2	2–2
1960	Luton Town	H	League Division 2	2–2
1963	Chelsea	A	League Division 1	3–1
1968	Queens Park Rangers	H	League Division 1	2–0
1971	Hull City	H	League Cup 2nd round	3–0
1974	Tottenham Hotspur	H	League Division 1	5–2

1977 The England team that faced Switzerland at Wembley included six players from Liverpool and ex-Anfield star Kevin Keegan, the highest number of players drawn from one club since Arsenal supplied seven against Italy at Highbury in 1934. Despite the familiarity of the team, they only drew 0–0. Terry McDermott won the first of his 25 caps, he was joined in the team on the night by Clemence, Neal, Hughes, Callaghan and Ray Kennedy.

1982	Nottingham Forest	H	League Division 1	4–3
1985	Watford	H	League Division 1	3–1

Not a fantastic performance, however, Molby was outstanding in midfield, something to do with the fact that new signing Steve McMahon was watching from the stands after his transfer from Aston Villa. Watford took the lead, the first goal to be scored at Anfield in the season, after a superb free kick by John Barnes was converted by Colin West who had run Lawrenson ragged all afternoon. Phil Neal had equalised through a penalty to put the teams level at half-time. Lady Luck shone on Liverpool in the second half and a couple of flukes earned Liverpool the points with Johnston and Rush being credited with the goals, with Johnston's taking two deflections before ballooning into the goal past the helpless Tony Coton.

1991	Notts County	A	League Division 1	2–1
1996	Southampton	H	Premier League	2–1

SEPTEMBER 8TH

1894	Aston Villa	H	League Division 1	1–2

Liverpool had entered the Second Division at the beginning of the 1893–94 season and won the League without losing a game. However, since automatic promotion and relegation had yet to be introduced, they were required to play in the Test Matches, beating Newton Heath (now known as Manchester United) to gain promotion. They had then drawn their first two games in the First Division, a run of 31 games without defeat that was finally brought to an end by this 1–2 defeat by Villa at Anfield. Villa had previously been responsible for ending Preston's unbeaten run from the start of the Football League in 1888.

1900	Stoke City	A	League Division 1	2–1
1906	Blackburn Rovers	A	League Division 1	1–1
1919	Arsenal	A	League Division 1	0–1

Dick Forshaw made his debut for the club.

1923	Preston North End	A	League Division 1	1–0
1926	Aston Villa	H	League Division 1	2–1
1928	Leicester City	H	League Division 1	6–3
1934	Portsmouth	H	League Division 1	0–1
1937	Portsmouth	A	League Division 1	1–1
1947	Sheffield United	A	League Division 1	1–3

Kevin Baron made his League debut for the club.

1948	Arsenal	A	League Division 1	1–1
1951	Wolves	A	League Division 1	1–2
1956	Doncaster Rovers	A	League Division 2	1–1
1962	Nottingham Forest	A	League Division 1	1–3
1970	Mansfield Town	A	League Cup 2nd round	0–0
1973	Chelsea	H	League Division 1	1–0
1979	Coventry City	H	League Division 1	4–0
1984	Arsenal	A	League Division 1	1–3
1990	Wimbledon	A	League Division 1	2–1

SEPTEMBER 9TH

1893	Lincoln City	H	League Division 2	3–0
1899	Sunderland	H	League Division 1	0–2
1905	Blackburn Rovers	H	League Division 1	1–3
1911	Manchester City	H	League Division 1	2–2
1912	Chelsea	A	League Division 1	2–1
1922	Preston North End	A	League Division 1	3–1
1931	Middlesbrough	A	League Division 1	1–4
1933	Aston Villa	A	League Division 1	2–4
1936	Portsmouth	H	League Division 1	0–0
1950	Derby County	H	League Division 1	1–0
1959	Scunthorpe United	H	League Division 2	2–0
1961	Scunthorpe United	H	League Division 2	2–1
1963	Wolves	A	League Division 1	3–1
1964	Leicester City	A	League Division 1	0–2
1967	Chelsea	H	League Division 1	3–1
1969	Sunderland	H	League Division 1	2–0
1972	Wolves	H	League Division 1	4–2
1978	Birmingham City	A	League Division 1	3–0
1989	Derby County	A	League Division 1	3–0
1995	Wimbledon	A	Premier League	0–1

SEPTEMBER 10TH

1898	Sunderland	A	League Division 1	0–1
1904	Chesterfield	A	League Division 2	1–1
1906	Bury	H	League Division 1	2–2
1910	Blackburn Rovers	A	League Division 1	2–1
1921	Sheffield United	A	League Division 1	1–0
1927	Sunderland	A	League Division 1	1–2
1928	Sheffield United	A	League Division 1	3–1
1930	Bolton Wanderers	H	League Division 1	7–2
1932	Aston Villa	H	League Division 1	0–0
1938	Charlton Athletic	H	League Division 1	1–0
1949	Bolton Wanderers	H	League Division 1	1–1
1952	Tottenham Hotspur	H	League Division 1	2–1
1955	Lincoln City	H	League Division 2	2–1
1956	Hibernian	A	Friendly	2–1
1958	Sheffield United	H	League Division 2	2–1
1960	Ipswich Town	A	League Division 2	0–1
1966	Sheffield Wednesday	H	League Division 1	1–1
1974	Brentford	H	League Cup 2nd round	2–1
1975	York City	A	League Cup 2nd round	1–0
1977	Coventry City	H	League Division 1	2–0
1983	Arsenal	A	League Division 1	2–0
1988	Aston Villa	A	League Division 1	1–1
1994	West Ham United	H	Premier League	0–0

SEPTEMBER 11TH

1897	Preston North End	H	League Division 1	0–0
1905	Aston Villa	A	League Division 1	0–5
1909	Blackburn Rovers	H	League Division 1	3–1
1920	Oldham Athletic	H	League Division 1	5–2
1926	Sheffield United	H	League Division 1	5–1
1935	Manchester City	A	League Division 1	0–6
1937	Preston North End	A	League Division 1	1–4
1946	Manchester United	A	League Division 1	0–5
1948	Bolton Wanderers	H	League Division 1	0–1
1954	Blackburn Rovers	A	League Division 2	3–4
1965	Fulham	H	League Division 1	2–1
1971	Southampton	H	League Division 1	1–0
1976	Derby County	A	League Division 1	3–2
1982	Luton Town	H	League Division 1	3–3

SEPTEMBER 12TH

1896	Derby County	H	League Division 1	2–0
1903	Sheffield Wednesday	H	League Division 1	1–3
1908	Blackburn Rovers	A	League Division 1	0–1
1914	Sunderland	A	League Division 1	2–2
1925	Arsenal	A	League Division 1	1–1

ABOVE: Billy Liddell
INSET: Elisha Scott

TOP: Programme from the 1989 FA Cup final between Liverpool and Everton, which Liverpool won 3–2 after extra time

BOTTOM: Programme from the 1986 FA Cup final between Liverpool and Everton. Liverpool won 3–1 to complete the double

The Hillsborough memorial at Anfield, recording the names of the fans who
lost their lives in the 1989 disaster

TOP: Kenny Dalglish
celebrates the double

BOTTOM: Alan Hansen

Ian Rush and Robbie Fowler celebrate after the 1995 Coca-Cola Cup final win over Bolton

Michael Owen collects the ball after scoring his first goal for
Liverpool

Ian St John

ABOVE: The Shankly gates at Anfield

LEFT: Bill Shankly

1931	Leicester City	A	League Division 1	1–2
1936	Grimsby Town	H	League Division 1	7–1
1951	Arsenal	H	League Division 1	0–0
1953	Tottenham Hotspur	A	League Division 1	1–2
1959	Middlesbrough	H	League Division 2	1–2
1962	West Ham United	H	League Division 1	2–1
1964	Sheffield Wednesday	A	League Division 1	0–1
1970	Newcastle United	A	League Division 1	0–0
1972	Eintracht Frankfurt	H	UEFA Cup 1st round 1st leg	2–0
1973	Derby County	A	League Division 1	1–3
1981	Ipswich Town	A	League Division 1	0–2

1984 Steve Nicol made his international debut for Scotland in the 6–1 win over Yugoslavia. John Wark who also played, made his 29th and last appearance, he scored seven goals in his international career.

| 1987 | Oxford United | H | League Division 1 | 2–0 |

John Barnes scored his first goal for the club.

| 1989 | Crystal Palace | H | League Division 1 | 9–0 |

Perry Suckling actually had a good game in the Crystal Palace goal during this game, it was the other ten men that let him down on the night, in one of the most bizarre games played at Anfield. Every time a Liverpool player shot it ended up in the net. Eight different players scored on the night, the most emotional one being John Aldridge. He was about to leave the club to sign for Real Sociedad in Spain, he stepped off the substitutes bench to take a penalty and scored his last goal in a Liverpool shirt. John only managed to play 86 games in total for the club but scored 61 times in that period. Will sadly be remembered for being the first player ever to miss a penalty in a Cup final.

1992	Sheffield United	A	Premier League	0–1
1993	Blackburn Rovers	H	Premier League	0–1
1995	Spartak Vladikavkaz	A	UEFA Cup 1st round 1st leg	2–1
1996	My Pa 47	A	European Cup-Winners' Cup 1st round 1st leg	1–0

SEPTEMBER 13TH

1894	Bolton Wanderers	H	League Division 1	1–2
1902	Sunderland	A	League Division 1	1–2
1913	Sunderland	H	League Division 1	1–3
1919	Aston Villa	H	League Division 1	2–1
1924	Manchester City	H	League Division 1	5–3
1930	Huddersfield Town	H	League Division 1	1–4
1947	Portsmouth	A	League Division 1	0–1
1952	Portsmouth	H	League Division 1	1–1
1958	Charlton Athletic	H	League Division 2	3–0
1967	Bolton Wanderers	H	League Cup 2nd round	1–1
1969	Manchester United	A	League Division 1	0–1
1975	Ipswich Town	A	League Division 1	0–2
1978	Nottingham Forest	A	European Cup 1st round 1st leg	0–2
1980	West Bromwich Albion	H	League Division 1	4–0
1986	Charlton Athletic	H	League Division 1	2–0
1997	Sheffield Wednesday	H	Premier League	2–1

SEPTEMBER 14TH

1895	Newcastle United	H	League Division 2	5–1

George Allan made his League debut.

1901	Everton	H	League Division 1	2–2
1907	Blackburn Rovers	H	League Division 1	2–0
1908	Sheffield United	A	League Division 1	2–0
1912	Bradford City	A	League Division 1	0–2
1929	West Ham United	H	League Division 1	3–1
1935	Grimsby Town	H	League Division 1	7–2
1938	Middlesbrough	H	League Division 1	3–1
1946	Bolton Wanderers	A	League Division 1	3–1
1957	Middlesbrough	A	League Division 2	2–2
1960	Luton Town	A	League Division 2	1–2
1963	West Ham United	H	League Division 1	1–2
1964	Reykjavik	H	European Cup 1st round 2nd leg	6–1
1968	Ipswich Town	A	League Division 1	2–0
1974	Manchester City	A	League Division 1	0–2
1976	Crusaders	H	European Cup 1st round 1st leg	2–0
1982	Dundalk	A	European Cup 1st round 1st leg	1–0
1983	BK Odense	A	European Cup 1st round 1st leg	1–0
1985	Oxford United	A	League Division 1	2–2

Another disappointing day as a last-minute own goal by Alan Kennedy gave Oxford a share of the spoils in a rather drab affair. John Aldridge had given Oxford the lead in the first half and that's how the score remained until Ian Rush scored from about two yards to level things up. Craig Johnston scored a superb goal to give Liverpool the lead, and it seemed only a formality to hold out and take home the points. On top of the dropped points Ronnie Whelan needed seven stitches in a head wound after a horrific challenge by John Trewick, which was bad enough to warrant a red card, but only received a yellow from the very lenient referee Mr Moules. Alan Kennedy played his last game for Liverpool, before his transfer to Sunderland (the own goal had no bearing on the move!) in a £100,000 deal. Alan had played 347 games for the club scoring on 21 occasions, the most memorable being the winner in the 1981 European Cup final against Real Madrid in Paris. He had amassed quite a considerable collection of medals in his seven years at Anfield winning two European Cup winners' medals plus one runners-up medal, five Championship medals and four consecutive League Cup winners' medals between 1981 and 1984. If it wasn't for the fact that Kenny Sansom was the England left-back Alan would have added many more caps to the two that he earned in 1984 against Wales and Northern Ireland.

1991	Aston Villa	H	League Division 1	1–1

SEPTEMBER 15TH

1894	West Bromwich Albion	A	League Division 1	0–5
1900	West Bromwich Albion	H	League Division 1	5–0
1906	Sunderland	H	League Division 1	1–2
1923	Preston North End	H	League Division 1	3–1
1924	Blackburn Rovers	A	League Division 1	1–3
1928	Manchester United	A	League Division 1	2–2

1934	Everton	A	League Division 1	0–1
1937	Stoke City	H	League Division 1	3–0
1948	Arsenal	H	League Division 1	0–1
1951	Sunderland	H	League Division 1	2–2
1952	Tottenham Hotspur	A	League Division 1	1–3
1954	Bristol Rovers	H	League Division 2	5–3

John Evans scored all five goals, the first time a Liverpool player had done so for over 45 years since Andy McGuigan's effort in 1902.

1956	Stoke City	H	League Division 2	0–2
1958	Sheffield United	A	League Division 2	0–2
1962	Ipswich Town	H	League Division 1	1–1
1965	West Ham United	H	League Division 1	1–1
1970	Ferencvaros	H	European Fairs Cup 1st round 1st leg	1–0
1971	Servette Geneva	A		

European Cup-Winners' Cup 1st round 1st leg 1–2

1973	Birmingham City	A	League Division 1	1–1
1979	Leeds United	A	League Division 1	1–1
1984	Sunderland	H	League Division 1	1–1
1987	Charlton Athletic	H	League Division 1	3–2
1996	Leicester City	A	Premier League	3–0

SEPTEMBER 16TH

1893	Ardwick	A	League Division 2	0–0
1899	West Bromwich Albion	A	League Division 1	0–2
1905	Sunderland	A	League Division 1	2–1
1907	Sheffield United	A	League Division 1	0–0
1911	Everton	A	League Division 1	1–2
1922	Preston North End	H	League Division 1	5–2
1929	Huddersfield Town	A	League Division 1	0–3
1931	Middlesbrough	H	League Division 1	7–2
1933	Leicester City	H	League Division 1	1–3
1936	Chelsea	A	League Division 1	0–2
1950	Everton	A	League Division 1	3–1
1953	Wolves	H	League Division 1	1–1
1961	Brighton & Hove Albion	A	League Division 2	0–0
1963	Wolves	H	League Division 1	6–0
1967	Southampton	A	League Division 1	0–1
1969	Dundalk	H	European Fairs Cup 1st round 1st leg	10–0

Ray Clemence made his senior debut for the club after spending two years as understudy to Tommy Lawrence. Fortunately he didn't have too much to worry about on the night as Liverpool recorded their second highest victory in their history. Only three outfield players plus Clemence failed to get on the score sheet against the part timers.

1972	Arsenal	A	League Division 1	0–0

The highlight of this game was when one of the linesmen fell injured during the game at Highbury, a loudspeaker appeal requested a qualified referee. When no fourth official was forthcoming, television commentator Jimmy Hill – who was in the crowd in preparation for *Match of the Day* which was screening the game that day – took over.

(On the same day, referee Jim Finn collapsed and died of a heart attack during the Exeter v Stockport match).

1978	Coventry City	H	League Division 1	1–0
1981	Oulu Palloseura	A	European Cup 1st round 1st leg	1–0
1986	Everton	H	Screen Sport Super Cup final 1st Leg	3–1

In March both clubs had won through to the final of the Super Cup, the competition organised to give the clubs who had qualified for Europe, but were banned by UEFA, some form of compensation. The competition had been a farce, unloved by the fans and players alike and the final held over to the following season. There was at last a sponsor for the tournament, Screen Sport, and a trophy to be won, with the final to be decided over two legs. At Anfield just 20,660 fans, indicative of both the esteem with which the competition was held and how frequently the two sides were being paired, saw Liverpool win 3–1 thanks to two goals from Ian Rush and one from Steve McMahon as opposed to one goal from Kevin Sheedy.

1989	Norwich City	H	League Division 1	0–0
1990	Manchester United	H	League Division 1	4–0
1992	Apollon	H	European Cup-Winners' Cup 1st round 1st leg	6–1

Ian Rush scored four goals.

| 1995 | Blackburn Rovers | H | Premier League | 3–0 |
| 1997 | Celtic | A | UEFA Cup 1st round 1st leg | 2–2 |

SEPTEMBER 17TH

1898	Wolves	H	League Division 1	1–0
1904	Bradford	H	League Division 2	4–1
1910	Nottingham Forest	H	League Division 1	2–3
1921	Sheffield United	H	League Division 1	1–1
1927	Derby County	H	League Division 1	5–2
1932	Middlesbrough	A	League Division 1	1–0
1938	Bolton Wanderers	A	League Division 1	1–3
1947	Charlton Athletic	A	League Division 1	0–2
1949	Birmingham City	A	League Division 1	3–2
1955	Leicester City	A	League Division 2	1–3
1959	Scunthorpe United	A	League Division 2	1–1
1960	Scunthorpe United	H	League Division 2	3–2
1966	Southampton	A	League Division 1	2–1
1974	Stroms Drammen	H	European Cup-Winners' Cup 1st round 1st leg	11–0

The highest score the club has ever recorded in a senior competition. Every player scored on the night except Brian Hall and Ray Clemence.

1975	Hibernian	A	UEFA Cup 1st round 1st leg	0–1
1977	Ipswich Town	A	League Division 1	1–1
1980	Oulu Palloseura	A	European Cup 1st round 1st leg	1–1
1983	Aston Villa	H	League Division 1	2–1
1985	Southampton	H	Screen Sport Super Cup 1st round 1st leg	2–1
1988	Tottenham Hotspur	H	League Division 1	1–1

1993   David Burrows, who spent five years at the club was sold to West Ham. The hard-tackling left-back made 178 appearances for the club even scoring on three occasions. He was a regular during the Championship-winning team of 1990 and the 1992 FA

Cup winning team. He also played in the Charity Shield in 1989 and 1990. Julian Dicks was signed from West Ham as replacement for Burrows, for £1.5 million. The West Ham skipper had spent five years at Upton Park where he hardly missed a game and played over 200 games and scored 36 goals. Part of the swap deal involving both players was Mike Marsh. The young midfielder played over 60 games for Liverpool and was part of the 1992 FA Cup-winning team that defeated Sunderland 2–0.

1994 Manchester United   A   Premier League   0–2
Phil Babb made his debut for the club.

SEPTEMBER 18TH

1897 Sheffield Wednesday   A   League Division 1   2–4
1909 Nottingham Forest   A   League Division 1   4–1
1917 Phil Taylor was born in Bristol. After playing for Bristol Rovers for just under a year Liverpool secured his services for £5,000.
1920 Oldham Athletic   A   League Division 1   0–0
1924 Bury   A   League Division 1   0–0
1926 Arsenal   A   League Division 1   0–2
1935 Stoke City   H   League Division 1   2–0
1937 Grimsby Town   H   League Division 1   2–1
1948 Everton   A   League Division 1   1–1
Liverpool attracted the biggest ever crowd seen at Goodison Park for a League match, 78,299. Joe Fagan scored Liverpool's goal.
1954 Fulham   H   League Division 2   4–1
1958 John Aldridge was born in Liverpool. John had started his career with Newport County with whom he won the Welsh Cup in 1980 before moving to Oxford United for £78,000 where he started to make his name as a top marksman scoring on average seven goals every 10 games he played, he was part of Oxford's Division Two winning side and their 3–0 League Cup final triumph over QPR at Wembley the following year. He joined Liverpool in a £750,000 deal in January 1987.
1965 Tottenham Hotspur   A   League Division 1   1–2
1968 Atletico Bilbao   A   European Fairs Cup 1st round 1st leg   1–2
1971 Leeds United   A   League Division 1   0–1
1976 Tottenham Hotspur   H   League Division 1   2–0
1982 Swansea Town   A   League Division 1   3–0
1991 Kuusysi Lahti   H   UEFA Cup 1st round 1st leg   6–1
Dean Saunders scored four goals in this one-sided cup tie.
1993 Everton   A   Premier League   0–2

SEPTEMBER 19TH

1896 Bury   A   League Division 1   2–1
1903 Sunderland   A   League Division 1   1–2
1908 Bradford City   H   League Division 1   4–0
1910 Sheffield United   A   League Division 1   0–2
1914 Sheffield Wednesday   H   League Division 1   2–1
1925 Manchester United   H   League Division 1   5–0
1927 Bury   A   League Division 1   2–5
1931 Everton   H   League Division 1   1–3

1936	Everton	A	League Division 1	0–2

1937 Geoff Strong was born in Northumberland. Geoff arrived from Arsenal in 1964.

1953	Burnley	H	League Division 1	4–0
1957	Rotherham United	A	League Division 2	2–2
1959	Derby County	A	League Division 2	2–1
1964	Everton	H	League Division 1	0–4
1967	Malmo	A	European Fairs Cup 1st round 1st leg	2–0
1970	Nottingham Forest	H	League Division 1	3–0
1972	Carlisle United	H	League Cup 2nd round replay	5–1
1973	Jeunesse D'esch	A	European Cup 1st round 1st leg	1–1
1977	Lancashire XI	H	Friendly	2–4
1979	Dynamo Tbilisi	H	European Cup 1st round 1st leg	2–1
1981	Aston Villa	H	League Division 1	0–0
1984	Lech Poznan	A	European Cup 1st round 1st leg	1–0
1989	Wigan Athletic	H	League Cup 2nd round 1st leg	5–2
1992	Aston Villa	A	Premier League	2–4

SEPTEMBER 20TH

1895 Tommy Lucas was born in St Helens. After playing for his local sides he moved to Anfield in 1916 where he was to enjoy 17 years of sterling service.

1902	Stoke City	H	League Division 1	1–1
1913	Everton	A	League Division 1	2–1
1919	Aston Villa	A	League Division 1	1–0

1920 John Shepherd was born in Liverpool. He joined the club shortly after the end of the First World War.

1930	Aston Villa	A	League Division 1	2–4
1947	Bolton Wanderers	H	League Division 1	0–0
1952	Middlesbrough	H	League Division 1	4–1
1958	Bristol Rovers	A	League Division 2	3–1
1961	Newcastle United	A	League Division 2	2–1
1969	Stoke City	H	League Division 1	3–1
1975	Aston Villa	H	League Division 1	3–0
1980	Southampton	A	League Division 1	2–2
1986	Southampton	A	League Division 1	1–2
1987	Newcastle United	A	League Division 1	4–1
1988	Arsenal	A	Mercantile Credit Trophy semi-final	1–2
1995	Sunderland	H	Coca-Cola Cup 2nd round 1st leg	2–0
1997	Southampton	A	Premier League	1–1

SEPTEMBER 21ST

1895	Loughborough Town	A	League Division 2	4–2
1901	Sunderland	A	League Division 1	1–1
1907	Bolton Wanderers	A	League Division 1	4–0
1912	Manchester City	H	League Division 1	1–2
1914	Blackburn Rovers	A	League Division 1	2–4
1929	Manchester United	A	League Division 1	2–1
1935	Leeds United	A	League Division 1	0–1

Jack Balmer made his League debut.

1946	Everton	H	League Division 1	0–0
1957	Leyton Orient	H	League Division 2	3–0
1960	international XI	H	Friendly	4–2
1963	Sheffield United	A	League Division 1	0–3
1968	Leicester City	H	League Division 1	4–0
1974	Stoke City	H	League Division 1	3–0
1985	Everton	A	League Division 1	3–2

51,500 witnessed the 133rd Merseyside derby. Dalglish played a master stroke by moving Molby back into a five-man defence to combat the reigning champions strike force of Lineker, Sharp and co. Dalglish opened the scoring after 20 seconds scoring one of the fastest goals in derby history, and he also became the first manager to score in a Mersey derby, with a stunning goal without an Everton player touching the ball. Ian Rush then increased the lead finishing off another fine move. Everton must have wondered what had hit them. Steve McMahon playing against his former club completed the first half destruction with a fine goal, scoring from outside the box after he had initiated the move. Everton came back in the second half and reverted to just three at the back and brought on Adrian Heath. They had nothing to lose by committing themselves to attack and they were rewarded with goals from Sharp and Lineker to produce an exciting finale. Liverpool held on and might have taken a two-goal lead when Dalglish hit the bar when it was easier to score, but the miss was not to prove costly. Phil Neal came on as a substitute to equal Ian Callaghan's record of 29 consecutive derby matches.

1991	Leeds United	A	League Division 1	0–1
1994	Burnley	H	League Cup 2nd round 1st leg	2–0
1996	Chelsea	H	Premier League	5–1

SEPTEMBER 22ND

1894	Blackburn Rovers	H	League Division 1	2–2
1900	Everton	A	League Division 1	1–1
1906	Birmingham City	A	League Division 1	1–2
1923	Burnley	A	League Division 1	0–2
1928	Leeds United	H	League Division 1	1–1
1934	Leeds United	A	League Division 1	3–0
1951	Aston Villa	A	League Division 1	0–2
1956	Middlesbrough	A	League Division 2	1–1
1962	Everton	A	League Division 1	2–2
1970	Mansfield Town	H	League Cup 2nd round replay	3–2
1973	Tottenham Hotspur	H	League Division 1	3–2
1979	Norwich City	H	League Division 1	0–0
1981	Coventry City	A	League Division 1	2–1
1984	Manchester United	A	League Division 1	1–1
1990	Everton	A	League Division 1	3–2
1992	Chesterfield	H	League Cup 2nd round 1st leg	4–4
1993	Fulham	A	League Cup 2nd round 1st leg	3–1

Robbie Fowler scored on his debut for the club.

| 1997 | Aston Villa | H | Premier League | 3–0 |

SEPTEMBER 23RD

1892	Southport	H	Lancashire Cup	2–0
1893	Small Heath	H	League Division 2	2–1
1895	Fred Hopkin was born in Dewsbury.			
1899	Everton	H	League Division 1	1–2
1905	Birmingham City	H	League Division 1	2–0

Jim Bradley made his senior debut for the club. The left half who was signed from Stoke City where he made his debut and held a first-team place at the age of 17.

1911	West Bromwich Albion	H	League Division 1	1–3
1922	Burnley	H	League Division 1	3–0
1933	Tottenham Hotspur	A	League Division 1	3–0
1950	Fulham	A	League Division 1	1–2
1957	Stoke City	A	League Division 2	2–1
1961	Bury	H	League Division 2	5–0
1967	Everton	H	League Division 1	1–0

1970 Steve Heighway made his debut for the Republic of Ireland in the 0–2 defeat by Poland in Dublin.

1972	Sheffield United	H	League Division 1	5–0
1978	West Bromwich Albion	A	League Division 1	1–1
1980	Swindon Town	H	League Cup 3rd round	5–0
1986	Fulham	H	Littlewoods Cup 2nd Round 1st Leg	10–0

Fulham were on the end of Liverpool's record victory in this competition.

1987	Blackburn Rovers	A	Littlewoods Cup 2nd Round 1st Leg	1–1
1989	Everton	A	League Division 1	3–1

1991 Peter Beardsley after four years service was sold to Everton. In his spell at the club Peter played 170 times, scoring on 58 occasions.

1995	Bolton	H	Premier League	5–2

Robbie Fowler scored four goals and Steve Harkness the other, in what was to be his only goal of the season.

SEPTEMBER 24TH

1889 Bill Lacey was born in Wexford. Joined Everton from his local side Shelbourne before moving to Liverpool in 1912 where he was to spend 12 glorious years.

1892	Bury	H	Lancashire League	4–0
1898	Everton	A	League Division 1	2–1
1904	Lincoln City	A	League Division 2	2–0
1910	Manchester City	A	League Division 1	2–1
1921	Chelsea	A	League Division 1	1–0
1927	West Ham United	A	League Division 1	1–3
1932	Bolton Wanderers	H	League Division 1	0–1
1938	Leeds United	H	League Division 1	3–0
1949	Derby County	H	League Division 1	3–1

Phil Boersma was born in Kirkby. Phil signed first as an amateur before turning professional for the club in September 1968.

1955	Middlesbrough	H	League Division 2	1–1
1958	Brighton & Hove Albion	A	League Division 2	2–2
1960	Leyton Orient	A	League Division 2	3–1

1966	Sunderland	H	League Division 1	2–2
1969	Manchester City	A	League Cup 3rd round	2–3
1974	Burnley	H	League Division 1	0–1
1977	Derby County	H	League Division 1	1–0

Alan Hansen made his debut.

1983	Manchester United	A	League Division 1	0–1
1984	Stockport County	A	League Cup 2nd round 1st leg	0–0
1985	Oldham Athletic	H	League Cup 2nd round 1st leg	3–0
1988	Southampton	A	League Division 1	3–1
1994	Newcastle United	A	Premier League	1–1

SEPTEMBER 25TH

1897	Everton	H	League Division 1	3–1
1909	Sunderland	H	League Division 1	1–4
1920	Preston North End	H	League Division 1	6–0
1926	Everton	A	League Division 1	0–1
1937	Leeds United	A	League Division 1	0–2
1948	Blackpool	A	League Division 1	0–1
1954	Swansea Town	A	League Division 2	2–3

1961 Ronnie Whelan was born in Dublin. Joined Liverpool from Home Farm in 1979.

1965	Everton	H	League Division 1	5–0
1968	Swansea Town	H	League Cup 3rd round	2–0
1971	Manchester United	H	League Division 1	2–2
1976	Newcastle United	A	League Division 1	0–1
1979	Chesterfield	H	League Cup 3rd round	3–1
1982	Southampton	H	League Division 1	5–0

Two goals apiece from Ronnie Whelan and Mark Lawrenson plus one from Souness sealed an easy win for Liverpool. Terry McDermott appeared as a substitute in what was to be the last time Anfield saw him in a Liverpool shirt. Terry played 310 games, scoring 75 goals in his eight years at Anfield. He won a host of honours including three European Cups, two League Cups and Four Division One Championship medals. He was also the first player in 1980 to win the Football Writers and PFA Player of the Year awards. He moved back to Newcastle for £100,000 a few weeks later.

1990	Crewe Alexandra	H	League Cup 2nd round 1st leg	5–1
1991	Stoke City	H	League Cup 2nd round 1st leg	2–2
1993	Chelsea	A	Premier League	0–1

SEPTEMBER 26TH

1896	West Bromwich Albion	H	League Division 1	0–0
1903	West Bromwich Albion	H	League Division 1	1–3
1908	Manchester United	A	League Division 1	2–3
1914	West Bromwich Albion	A	League Division 1	0–4
1925	Everton	H	League Division 1	5–1
1931	Grimsby Town	H	League Division 1	4–0
1936	Leeds United	A	League Division 1	0–2
1953	Charlton Athletic	A	League Division 1	0–6
1959	Plymouth Argyle	H	League Division 2	4–1

1964	Aston Villa	H	League Division 1	5–1

Bob Graham scored a hat-trick on his debut for the club.

1970	Southampton	A	League Division 1	0–1
1972	Eintracht Frankfurt	A	UEFA Cup 1st round 2nd leg	0–0
1981	West Ham United	A	League Division 1	1–1
1992	Wimbledon	H	Premier League	2–3
1995	Spartak Vladikavkaz	H	UEFA Cup 1st round 2nd leg	0–0
1996	My Pa 47	H	European Cup-Winners' Cup 1st round 2nd leg	3–1

SEPTEMBER 27TH

1902	Everton	A	League Division 1	1–3
1913	West Bromwich Albion	H	League Division 1	0–0
1919	Newcastle United	H	League Division 1	1–1
1924	Nottingham Forest	H	League Division 1	3–0
1930	Chelsea	H	League Division 1	3–1
1947	Everton	A	League Division 1	3–0

Two goals inside a minute early in the second half by Jack Balmer and Alf Stubbins set up a comfortable victory over Everton at Goodison.

1952	West Bromwich Albion	A	League Division 1	0–3
1958	Cardiff City	H	League Division 2	1–2
1967	Bolton Wanderers	A	League Cup 2nd round replay	2–3
1969	West Bromwich Albion	A	League Division 1	2–2
1975	Everton	A	League Division 1	0–0
1977	IFK Goteborg	A	Friendly	3–2
1978	Nottingham Forest	H	European Cup 1st round 2nd leg	0–0
1980	Brighton & Hove Albion	H	League Division 1	4–1
1986	Aston Villa	H	League Division 1	3–3
1988	Walsall	H	League Cup 2nd round 1st leg	1–0
1997	West Ham United	A	Premier League	1–2

SEPTEMBER 28TH

1884 The first game ever to be played at Anfield, which at the time was home for Everton. They beat Earlstown 5–0 and they were to stay for the next eight years as they became founder members of the League. Behind the scenes problems started when the owner John Orrell and founder of Everton John Holding, disagreed over rent for the ground which had been redeveloped and often attracted crowds of over 8,000. The matter was resolved at a meeting in 1892 when the club were given notice to quit Anfield which they duly did [see March 15th 1892].

1895	Burslem P.Vale	H	League Division 2	5–1
1901	Small Heath	H	League Division 1	3–1
1907	Birmingham City	H	League Division 1	3–4
1912	West Bromwich Albion	A	League Division 1	1–3
1929	Grimsby Town	H	League Division 1	2–0
1935	West Bromwich Albion	H	League Division 1	5–0
1946	Leeds United	H	League Division 1	2–0
1957	Charlton Athletic	A	League Division 2	1–5

Gerry Byrne made his senior debut for the club.

1963	Everton	H	League Division 1	2–1
1966	Petrolul Ploesti	H	European Cup Preliminary Round 1st leg	2–0
1968	Wolves	A	League Division 1	6–0
1974	Sheffield United	A	League Division 1	0–1
1976	Crusaders	A	European Cup 1st round 2nd leg	5–0
1982	Dundalk	H	European Cup 1st round 2nd leg	1–0
1983	BK Odense	H	European Cup 1st round 2nd leg	5–0
1985	Tottenham Hotspur	H	League Division 1	4–1

After the victory over Everton in the last game, it was a test of the team's character in the way they responded to a Tottenham team that came to Anfield with the apparent sole intention of kicking their way to victory. A first half that was littered with fouls and stoppages was in its 4th minute of injury time when Lawrenson scored one of his rare goals, from almost the by-line, catching Ray Clemence in the Spurs goal unaware, it was no more than they deserved. Spurs scored shortly after the interval with a fine effort by winger Chiedozie only for Ian Rush to restore the lead with a typical 'Rushie' goal from the angle of the box. The game drifted on and Liverpool were awarded two penalties, one which seemed harsh but none the less was converted in his typically thunderbolt style by Jan Molby. With nearly a quarter of the season gone Liverpool moved into second place nine points behind Manchester United who had started with 10 straight victories. Alan Hansen was confirmed officially as club captain in place of Phil Neal before the game.

1991	Sheffield Wednesday	H	League Division 1	1–1

SEPTEMBER 29TH

1894	Wolves	A	League Division 1	1–3
1900	Sunderland	H	League Division 1	1–2
1906	Everton	H	League Division 1	1–2
1923	Burnley	H	League Division 1	1–0
1928	Everton	A	League Division 1	0–1
1934	West Bromwich Albion	H	League Division 1	3–2
1951	Derby County	H	League Division 1	2–0
1956	Leicester City	H	League Division 2	2–0
1962	Wolves	A	League Division 1	2–3
1965	Juventus	A	European Cup-Winners' Cup	0–1
1970	Ferencvaros	A	European Fairs Cup 1st round 2nd leg	1–1
1971	Servette Geneva	H	European Cup-Winners' Cup 1st round 2nd leg	2–0
1973	Manchester United	A	League Division 1	0–0
1979	Nottingham Forest	A	League Division 1	0–1

1981 The football world mourned the passing of the great Bill Shankly who died aged 68. Born in Glenbuck in 1913 he is perhaps best remembered as one of the greatest managers of British football let alone Liverpool. As a player he was a tough tackling wing-half with Carlisle and Preston and won an FA Cup winners' medal with the latter in 1938 when George Mutchs last-minute penalty won the trophy. Even then his acid wit was well sharpened: at the final whistle he made his way over to the sad-looking Huddersfield team and told them it was their own fault they'd lost! With five Scottish caps also safely tucked away he moved into management with Carlisle in 1949 before moving on to Grimsby, Workington and Huddersfield before being appointed manager at Liverpool in December 1959. On July 12th 1974, with the FA Cup safely in the trophy room, Shankly called a press conference and paraded his latest signing, Ray Kennedy of Arsenal. Then the Liverpool chairman announced that Shankly had decided to retire. Those present thought it was a joke, but Shankly was adamant; he was tired and wanted a rest from League football (echoes, perhaps, of his famous quote: 'Some people think football is a matter of life and death; it's much more serious than that.'). Although Shankly sat in on the board meeting that made Bob Paisley his successor, there was little else for him to do at Anfield; no directorship, no general manager's role. Retirement was therefore seven years in the wilderness for Bill Shankly. Although he was admitted to hospital earlier in the month no one realised his illness was so serious until his death was announced [see July 12th].

1984	Sheffield Wednesday	H	League Division 1	0–2
1987	Derby County	H	League Division 1	4–0
1990	Sunderland	A	League Division 1	1–0
1992	Apollon	A	European Cup-Winners' Cup 1st round 2nd leg	2–1
1996	West Ham United	A	Premier League	2–1

SEPTEMBER 30TH

1893	Notts County	A	League Division 2	0–1
1895	Burton Wand	H	League Division 2	4–1
1899	Blackburn Rovers	A	League Division 1	0–2
1905	Everton	A	League Division 1	2–4
1911	Sunderland	A	League Division 1	2–1

Bob Pursell made his debut after his transfer from Queen's Park. However the Scottish club protested that he had been poached and Liverpool were later fined £250 for their actions.

Harold Barton was born.

| 1922 | Burnley | A | League Division 1 | 2–0 |
| 1933 | Everton | H | League Division 1 | 3–2 |

1934 Alan A'Court was born in Rainhill, Lancs.

1950	Bolton Wanderers	H	League Division 1	3–3
1961	Charlton Athletic	A	League Division 2	4–0
1967	Stoke City	H	League Division 1	2–1
1969	Dundalk	A	European Fairs Cup 1st round 2nd leg	4–0
1972	Leeds United	A	League Division 1	2–1
1975	Hibernian	H	UEFA Cup 1st round 2nd leg	3–1
1978	Bolton Wanderers	H	League Division 1	3–0
1981	Oulu Palloseura	H	European Cup 1st round 2nd leg	7–0

This is where it all began. Ian Rush scored his first-ever goal for the club, something he never stopped doing until he left. Just one year on after hammering the same opposition for ten goals Liverpool scored another seven to comfortably go through to the next round.

| 1986 | Everton | A | Screen Sport Super Cup final 2nd Leg | 4–1 |

Goodison Park staged the second leg of the Screen Sport Super Cup final, with Liverpool 3–1 ahead after the first leg. A crowd of 26,068, almost six thousand more than had seen the first leg, were present to see Liverpool complete a 7–2 aggregate win. Ian Rush scored the 10th hat-trick of his career and Steve Nichol the other for

Liverpool, whilst Everton's reply came from Graeme Sharp from the penalty spot. Liverpool thus collected the trophy in the only season it has been contested and are thus the reigning holders, although one suspects the tankards each player received for taking part have proved rather more useful over the years!

| 1997 | Celtic | H | UEFA Cup 1st round 2nd leg | 0–0 |

OCTOBER 1ST

| 1892 | West Manchester | H | Lancashire League | 3–1 |
| 1898 | Notts County | H | League Division 1 | 0–0 |

Harold Wadsworth was born in Bootle.

1903	Notts County	A	League Division 1	2–4
1904	Leicester Fosse	H	League Division 2	4–0
1908	Nottingham Forest	A	League Division 1	1–5
1910	Everton	H	League Division 1	0–2
1921	Chelsea	H	League Division 1	1–1
1925	Notts County	A	League Division 1	2–1
1927	Portsmouth	H	League Division 1	8–2
1932	Everton	A	League Division 1	1–3
1938	Everton	A	League Division 1	1–2

Prime Minister Neville Chamberlain was present at this game after he returned from Munich with the promise that war had been averted. The crowd responded to his presence by singing the National Anthem. National fervour didn't help Liverpool, as a penalty by Joe Fagan wasn't enough to stop Everton winning.

1949	West Bromwich Albion	A	League Division 1	1–0
1955	Plymouth Argyle	H	League Division 2	4–1
1958	Everton	A	Friendly	2–1
1960	Derby County	H	League Division 2	1–0

1962 Paul Walsh was born in London. Started his career with Charlton Athletic before moving to Luton in 1982 for £250,000. He enjoyed two years at Kenilworth Road before moving to Anfield for £700,000 in May 1984.

1966	Aston Villa	A	League Division 1	3–2
1974	Stroms Drammen	A	European Cup-Winners' Cup 1st round 2nd leg	1–0
1977	Manchester United	A	League Division 1	0–2
1980	Oulu Palloseura	H	European Cup 1st round 2nd leg	10–1
1983	Sunderland	H	League Division 1	0–1

Whilst the scoreline was a big shock to everyone, the bigger shock was the fact that Phil Neal for the first time in over eight years wasn't in the team. He had been an ever-present in League matches since the 14th December 1974.

1988	Newcastle United	H	League Division 1	1–2
1994	Sheffield Wednesday	H	Premier League	4–1
1995	Manchester United	A	Premier League	2–2

OCTOBER 2ND

1887 Ephraim Longworth joined Liverpool in 1910 from Leyton.
1891 Archie Rawlings was born in Leicester.

| 1897 | Preston North End | A | League Division 1 | 1–1 |
| 1909 | Everton | A | League Division 1 | 3–2 |

1920	Preston North End	A	League Division 1	3–2
1926	Leeds United	H	League Division 1	2–4
1937	Everton	H	League Division 1	1–2
1948	Derby County	H	League Division 1	0–0
1954	Notts County	H	League Division 2	3–1
1965	Aston Villa	H	League Division 1	3–1
1968	Atletico Bilbao	H	European Fairs Cup 1st round 2nd leg	2–1
1971	Stoke City	A	League Division 1	0–0
1976	Middlesbrough	H	League Division 1	0–0
1978	Saudi Arabia	Jeddah	Friendly	1–1
1982	Ipswich Town	A	League Division 1	0–1
1991	Kuusysi Lahti	A	UEFA Cup 1st round 2nd leg	0–1
1993	Arsenal	H	Premier League	0–0

OCTOBER 3RD

1896	Everton	A	League Division 1	1–2
1903	Small Heath	A	League Division 1	2–1

John Parkinson made his debut to start his long and distinguished career with the club.

1908	Everton	H	League Division 1	0–1
1914	Everton	H	League Division 1	0–5
1925	Burnley	A	League Division 1	1–2

Tony McNamara born in Liverpool. He joined Everton in May 1950 and went on to make 111 appearances at outside right, scoring 21 goals for the club. He was sold to Liverpool in December 1957 where he played only 11 games during 1957/8 season and later played for Crewe and Bury before retiring.

1931	Chelsea	A	League Division 1	0–2
1936	Birmingham City	H	League Division 1	2–0
1953	Sheffield Wednesday	H	League Division 1	2–2
1959	Swansea Town	A	League Division 2	4–5
1970	Chelsea	H	League Division 1	1–0
1972	West Bromwich Albion	A	League Cup 3rd round	1–1
1973	Jeunesse D'esch	H	European Cup 1st round 2nd leg	2–0
1979	Dynamo Tbilisi	A	European Cup 1st round 2nd leg	0–3
1981	Swansea Town	H	League Division 1	2–2
1984	Lech Poznan	H	European Cup 1st round 2nd leg	4–0
1987	Portsmouth	H	League Division 1	4–0

1990 Jim Magilton was sold to Oxford United for £100,000. Jim who was at Anfield as a trainee never played for the first team but showed great potential. He has since gone on and won over 35 caps for Northern Ireland.

1992	Sheffield Wednesday	H	Premier League	1–0

OCTOBER 4TH

1902	Sheffield Wednesday	H	League Division 1	4–2
1913	Sheffield Wednesday	A	League Division 1	1–4
1919	Newcastle United	A	League Division 1	0–3
1924	Everton	A	League Division 1	1–0
1930	Newcastle United	A	League Division 1	4–0

1947	Middlesbrough	A	League Division 1	1–3
1951	Rhyl	A	Friendly	3–0
1952	Newcastle United	H	League Division 1	5–3
1958	Huddersfield Town	A	League Division 2	0–5
1961	Newcastle United	H	League Division 2	2–0
1967	Malmo	H	European Fairs Cup 1st round 2nd leg	2–1
1969	Nottingham Forest	H	League Division 1	1–1
1975	Wolves	H	League Division 1	2–0
1977	Arsenal	A	League Division 1	0–0
1980	Manchester City	A	League Division 1	3–0
1986	Wimbledon	A	League Division 1	3–1
1989	Wigan Athletic	A	League Cup 2nd round 2nd leg	3–0
1991	Rob Jones was bought from Crewe Alexandra for £300,000.			
1995	Sunderland	A	Coca-Cola Cup 2nd round 2nd leg	1–0

OCTOBER 5TH

1895	Newcastle United	A	League Division 2	0–1
1899	Notts County	A	League Division 1	1–2
1901	Derby County	A	League Division 1	1–1
1905	David Wright made his debut.			
1907	Everton	A	League Division 1	4–2
1912	Everton	H	League Division 1	0–2
1929	Leicester City	A	League Division 1	1–2
1935	Sunderland	A	League Division 1	0–2
1946	Grimsby Town	A	League Division 1	6–1
1957	Doncaster Rovers	H	League Division 2	5–0
1960	Everton	H	Friendly	3–1
1963	Aston Villa	H	League Division 1	5–2
1968	Burnley	A	League Division 1	4–0
1971	Southampton	H	League Cup 3rd round	1–0
1974	Carlisle United	A	League Division 1	1–0
1982	Ipswich Town	A	League Cup 2nd round 2nd leg	2–1
1983	Brentford	A	League Cup 2nd round 1st leg	4–1
1985	Queens Park Rangers	A	League Division 1	1–2

Kenny Dalglish dropped himself from the team line-up and brought in Paul Walsh to play on the Astroturf pitch at Loftus Road. History will show that Loftus Road is a favourite away ground for Liverpool. This was not going to be one of those days, however. Despite an equalising goal from Walsh, Liverpool were always second best and got what they deserved from the game: nothing. What was even more disappointing was the news that Manchester United had dropped a point in their game with Luton.

1993	Fulham	H	League Cup 2nd round 2nd leg	5–0

Robbie Fowler scored all the goals in this one-sided League cup game. Only four other players have achieved the feat of scoring five goals in one game in a Liverpool shirt.

1994	Burnley	A	League Cup 2nd round 2nd leg	4–1

OCTOBER 6TH

1894	Sheffield United	H	League Division 1	2–2
1900	Derby County	A	League Division 1	3–2
1906	Arsenal	A	League Division 1	1–2
1923	Everton	A	League Division 1	0–1
1928	West Ham United	A	League Division 1	1–1
1934	Sheffield Wednesday	A	League Division 1	1–4

1948 Larry 'Valentine' Lloyd was born in Bristol. The rugged centre-half joined the club for £50,000 from Bristol Rovers in 1969.

1951	Charlton Athletic	A	League Division 1	0–2
1955	Bristol Rovers	A	League Division 2	1–2
1956	Blackburn Rovers	H	League Division 2	2–3

1957 Bruce Grobbelaar was born in Durban, South Africa. Bruce started his career with Vancouver Whitecaps but gained immediate attention when he spent a few months on trial at Crewe. He joined Liverpool in March 1981.

1962	Bolton Wanderers	H	League Division 1	1–0
1970	Swindon Town	A	League Cup 3rd round	0–2
1973	Newcastle United	H	League Division 1	2–1
1979	Bristol City	H	League Division 1	4–0
1984	West Bromwich Albion	H	League Division 1	0–0
1987	Blackburn Rovers	H	Littlewoods Cup 2nd Round 2nd Leg	1–0
1990	Derby County	H	League Division 1	2–0
1991	Manchester United	A	League Division 1	0–0

Rob Jones made his debut nearly three years after he signed from Crewe. Seven years on and approaching 200 games for the club he is yet to find the net.

1992	Chesterfield	A	League Cup 2nd round 2nd leg	4–1

OCTOBER 7TH

1893	Middlesbrough	H	League Division 2	4–0

Jimmy Stott had the honour of becoming the first Liverpool player to score a hat-trick. He was to play a key part in the club winning promotion in its first year in the Football League.

1894 Tommy Bromilow was born in Liverpool. Tommy started his career at local level and then represented the Army before moving to Anfield in October 1919.

1895	Crewe Alexandra	H	League Division 2	6–1
1899	Derby County	H	League Division 1	0–2
1905	Derby County	H	League Division 1	4–1
1911	Blackburn Rovers	H	League Division 1	1–2
1922	Everton	H	League Division 1	5–1
1933	Chelsea	H	League Division 1	3–0
1950	Stoke City	H	League Division 1	0–0

John Heydon was born in Birkenhead.

1953	South Africa XI	H	Friendly	3–2
1959	Everton	A	Friendly	3–0
1961	Middlesbrough	A	League Division 2	0–2
1964	Sheffield United	H	League Division 1	3–1
1967	Leicester City	A	League Division 1	1–2
1969	Tottenham Hotspur	H	League Division 1	0–0

1972	Everton	H	League Division 1	1–0
1975	Burnley	H	League Cup 3rd round	1–1
1978	Norwich City	A	League Division 1	4–1
1980	Middlesbrough	H	League Division 1	4–2
1981	Exeter City	H	League Cup 2nd round 1st leg	5–0
1986	Fulham	A	Littlewoods Cup 2nd Round 2nd Leg	3–2

OCTOBER 8TH

1892	West Manchester	A	Lancashire Cup	3–1
1898	Stoke City	H	League Division 1	1–2
1904	Leicester Fosse	A	League Division 2	2–0
1910	Sheffield Wednesday	A	League Division 1	0–1
1921	Preston North End	A	League Division 1	1–1
1927	Leicester City	A	League Division 1	1–1
1932	Leicester City	A	League Division 1	2–1
1938	Leicester City	A	League Division 1	2–2
1949	Middlesbrough	H	League Division 1	2–0
1960	Lincoln City	A	League Division 2	2–1
1966	Fulham	H	League Division 1	2–2
1968	Everton	H	League Division 1	1–1

The 100th League meeting between the two clubs. Tommy Smith and Alan Ball were the goalscorers.

1973	West Ham United	A	League Cup 2nd round	2–2
1974	Bristol City	A	League Cup 3rd round	0–0
1977	Chelsea	H	League Division 1	2–0
1988	Luton Town	A	League Division 1	0–1
1994	Aston Villa	H	Premier League	3–2
1997	Chelsea	H	Premier League	4–0

OCTOBER 9TH

| 1897 | Stoke City | H | League Division 1 | 4–0 |

1899 George Allan died aged 24 from tuberculosis. George was a great centre forward who in his two spells at the club scored 60 goals in 97 games.

1909	Manchester United	H	League Division 1	3–2
1920	Sheffield United	H	League Division 1	2–2
1926	Newcastle United	A	League Division 1	0–1
1929	Blackburn Rovers	H	League Division 1	1–1

Harold Barton made his League debut.

1937	West Bromwich Albion	H	League Division 1	0–1
1946	Middlesbrough	A	League Division 1	2–2
1948	Chelsea	H	League Division 1	1–1
1954	Rotherham United	H	League Division 2	3–1
1957	Everton	A	Friendly	0–2

The floodlights were switched on at Goodison Park for the first time in a match to celebrate the 75th anniversary of the Liverpool County FA.

| 1963 | Sheffield Wednesday | H | League Division 1 | 3–1 |
| 1965 | Manchester United | A | League Division 1 | 0–2 |

1971	Chelsea	H	League Division 1	0–0
1979	Bolton Wanderers	A	League Division 1	1–1
1982	West Ham United	A	League Division 1	1–3
1984	Stockport County	H	League Cup 2nd round 2nd leg	2–0
1985	Oldham Athletic	A	League Cup 2nd round 2nd leg	5–2
1990	Crewe Alexandra	A	League Cup 2nd round 2nd leg	1–4
1991	Stoke City	A	League Cup 2nd round 2nd leg	3–2
1994	Chelsea	H	Premier League	3–1

1996 Jamie Carragher signed professional forms for the club. Jamie was a member of the 1996 Youth Cup winning team.

OCTOBER 10TH

1896	Nottingham Forest	H	League Division 1	3–0
1903	Everton	H	League Division 1	2–2
1908	Leicester Fosse	A	League Division 1	2–3
1914	Chelsea	A	League Division 1	1–3
1925	Leeds United	H	League Division 1	1–1
1931	West Ham United	H	League Division 1	2–2
1936	Middlesbrough	A	League Division 1	3–3
1953	Aston Villa	H	League Division 1	6–1
1959	Brighton & Hove Albion	H	League Division 2	2–2
1964	Birmingham City	A	League Division 1	0–0
1970	Tottenham Hotspur	A	League Division 1	0–1
1972	West Bromwich Albion	H	League Cup 3rd round replay	2–1
1981	Leeds United	H	League Division 1	3–0
1984	Southampton	H	League Division 1	1–1

1991 Jimmy Carter was sold to Arsenal for £500,000. Jimmy never really showed he had the makings of a top-flight winger and only made four full appearances for the club. Arsenal who had originally wanted him took him back to London where he was an equal failure.

1992	Everton	H	Friendly	2–2
1993	Great Britain XI	H	Friendly	1–2

OCTOBER 11TH

1902	West Bromwich Albion	A	League Division 1	2–1
1913	Bolton Wanderers	H	League Division 1	2–1
1919	Chelsea	A	League Division 1	0–1
1924	Newcastle United	A	League Division 1	0–0
1930	Sheffield Wednesday	H	League Division 1	1–2
1947	Chelsea	H	League Division 1	3–0
1952	Bolton Wanderers	A	League Division 1	2–2
1958	Lincoln City	H	League Division 2	3–2

1963 Ronny Rosenthal was born in Haifa, Israel.

1969	Newcastle United	A	League Division 1	0–1
1975	Birmingham City	H	League Division 1	3–1
1978	Swansea City	H	Friendly	3–2
1980	Ipswich Town	H	League Division 1	1–1

| 1986 | Tottenham Hotspur | H | League Division 1 | 0–1 |

OCTOBER 12TH

1895	Newton Heath	H	League Division 2	7–1
1901	Sheffield Wednesday	H	League Division 1	1–2
1907	Sunderland	H	League Division 1	1–0
1912	Sheffield Wednesday	A	League Division 1	0–1
1929	Birmingham City	H	League Division 1	1–1
1935	Birmingham City	H	League Division 1	1–2
1946	Charlton Athletic	H	League Division 1	1–1

Cyril Done was born in Liverpool.

1957	Swansea Town	H	League Division 2	4–0
1966	Petrolul Ploesti	A	European Cup Preliminary Round 2nd leg	1–3
1968	Manchester United	H	League Division 1	2–0
1974	Middlesbrough	H	League Division 1	2–0

1977 A packed Anfield saw Scotland beat Wales 2–0 to qualify for the World Cup finals in Argentina.

| 1984 | Tottenham Hotspur | A | League Division 1 | 0–1 |
| 1985 | Southampton | H | League Division 1 | 1–0 |

It was important after the hiccup in the last game away to QPR that Liverpool bounced back with a victory no matter what and this, like the previous home game against Spurs, was a contest when the opposition came to Anfield to kick their way to victory. Justice was served when in the second half Steve McMahon scored what was to be the decisive goal, on the hour mark. Southampton had six players booked in a 30-minute period, including Mark Wright and Jimmy Case.

| 1988 | Walsall | A | League Cup 2nd round 2nd leg | 3–1 |
| 1996 | Manchester United | A | Premier League | 0–1 |

OCTOBER 13TH

| 1894 | Everton | A | League Division 1 | 0–3 |

The first League derby between the two teams watched by a huge crowd of nearly 45,000 paying spectators.

1900	Bolton Wanderers	H	League Division 1	2–1
1906	Sheffield Wednesday	H	League Division 1	1–2
1923	Everton	H	League Division 1	1–2
1928	Newcastle United	H	League Division 1	2–1
1934	Birmingham City	H	League Division 1	5–4
1951	Fulham	H	League Division 1	4–0
1956	Bristol Rovers	A	League Division 2	1–2
1962	Leicester City	A	League Division 1	0–3
1964	Leicester City	H	League Division 1	0–1
1965	Juventus	H	European Cup-Winners' Cup	2–0
1973	Southampton	A	League Division 1	0–1
1979	Ipswich Town	A	League Division 1	2–1

1893	Small Heath	A	League Division 2	3–2
1899	Bury	A	League Division 1	1–2
1905	Sheffield Wednesday	A	League Division 1	2–3
1911	Sheffield Wednesday	A	League Division 1	2–2
1912	Sheffield United	A	League Division 1	1–4
1922	Everton	A	League Division 1	1–0
1933	Sunderland	A	League Division 1	1–4
1950	West Bromwich Albion	A	League Division 1	1–1
1961	Walsall	H	League Division 2	6–1

Roger Hunt continued his fine run of goalscoring with his second hat-trick of the season.

1967	West Ham United	H	League Division 1	3–1
1972	Southampton	A	League Division 1	1–1
1975	Burnley	A	League Cup 3rd round replay	0–1
1978	Derby County	H	League Division 1	5–0

A four-goal blitz in a twenty-minute period during the second half earned Liverpool the points. Ray Kennedy and Kenny Dalglish scoring two each to add to Craig Johnston's first-half goal.

1989	Wimbledon	A	League Division 1	2–1
1995	Coventry	H	Premier League	0–0

1892	Nantwich	A	FA Cup Qualifying round	4–0
1898	Aston Villa	H	League Division 1	0–3
1904	West Bromwich Albion	H	League Division 2	3–2
1910	Bristol City	H	League Division 1	4–0
1921	Preston North End	H	League Division 1	4–0
1924	Blackburn Rovers	H	League Division 1	0–0
1927	Everton	A	League Division 1	1–1
1932	Portsmouth	H	League Division 1	4–3

A twenty-minute hat-trick in the second half by Gordon Hodgson sealed the victory in a seven-goal epic at Anfield.

1938	Aston Villa	H	League Division 1	3–0
1949	Blackpool	A	League Division 1	0–0
1955	West Ham United	H	League Division 2	3–1
1960	Portsmouth	H	League Division 2	3–3
1966	Nottingham Forest	A	League Division 1	1–1
1968	Arsenal	A	League Cup 4th Round	1–2
1977	Leeds United	A	League Division 1	2–1
1983	West Ham United	A	League Division 1	3–1
1994	Blackburn Rovers	A	Premier League	2–3
1997	West Bromwich Albion	A	League Cup 3rd round	2–0

1897	Everton	A	League Division 1	0–3
1909	Bradford City	A	League Division 1	2–1
1920	Sheffield United	A	League Division 1	1–0

1926	Sheffield Wednesday	A	League Division 1	2–3
1937	Wolves	A	League Division 1	0–2
1948	Birmingham City	A	League Division 1	1–0
1954	Stoke City	A	League Division 2	0–2
1965	Newcastle United	H	League Division 1	2–0
1968	Sheffield Wednesday	A	League Division 1	2–1
1971	Nottingham Forest	A	League Division 1	3–2
1974	Bristol City	H	League Cup 3rd round replay	4–0

After struggling in the first game at Ashton Gate, Liverpool made no mistake in the replay thanks to two goals each from Steve Heighway and Ray Kennedy.

1976	Everton	H	League Division 1	3–1
1982	Manchester United	H	League Division 1	0–0
1993	Oldham Athletic	H	Premier League	2–1

OCTOBER 17TH

1896	Sunderland	A	League Division 1	3–4
1903	Stoke City	A	League Division 1	2–5
1908	Leicester Fosse	H	League Division 1	2–2
1914	Bradford City	H	League Division 1	2–1
1925	Manchester City	H	League Division 1	2–1
1931	West Bromwich Albion	A	League Division 1	2–1
1936	Bolton Wanderers	H	League Division 1	0–0
1953	Huddersfield Town	A	League Division 1	0–2
1959	Stoke City	A	League Division 2	1–1
1964	West Ham United	H	League Division 1	2–2
1970	Burnley	H	League Division 1	2–0
1981	Brighton & Hove Albion	A	League Division 1	3–3
1987	Queens Park Rangers	H	League Division 1	4–0
1994	Brighton & Hove Albion	A	Friendly	2–1
1995	Brondby IF	A	UEFA Cup 2nd round 1st leg	0–0
1996	FC Sion	A	European Cup-Winners' Cup 2nd round 1st leg	2–1

OCTOBER 18TH

1902	Notts County	H	League Division 1	0–2
1913	Chelsea	A	League Division 1	0–3
1919	Chelsea	H	League Division 1	0–1

Tom Bromilow made his first outing for the club. Tom had asked the club for a trial and proved his worth by gaining a contract.

1924	Sheffield United	H	League Division 1	4–1
1930	Leeds United	H	League Division 1	2–0
1947	Huddersfield Town	A	League Division 1	1–1
1952	Aston Villa	H	League Division 1	0–2
1958	Fulham	A	League Division 2	1–0
1961	Everton	A	Friendly	2–2
1969	Ipswich Town	A	League Division 1	2–2
1975	Coventry City	A	League Division 1	0–0
1978	Manchester City	H	League Division 1	1–0

1980	Everton	A	League Division 1	2–2
1986	Oxford United	H	League Division 1	4–0
1992	Manchester United	A	Premier League	2–2
1997	Everton	A	Premier League	0–2

OCTOBER 19TH

1895	Grimsby Town	A	League Division 2	0–1
1896	Sheffield United	A	League Division 1	1–1
1901	Notts County	A	League Division 1	2–2
1907	Arsenal	A	League Division 1	1–2
1912	Blackburn Rovers	H	League Division 1	4–1
1929	Derby County	A	League Division 1	2–2
1935	Bolton Wanderers	A	League Division 1	0–0
1946	Huddersfield Town	A	League Division 1	4–1

Billy Liddell made his debut for Scotland in the 1-3 defeat by Wales in Wrexham. Ray Lambert made his debut for Wales.

1957	Derby County	A	League Division 2	1–2
1960	Luton Town	H	League Cup 2nd round	1–1
1963	West Bromwich Albion	H	League Division 1	1–0
1966	Petrolul Ploesti	N	European Cup preliminary round play-off	2–0
1968	Tottenham Hotspur	A	League Division 1	1–2
1974	Queens Park Rangers	A	League Division 1	1–0
1977	Dynamo Dresden	H	European Cup 2nd round 1st leg	5–1
1982	JK Helsinki	A	European Cup 2nd round 1st leg	0–1
1983	Athletic Bilbao	H	European Cup 2nd round 1st leg	0–0
1985	Manchester United	A	League Division 1	1–1

Liverpool arrived at Old Trafford 10 points behind and left still 10 points behind, but those who witnessed the game will have no doubts that Liverpool deserved to have won this game. Craig Johnston had given Liverpool the lead, a reward for a fine performance, from an Ian Rush cross. Rush had still never scored against the opposition. It was also the first goal that Manchester United had conceded at Old Trafford that season. Paul McGrath grabbed an equaliser for the home side after Lawrenson had misjudged a long clearance from Bailey.

1987	Dundee	A	Friendly	4–0

Ray Houghton was signed from Oxford United for £825,000.

1988	Steve Staunton made his international debut for the Republic of Ireland in the 4–0 victory over Tunisia in Dublin. Ten years on and Steve has hardly missed a game for his country, winning nearly 70 caps.

1991	Chelsea	A	League Division 1	2–2
1993	Bord Gais League	Dublin	Friendly	2–1

OCTOBER 20TH

1894	Stoke City	H	League Division 1	2–0
1900	Notts County	A	League Division 1	0–3
1906	Bury	A	League Division 1	3–1
1923	Nottingham Forest	H	League Division 1	4–2
1928	Huddersfield Town	H	League Division 1	2–3

1934	Grimsby Town	H	League Division 1	1–1

1943 Chris Lawler was born in Liverpool. He joined the club as an amateur in 1959.

1951	Middlesbrough	A	League Division 1	3–3
1956	Fulham	H	League Division 2	4–3

1961 Ian Rush was born in St Asaph. Ian started his career with Chester City where he made an instant impact, scoring 17 goals in 38 games, a trend he was to continue for the next 20 years of his career.

1971	Bayern Munich	H	European Cup-Winners' Cup 2nd round 1st leg	0–0
1973	Leeds United	A	League Division 1	0–1
1976	Trabzonspor	A	European Cup 2nd round 1st leg	0–1
1979	Everton	H	League Division 1	2–2
1984	Everton	H	League Division 1	0–1

1988 David Burrows was signed from West Bromwich Albion for £550,000.

1990	Norwich City	A	League Division 1	1–1

1994 Julian Dicks was sold back to West Ham for £1 million after just one season at Anfield. Julian never quite settled in and made 31 appearances scoring 3 goals in his all-too-brief Liverpool career.

OCTOBER 21ST

1893	Burton Swifts	A	League Division 2	1–0
1895	Burslem Port Vale	A	League Division 2	4–5
1899	Notts County	H	League Division 1	3–1
1905	Nottingham Forest	H	League Division 1	4–1

Goalkeeper Sam Hardy made his debut for the club after his summer signing from Chesterfield Town for £500.

1911	Bury	H	League Division 1	1–1

1920 Cyril Done was born in Liverpool. After playing for the local boys side in Bootle Cyril joined the playing staff at Liverpool in January 1938.

1922	Cardiff City	H	League Division 1	3–1
1933	Middlesbrough	A	League Division 1	1–4

Roy Evans was born in Bootle.

1950	Middlesbrough	H	League Division 1	0–0

Goalkeeper Russell Crossley was born in Yorkshire. After building a reputation as a brave keeper during his time in the army, Crossley signed for Liverpool in June 1947.

1961	Derby County	A	League Division 2	0–2

1967 Paul Ince born in Ilford in Essex. Signed by West Ham as a professional in July 1985 he soon established himself as a commander in the midfield for the Hammers and was soon the subject of numerous transfer enquiries. At the end of the 1988–89 season he announced his wish to leave Upton Park, although the circumstances surrounding his departure to Old Trafford in September 1989 ensured a hostile reception whenever he has returned to West Ham. Surprisingly he was allowed to join Inter Milan in 1995 but later returned home to Liverpool in the summer of 1997 where he was immediately appointed captain.

1970	Dinamo Bucharest	H	European Fairs Cup 2nd round 1st leg	3–0
1972	Stoke City	H	League Division 1	2–1
1978	Chelsea	H	League Division 1	2–0
1981	AZ 67 Alkmaar	A	European Cup 2nd round 1st leg	2–2

1986	Blackburn Rovers	A	Friendly	3–2
1989	Southampton	A	League Division 1	1–4
1997	R.C.Strasbourg	A	UEFA Cup 2nd round 1st leg	0–3

OCTOBER 22ND

1892	Higher Walton	A	Lancashire League	2–0
1898	Burnley	A	League Division 1	1–2
1904	Burnley	A	League Division 2	2–0
1910	Newcastle United	A	League Division 1	1–6
1921	Tottenham Hotspur	A	League Division 1	1–0
1927	Bolton Wanderers	A	League Division 1	1–2
1932	Arsenal	H	League Division 1	2–3
1938	Wolves	A	League Division 1	2–2
1949	Newcastle United	H	League Division 1	2–2
1955	Bury	A	League Division 2	4–1
1960	Huddersfield Town	A	League Division 2	4–2
1975	Real Sociedad	A	UEFA Cup 2nd round 1st leg	3–1
1977	Everton	H	League Division 1	0–0
1978	Tottenham Hotspur	A	League Division 1	0–0
1980	Aberdeen	A	European Cup 2nd round 1st leg	1–0
1983	Queens Park Rangers	A	League Division 1	1–0
1985	Southampton	A	Screen Sport Super Cup 1st round 2nd leg	1–1
1988	Coventry City	H	League Division 1	0–0
1992	Spartak Moscow	A	European Cup-Winners' Cup 2nd round 1st leg	2–4
1994	Wimbledon	H	Premier League	3–0
1995	Southampton	A	Premier League	3–1

OCTOBER 23RD

1897	Derby County	H	League Division 1	4–2
1909	Sheffield Wednesday	H	League Division 1	3–1
1920	Everton	H	League Division 1	1–0
1926	Leicester City	H	League Division 1	1–0
1937	Leicester City	H	League Division 1	1–1
1948	Middlesbrough	H	League Division 1	4–0

1951 David Johnson was born in Liverpool. Started his career on Everton's books before moving to Ipswich Town in 1972. He stayed there for four years before arriving at Anfield in August 1976 for a club record fee at the time of £200,000.

1954	Bury	H	League Division 2	1–1
1965	West Bromwich Albion	A	League Division 1	0–3
1968	Coventry City	H	League Division 1	2–0
1971	Huddersfield Town	H	League Division 1	2–0
1974	Ferencvaros	H	European Cup-Winners' Cup 2nd round 1st leg	1–1
1976	Leeds United	A	League Division 1	1–1
1982	Stoke City	A	League Division 1	1–1
1991	Auxerre	A	UEFA Cup 2nd round 1st leg	0–2
1993	Manchester City	A	Premier League	1–1

Dominic Matteo made his first senior appearance for the club.

| 1996 | Charlton Athletic | A | League Cup 3rd round | 1–1 |

OCTOBER 24TH

1896	Blackburn Rovers	H	League Division 1	4–0
1903	Derby County	H	League Division 1	3–1
1908	Notts County	A	League Division 1	2–1
1914	Burnley	A	League Division 1	0–3
1925	Tottenham Hotspur	A	League Division 1	1–3

Arthur Riley replaced Elisha Scott in goal to make his debut for the club. Even though it was another four years before he was to take over on a permanent basis, Riley stayed loyal to the club that brought him over from South Africa. He was to remain an ever-present until the outbreak of the War playing 338 games in all for the club.

1931	Blackpool	H	League Division 1	3–2
1936	Brentford	A	League Division 1	2–5
1953	Sheffield United	H	League Division 1	3–0
1959	Portsmouth	H	League Division 2	1–1
1960	Luton Town	A	League Cup 2nd round replay	5–2
1964	West Bromwich Albion	A	League Division 1	0–3
1967	Burnley	A	League Division 1	1–1
1970	Ipswich Town	A	League Division 1	0–1
1972	AEK Athens	H	UEFA Cup 2nd round 1st leg	3–0
1973	Red Star Belgrade	A	European Cup 2nd round 1st leg	1–2
1981	Manchester United	H	League Division 1	1–2
1984	Benfica	H	European Cup 2nd round 1st leg	3–1
1987	Luton Town	A	League Division 1	1–0
1995	Manchester City	H	Coca-Cola Cup 3rd round	4–0

OCTOBER 25TH

1902	Bolton Wanderers	A	League Division 1	1–1
1913	Oldham Athletic	H	League Division 1	0–3
1919	Burnley	A	League Division 1	2–1
1924	Sunderland	H	League Division 1	3–1
1930	Blackpool	A	League Division 1	3–1
1947	Derby County	H	League Division 1	2–2
1952	Sunderland	A	League Division 1	1–3
1958	Sheffield United	H	League Division 2	3–2

1968 David Burrows born in Dudley. He first made his name with West Bromwich Albion before joining Liverpool for £550,000 in 1988. In 1993 he joined West Ham but a little less than a year later returned to the city of Liverpool, signing for Everton. Six months later he was sold to Coventry for £1.1 million.

1969	Southampton	H	League Division 1	4–1
1975	Derby County	H	League Division 1	1–1
1978	Middlesbrough	H	League Division 1	2–0
1980	Arsenal	H	League Division 1	1–1
1983	Brentford	H	League Cup 2nd round 2nd leg	4–0
1986	Luton Town	A	League Division 1	1–4
1989	Arsenal	A	League Cup 3rd round	0–1

1992	Norwich City	H	Premier League	4–1
1994	Stoke City	H	League Cup 3rd round	2–1
1997	Derby County	H	Premier League	4–0

OCTOBER 26TH

1895	Notts County	H	League Division 2	3–0
1901	Bolton Wanderers	H	League Division 1	1–1
1907	Sheffield Wednesday	H	League Division 1	3–0
1912	Derby County	A	League Division 1	2–4
1929	Manchester City	H	League Division 1	1–6
1935	Huddersfield Town	H	League Division 1	3–0

1939 Willie Stephenson was born in Edinburgh. After playing for Glasgow Rangers Willie moved to Australia before coming back to Britain and Liverpool in October 1962.

1946	Brentford	H	League Division 1	1–0
1957	Bristol Rovers	H	League Division 2	2–0
1963	Ipswich Town	A	League Division 1	2–1
1968	Newcastle United	H	League Division 1	2–1
1974	Leeds United	H	League Division 1	1–0
1977	Derby County	H	League Cup 3rd round	2–0

1981 Steve Nicol was signed from Ayr United for a fee of £300,000.

| 1982 | Ipswich Town | H | League Cup 2nd round replay | 2–0 |
| 1985 | Luton Town | H | League Division 1 | 3–2 |

Paul Walsh who had asked for a transfer was recalled to the team in place of the injured Ian Rush, and completely stole the show with a virtuoso performance against his former club. He scored two goals and also had a hand in the other from Molby, who played in the back five again.

| 1988 | Nottingham Forest | A | League Division 1 | 1–2 |
| 1991 | Coventry City | H | League Division 1 | 1–0 |

OCTOBER 27TH

1894	Aston Villa	A	League Division 1	0–5
1900	Preston North End	H	League Division 1	3–2
1906	Manchester City	H	League Division 1	5–4

Bobby Robinson scored a hat-trick to edge out City in a nine goal thriller.

| 1923 | Nottingham Forest | A | League Division 1 | 1–0 |
| 1928 | Arsenal | A | League Division 1 | 4–4 |

Over 50,000 witnessed one of the finest matches seen at Highbury between the Wars. Gordon Hodgson scored a hat-trick in 13 minutes in the first half to add to Dick Edmed's first minute goal to give Liverpool a 4–2 half-time lead. However Arsenal rallied in the second half and scored two goals to level things.

1934	Preston North End	A	League Division 1	2–2
1951	West Bromwich Albion	H	League Division 1	2–5
1956	Barnsley	A	League Division 2	1–4
1962	West Bromwich Albion	A	League Division 1	0–1
1971	West Ham United	A	League Cup 4th Round	1–2
1973	Sheffield United	H	League Division 1	1–0
1976	Leicester City	A	League Division 1	1–0

1979	Manchester City	A	League Division 1	4–0
1990	Chelsea	H	League Division 1	2–0
1993	Ipswich Town	H	League Cup 3rd round	3–2
1996	Derby County	H	Premier League	2–1

OCTOBER 28TH

| 1893 | Arsenal | A | League Division 2 | 5–0 |

This result is the highest score Liverpool have ever recorded against the north London giants.

1899	Manchester City	A	League Division 1	1–0
1905	Manchester City	A	League Division 1	1–0
1911	Middlesbrough	A	League Division 1	2–3
1922	Cardiff City	A	League Division 1	0–3
1933	Blackburn Rovers	H	League Division 1	4–0
1950	Sheffield Wednesday	A	League Division 1	1–4
1959	Everton	H	Friendly	0–2
1961	Leyton Orient	H	League Division 2	3–3
1967	Sheffield Wednesday	H	League Division 1	1–0
1972	Norwich City	A	League Division 1	1–1
1978	Everton	A	League Division 1	0–1
1980	Portsmouth	H	League Cup 4th Round	4–1
1981	Exeter City	A	League Cup 2nd round 2nd leg	6–0
1984	Nottingham Forest	A	League Division 1	2–0
1987	Everton	H	Littlewoods Cup 3rd Round	0–1

The previous season Liverpool had ended Everton's hopes of the Littlewoods Cup with a 1–0 win at Goodison. Everton exacted their revenge with a similar scoreline at Anfield in front of a crowd of 44,071. Defender Gary Stevens scored the vital goal in the second half and Neville Southall pulled off a string of saves to thwart Liverpool throughout.

| 1992 | Sheffield United | A | League Cup 3rd round | 0–0 |
| 1995 | Manchester City | H | Premier League | 6–0 |

OCTOBER 29TH

1892	Newtown	H	FA Cup Qualifying round	9–0
1898	Sheffield United	H	League Division 1	2–1
1904	Grimsby Town	H	League Division 2	5–0

Goalkeeper John Ned Doig was born in Letham. Ned was a regular for Sunderland where he was ever present in their Championship-winning teams of 1892, 1893, 1895 and 1902 before moving to Anfield after 14 years at Roker Park in June 1904.

1910	Tottenham Hotspur	H	League Division 1	1–2
1921	Tottenham Hotspur	H	League Division 1	1–1
1927	Blackburn Rovers	H	League Division 1	4–2
1932	Manchester City	A	League Division 1	1–1
1938	Huddersfield Town	H	League Division 1	3–3
1949	Fulham	A	League Division 1	1–0
1955	Rotherham United	H	League Division 2	2–0
1958	Everton	H	Friendly	3–2

1960	Sunderland	H	League Division 2	1–1
1962	New Brighton	A	Friendly	5–2
1966	Stoke City	A	League Division 1	0–2
1973	West Ham United	H	League Cup 2nd round replay	1–0
1977	Manchester City	A	League Division 1	1–3
1983	Luton Town	H	League Division 1	6–0

Ian Rush scored five goals in the game, not surprisingly the only time he achieved this in his glittering career. He is the third player (out of five) to achieve this remarkable feat in the club's history. Kenny Dalglish managed to score the other goal in the game.

1985	Brighton & Hove Albion	H	League Cup 3rd round	4–0
1986	Leicester City	H	Littlewoods Cup 3rd Round	4–1
1988	West Ham United	A	League Division 1	2–0
1989	Tottenham Hotspur	H	League Division 1	1–0
1991	Port Vale	H	League Cup 3rd round	2–2
1994	Ipswich Town	A	Premier League	3–1

OCTOBER 30TH

1897	Aston Villa	A	League Division 1	1–3
1909	Bristol City	A	League Division 1	1–0
1920	Everton	A	League Division 1	3–0
1926	Blackburn Rovers	A	League Division 1	1–2

Dave Hickson born in Ellesmere Port. Signed by Everton in May 1948 from Ellesmere Port he remained at Goodison until September 1955. He was sold to Aston Villa for £17,500 but remained only two months before switching to Huddersfield for £16,000 and then returned to Everton in August 1957 for £7,500. Just over two years later he was on the move again, making the relatively short trip across Stanley Park to sign for Liverpool where he stayed for a further two years, scoring 38 goals in 67 games. He later finished his playing career with Bury and Tranmere.

1937	Sunderland	A	League Division 1	3–2
1948	Newcastle United	A	League Division 1	0–1
1954	Lincoln City	A	League Division 2	3–3
1957	Everton	H	Friendly	3–2

Liverpool spent nearly £15,000 on installing floodlights at Anfield and the friendly was to mark their use for the first time. The opportunity of beating Everton again had not been possible due to the fact that the clubs were in different divisions for such a long time.

1965	Nottingham Forest	H	League Division 1	4–0
1968	Nottingham Forest	A	League Division 1	1–0
1971	Sheffield United	A	League Division 1	1–1
1976	Aston Villa	H	League Division 1	3–0
1979	Exeter City	H	League Cup 4th Round	2–0
1982	Brighton & Hove Albion	H	League Division 1	3–1
1993	Southampton	H	Premier League	4–2

OCTOBER 31ST

| 1896 | West Bromwich Albion | A | League Division 1 | 1–0 |

1903	Manchester City	A	League Division 1	2–3
1908	Newcastle United	H	League Division 1	2–1
1914	Tottenham Hotspur	H	League Division 1	7–2

Fred Pagnam scored four goals in this demolition of the north London club.

1925	Sunderland	H	League Division 1	2–2
1931	Sheffield United	A	League Division 1	0–3
1936	Arsenal	H	League Division 1	2–1
1953	Chelsea	A	League Division 1	2–5
1959	Sunderland	A	League Division 2	1–1
1964	Manchester United	H	League Division 1	0–2
1966	Representative XI	Doncaster	Friendly	4–3
1970	Wolves	H	League Division 1	2–0
1972	Leeds United	H	League Cup 4th Round	2–2
1981	Sunderland	A	League Division 1	2–0
1984	Tottenham Hotspur	A	League Cup 3rd round	0–1
1990	Manchester United	A	League Cup 3rd round	3–1
1992	Tottenham Hotspur	A	Premier League	0–2
1994	Queens Park Rangers	A	Premier League	1–2
1995	Brondby IF	H	UEFA Cup 2nd round 2nd leg	0–1
1996	FC Sion	H	European Cup-Winners' Cup 2nd round 2nd leg	6–3

In a remarkable game Liverpool ran out comfortable winners. Leading 2–1 from the first leg this should have been an easy passage into the next round. Liverpool ended up going into the half-time break losing 1–2 which meant the scores were level on aggregate. Three quick goals in a five-minute spell, however, ensured the victory, which was great for the watching TV audience.

NOVEMBER 1ST

1902	Middlesbrough	H	League Division 1	5–0

Steve Raybould scored a hat-trick. This took his tally to 13 in the first ten games of the season.

1913	Manchester United	A	League Division 1	0–3
1919	Burnley	H	League Division 1	0–1
1930	Manchester City	H	League Division 1	0–2

1937 Jimmy Melia was born in Liverpool. Joined the club from schoolboy level and spent the next 11 years playing in the first team.

1947	Blackpool	A	League Division 1	0–2
1952	Wolves	H	League Division 1	2–1
1958	Stoke City	A	League Division 2	2–0
1969	Derby County	A	League Division 1	0–4
1975	Middlesbrough	A	League Division 1	1–0
1980	Stoke City	A	League Division 1	2–2
1986	Norwich City	H	League Division 1	6–2
1987	Everton	H	League Division 1	2–0
1988	Arsenal	H	League Cup 3rd round	1–1
1997	Bolton Wanderers	A	Premier League	1–1

NOVEMBER 2ND

1895	Newton Heath	A	League Division 2	2–5
1901	Manchester City	A	League Division 1	3–2
1907	Bristol City	A	League Division 1	0–2
1912	Tottenham Hotspur	H	League Division 1	4–1
1929	Portsmouth	A	League Division 1	3–3
1935	Middlesbrough	A	League Division 1	2–2
1946	Blackburn Rovers	A	League Division 1	0–0
1957	Lincoln City	A	League Division 2	1–0
1963	Leicester City	H	League Division 1	0–1
1968	West Bromwich Albion	A	League Division 1	0–0
1974	Ipswich Town	A	League Division 1	0–1
1977	Dynamo Dresden	A	European Cup 2nd round 2nd leg	1–2
1982	JK Helsinki	H	European Cup 2nd round 2nd leg	5–0
1983	Athletic Bilbao	A	European Cup 2nd round 2nd leg	1–0
1985	Leicester City	H	League Division 1	1–0

Every now and again teams play against opposition and no matter what happens you know you may never score if you played until the following day, and this game looked like it was going to fall into that category, thanks to a fine display of goalkeeping from youngster Ian Andrews in the Leicester goal. No matter what Liverpool threw at him he saved, one in the second half from Molby described by some as good as Banks's from Pele. So it was a huge surprise to the Anfield crowd when Rush scored with probably the softest shot of the afternoon with five minutes to go, leaving the wonderful Andrews and the plucky Leicester with nothing from the game. With 15 League games gone Liverpool were still 10 points behind leaders Manchester United.

1991	Crystal Palace	H	League Division 1	1–2

NOVEMBER 3RD

1894	Burnley	H	League Division 1	0–3
1900	Wolves	A	League Division 1	1–2
1906	Middlesbrough	A	League Division 1	1–0
1923	Huddersfield Town	H	League Division 1	1–1
1928	Birmingham City	H	League Division 1	1–2
1934	Wolves	H	League Division 1	2–1
1951	Newcastle United	A	League Division 1	1–1
1956	Port Vale	H	League Division 2	4–1
1962	Burnley	H	League Division 1	1–2
1971	Bayern Munich	A	European Cup-Winners' Cup 2nd round 2nd leg	1–3
1973	Arsenal	A	League Division 1	2–0
1976	Trabzonspor	H	European Cup 2nd round 2nd leg	3–0
1979	Wolves	H	League Division 1	3–0
1984	Stoke City	A	League Division 1	1–0
1986	Motherwell	A	Friendly	1–1
1996	Blackburn Rovers	A	Premier League	0–3

NOVEMBER 4TH

1893	Newcastle United	H	League Division 2	5–1
1899	Sheffield United	H	League Division 1	2–2
1905	Bury	H	League Division 1	3–1
1911	Notts County	H	League Division 1	3–0
1922	Tottenham Hotspur	A	League Division 1	4–2
1933	Birmingham City	A	League Division 1	2–1
1950	Newcastle United	H	League Division 1	2–4
1961	Preston North End	A	League Division 2	3–1
1967	Tottenham Hotspur	A	League Division 1	1–1
1970	Dinamo Bucharest	A	European Fairs Cup 2nd round 2nd leg	1–1
1972	Chelsea	H	League Division 1	3–1
1975	Real Sociedad	H	UEFA Cup 2nd round 2nd leg	6–0

The debut appearance in the first team for David Fairclough when he came on as substitute and scored. Something he was to repeat on many more occasions. He was to make a total of 88 appearances in all with 62 of those with him sitting in the dug-out at kick-off, and had scored an amazing 52 goals to give him one of the highest ratios in the club's goalscoring history.

1978	Leeds United	H	League Division 1	1–1
1981	AZ67 Alkmaar	H	European Cup 2nd round 2nd leg	3–2
1987	Wimbledon	A	League Division 1	1–1
1989	Coventry City	H	League Division 1	0–1
1990	Tottenham Hotspur	A	League Division 1	3–1
1992	Spartak Moscow	H	European Cup-Winners' Cup 2nd round 2nd leg	0–2
1995	Newcastle United	A	Premier League	1–2
1997	R.C.Strasbourg	H	UEFA Cup 2nd round 2nd leg	2–0

NOVEMBER 5TH

1892	Blackpool	A	Lancashire League	0–3
1898	Newcastle United	A	League Division 1	0–3
1904	Blackpool	A	League Division 2	3–0
1910	Middlesbrough	A	League Division 1	2–2

1911 'Nivvy' Nieuwenhuys was born in Transvaal. One of the first South Africans to arrive at Anfield in the autumn of 1933.

1921	Everton	A	League Division 1	1–1
1927	Cardiff City	A	League Division 1	1–1
1932	Leeds United	H	League Division 1	0–1
1938	Portsmouth	A	League Division 1	1–1
1949	Manchester City	H	League Division 1	4–0
1955	Swansea Town	A	League Division 2	1–2
1960	Plymouth Argyle	A	League Division 2	4–0
1966	Nottingham Forest	H	League Division 1	4–0

1969 Emlyn Hughes started his distinguished international career for England in the 1–0 victory over Holland in Amsterdam.

1971 Rob Jones was born in Wrexham. Another product of the Dario Gradi academy at Crewe Alexandra, Rob played over 90 games for the club, even managing to score two goals before joining Liverpool in October 1991.

1974	Ferencvaros	A	European Cup-Winners' Cup 2nd round 2nd leg	0–0
1977	Aston Villa	H	League Division 1	1–2
1980	Aberdeen	H	European Cup 2nd round 2nd leg	4–0
1988	Middlesbrough	H	League Division 1	3–0
1994	Nottingham Forest	H	Premier League	1–0

NOVEMBER 6TH

1897	Nottingham Forest	H	League Division 1	1–2
1909	Bury	H	League Division 1	2–2
1920	Bradford	H	League Division 1	0–1
1926	Huddersfield Town	H	League Division 1	2–3
1937	Brentford	H	League Division 1	3–4
1948	Portsmouth	H	League Division 1	3–1
1954	Hull City	H	League Division 2	2–1

1957 Alan A'Court made his international debut for England in the 2–3 defeat by Northern Ireland at Wembley. He was to win another four caps in his career.

1965	Sheffield Wednesday	A	League Division 1	2–0
1971	Arsenal	H	League Division 1	3–2
1973	Red Star Belgrade	H	European Cup 2nd round 2nd leg	1–2
1976	Sunderland	A	League Division 1	1–0
1979	Lille OSC	A	Friendly	1–3
1982	Everton	A	League Division 1	5–0

Ian Rush equalled the individual goalscoring record for the Merseyside derby with a four-goal blast at Goodison, with Mark Lawrenson adding the other in a complete rout by Liverpool. Everton had Glenn Keeley sent off for a professional foul on Dalglish.

1983	Everton	H	League Division 1	3–0
1991	Auxerre	H	UEFA Cup 2nd round 2nd leg	3–0
1993	West Ham United	H	Premier League	2–0

NOVEMBER 7TH

1896	Sunderland	H	League Division 1	3–0
1903	Notts County	H	League Division 1	2–1
1908	Bristol City	A	League Division 1	0–1
1914	Newcastle United	A	League Division 1	0–0

1929 Dave Hickson was born in Cheshire. Dave joined from Everton for a fee of £10,000 in the winter of 1959.

1931	Blackburn Rovers	H	League Division 1	4–2
1936	Preston North End	A	League Division 1	1–3
1953	Manchester City	H	League Division 1	2–2
1959	Aston Villa	H	League Division 2	2–1

Liverpool against Aston Villa in the Second Division had an unfamiliar ring to it, but at Anfield 49,981 saw Villa go down 2–1 for their first defeat in 15 matches, thanks to two goals by Dave Hickson.

1963 John Barnes was born in Jamaica. He signed for Watford as a 14-year-old and later helped them rise through the divisions and played in the 1984 FA Cup final defeat by Everton. He moved to Liverpool in the summer of 1987 for £900,000 after Arsenal, who were also keen to sign him, weren't prepared to meet his wage demands under their strict pay structure. This, of course, turned out to be Liverpool's gain and Arsenal's loss. John had played over 280 games for Watford scoring just over 80 goals.

1964	Fulham	A	League Division 1	1–1
1967	TSV Munchen 1860	H	European Fairs Cup 2nd round 1st leg	8–0
1970	Derby County	A	League Division 1	0–0
1972	AEK Athens	A	UEFA Cup 2nd round 2nd leg	3–1
1981	Everton	H	League Division 1	3–1
1984	Benfica	A	European Cup 2nd round 2nd leg	0–1
1992	Middlesbrough	H	Premier League	4–1

NOVEMBER 8TH

1902	Newcastle United	A	League Division 1	2–1
1913	Burnley	H	League Division 1	1–1
1917	Barney Ramsden was born in Sheffield.			
1919	Bradford	A	League Division 1	2–1
1924	Preston North End	H	League Division 1	3–1
1930	Derby County	A	League Division 1	2–2
1947	Grimsby Town	H	League Division 1	3–1
1952	Charlton Athletic	A	League Division 1	2–3
1958	Leyton Orient	H	League Division 2	3–0
1969	Wolves	H	League Division 1	0–0
1975	Manchester United	H	League Division 1	3–1
1980	Nottingham Forest	H	League Division 1	0–0
1983	Fulham	A	League Cup 3rd round	1–1
1986	Queens Park Rangers	A	League Division 1	3–1

1994   One of the most astonishing stories in football broke. *The Sun* printed a story in which former Liverpool goalkeeper and Southampton custodian Bruce Grobbelaar was accused of accepting bribes to 'throw' games. There were five games, they claimed, that Grobbelaar attempted or succeeded in throwing. These were: Newcastle United v Liverpool on 21 November 1993, which resulted in a 3–0 win for Newcastle; Liverpool v Manchester United on 4 January 1994, 3–3; Norwich City v Liverpool on 5 February 1994, 2–2; Coventry City v Southampton on 24 September 1994, a 3–1 win for Southampton; and Manchester City v Southampton on 5 November 1994, 3–3. Additionally, the newspaper alleged they had evidence that Grobbelaar agreed to influence the result of the Liverpool v Southampton game that was to be played the following March. It was claimed that Grobbelaar was paid £40,000 for the game against the Magpies and that a Far East betting syndicate had staked £150,000 at odds of 20–1 that Newcastle would win 3–0, thereby collecting £3–million winnings. It was also claimed that had Manchester United won their game in January, Grobbelaar would have collected £125,000, as well as a further £80,000 from the Norwich City game, an undisclosed fee for the Coventry game and £50,000 from a recent game with Manchester City. His fee, which it is claimed was accepted, for throwing the Liverpool v Southampton game in March 1995 was to be £100,000, plus a retainer of £2,000 which would be paid fortnightly up until the match, netting him a further £34,000. *The Sun*, who also claimed to have videotaped evidence of the various transactions taking place, handed their dossier over to the Football Association, which in turn announced an immediate investigation into the claims. The affair ended in the Criminal Court where the case against Grobbelaar was dismissed.

| 1997 | Tottenham Hotspur | H | Premier League | 4–0 |

NOVEMBER 9TH

1895	Leicester Fosse	H	League Division 2	3–1
1901	Wolves	H	League Division 1	4–1
1907	Notts County	H	League Division 1	6–0
1912	Middlesbrough	A	League Division 1	4–3
1929	Bolton Wanderers	H	League Division 1	3–0
1935	Aston Villa	H	League Division 1	3–2
1946	Portsmouth	H	League Division 1	3–0

Jack Balmer scored a hat-trick.

1957	Notts County	H	League Division 2	4–0
1963	Bolton Wanderers	A	League Division 1	2–1
1966	Burnley	H	League Division 1	2–0
1968	Chelsea	H	League Division 1	2–1

1972 Larry Lloyd became the first player to fight a ban before the newly formed independent disciplinary tribunal. Lloyd had previously been sent off in the opening game of the season for chopping down and then kicking Wyn Davies of Manchester City. Although the tribunal did not call the referee (Gordon Kew) or his linesmen to give evidence, they did watch a television film of the incident and found: 'The tribunal is satisfied that Lloyd is not free from blame. It does, however, regard his sending-off as sufficient punishment and therefore quashes the sentence of a three-match suspension imposed by the Football Association.' More than a quarter of a century later there still is no hard and fast rules about when video evidence may be used. The men in grey suits at Lancaster Gate take action against certain individuals only, whilst others seem to escape punishment.

1974	Arsenal	H	League Division 1	1–3
1976	Leicester City	H	League Division 1	5–1
1985	Coventry City	A	League Division 1	3–0

This was to be one of the key days in the season for Liverpool, as they coasted to a comfortable victory thanks to goals from Beglin, Walsh and Rush. Grobbelaar hardly had a save to make and Liverpool bossed the game at their own pace with ease. What made the victory even sweeter was the news that Manchester United had been beaten for the first time, 1–0 away to Sheffield Wednesday, and that the margin at the top of the league was now only seven points. This was to be the last game that Phil Neal was to play in a Liverpool shirt before he took over as player-manager at Bolton. After nearly eleven years to the day, Phil hardly missed a game during his time at Anfield and proved to be not only Bob Paisley's first signing but also possibly the shrewdest. He played a total of 635 games, scoring 60 goals. His medal collection was pretty impressive and during his eleven years he won: seven Division 1 Championship medals, four FA Cup medals, four consecutive League Cup winners' medals, four European Cup winners' medals and one UEFA Cup medal. In addition he won 50 caps for England whilst at the club. A true Anfield legend.

| 1988 | Arsenal | A | League Cup 3rd round replay | 0–0 |

NOVEMBER 10TH

1894	Stoke City	A	League Division 1	1–3
1900	Aston Villa	H	League Division 1	5–1
1906	Preston North End	H	League Division 1	6–1
1923	Huddersfield Town	A	League Division 1	1–3
1928	Portsmouth	A	League Division 1	1–0
1934	Huddersfield Town	A	League Division 1	0–8
1951	Bolton Wanderers	H	League Division 1	1–1
1956	Rotherham United	A	League Division 2	2–2
1962	Manchester United	A	League Division 1	3–3
1973	Wolves	H	League Division 1	1–0

Patrik Berger was born in Prague, Czechoslovakia. Patrik was one of the stars of Euro 96 for his country, who ultimately reached the final and attracted immediate attention from a host of clubs throughout Europe. He joined Liverpool in the summer of 1996.

1979	Brighton & Hove Albion	A	League Division 1	4–1
1981	Middlesbrough	H	League Cup 3rd round	4–1

1987 Mark Lawrenson won his 38th and last cap for the Republic of Ireland in the 5–0 win over Israel.

1990	Luton Town	H	League Division 1	4–0

NOVEMBER 11TH

1893	Walsall Town Swifts	A	League Division 2	1–1
1899	Newcastle United	A	League Division 1	1–1
1905	Middlesbrough	A	League Division 1	5–1

Joe Hewitt scored his first hat-trick of his Liverpool career.

1911	Tottenham Hotspur	A	League Division 1	0–2
1922	Tottenham Hotspur	H	League Division 1	0–0
1933	Leeds United	H	League Division 1	4–3

Sam English scored two goals in a run that was to see him score in five successive games with eight goals during that time.

1950	Huddersfield Town	A	League Division 1	2–2
1961	Luton Town	H	League Division 2	1–1
1967	Manchester United	H	League Division 1	1–2
1972	Manchester United	A	League Division 1	0–2
1978	Queens Park Rangers	A	League Division 1	3–1
1980	Coventry City	H	League Division 1	2–1
1982	Rotherham United	H	League Cup 3rd round	1–0
1989	Queens Park Rangers	A	League Division 1	2–3
1992	Sheffield United	H	League Cup 3rd round replay	3–0

NOVEMBER 12TH

1892	Fleetwood Rovers	A	Lancashire League	4–1
1898	Preston North End	H	League Division 1	3–1
1904	Burslem Port Vale	A	League Division 2	2–1
1910	Preston North End	H	League Division 1	3–0
1921	Everton	H	League Division 1	1–1
1924	Huddersfield Town	H	League Division 1	2–3

1927	Sheffield Wednesday	H	League Division 1	5–2
1932	Blackburn Rovers	A	League Division 1	2–2
1938	Arsenal	H	League Division 1	2–2
1949	Charlton Athletic	A	League Division 1	3–1
1955	Notts County	H	League Division 2	2–1
1960	Norwich City	H	League Division 2	2–1
1966	Newcastle United	A	League Division 1	2–0
1969	Vitoria Setubal	A	European Fairs Cup 2nd round 1st leg	0–1
1974	Middlesbrough	H	League Cup 4th Round	0–1
1977	Queens Park Rangers	A	League Division 1	0–2
1983	Tottenham Hotspur	A	League Division 1	2–2
1988	Millwall	H	League Division 1	1–1

NOVEMBER 13TH

1897	West Bromwich Albion	A	League Division 1	1–2
1909	Tottenham Hotspur	A	League Division 1	0–1
1920	Bradford	A	League Division 1	3–1
1926	Sunderland	A	League Division 1	1–2
1937	Manchester City	A	League Division 1	3–1
1948	Manchester City	A	League Division 1	4–2
1954	Luton Town	A	League Division 2	2–3
1957	Hibernian	H	Friendly	3–3
1965	Northampton Town	H	League Division 1	5–0
1971	Everton	A	League Division 1	0–1
1981	Irish Internationals	Dublin	Friendly	1–0
1982	Coventry City	H	League Division 1	4–0
1996	Charlton Athletic	H	League Cup 3rd round replay	4–1

NOVEMBER 14TH

1896	Preston North End	A	League Division 1	1–1
1903	Sheffield United	A	League Division 1	1–2
1908	Preston North End	H	League Division 1	2–1
1914	Middlesbrough	H	League Division 1	1–1
1925	West Bromwich Albion	H	League Division 1	2–0
1931	Sunderland	A	League Division 1	3–1
1936	Sheffield Wednesday	H	League Division 1	2–2
1953	Sunderland	A	League Division 1	2–3
1959	Lincoln City	A	League Division 2	2–4
1962	Arsenal	H	League Division 1	2–1
1964	Nottingham Forest	H	League Division 1	2–0
1967	TSV Munchen 1860	A	European Fairs Cup 2nd round 2nd leg	1–2
1970	Coventry City	H	League Division 1	0–0

NOVEMBER 15TH

1895   Neil McBain born in Campbeltown. He is assured of his place in the history books for becoming the oldest player to have appeared in the Football League in 1947, at the age of 51 years and four months. He was forced to select himself as emergency goalkeeper for New Brighton, where he was manager, conceding three goals as Hartlepool's United won 3–0. He began his career with Manchester United in November 1921 shortly after his £6,250 transfer from Ayr United. He requested a transfer in January 1923 and was sold to Everton, spending four seasons at Goodison, later playing for St Johnstone, Liverpool (he only played 12 games in the two seasons he was at the club) and Watford before moving into management. His last position was back at Ayr United in 1963. He died on 13th May 1974.

1902	Wolves	H	League Division 1	4–1
1913	Preston North End	A	League Division 1	1–0
1919	Bradford	H	League Division 1	3–3
1924	Burnley	A	League Division 1	1–2
1930	Leicester City	H	League Division 1	3–1

1937 Ron Yeats was born in Aberdeen. After playing for his local boys club Ron moved to Dundee United before Liverpool bought him for £22,000.

1947	Sunderland	A	League Division 1	1–5
1952	Arsenal	H	League Division 1	1–5
1958	Derby County	A	League Division 2	2–3
1969	West Ham United	H	League Division 1	2–0

The BBC's *Match of the Day* broadcasted in colour for the first time. Fittingly, Liverpool, who were one of the clubs to have been featured when the programme first aired in 1964 against Arsenal, were again featured, this time beating West Ham.

1972 Ray Clemence and Kevin Keegan both made their international debuts for England in the 1–0 victory over Wales in Cardiff.

1975	Newcastle United	A	League Division 1	2–1
1980	Crystal Palace	A	League Division 1	2–2
1987	Manchester United	A	League Division 1	1–1

NOVEMBER 16TH

1895	Arsenal	A	League Division 2	2–0
1907	Manchester City	A	League Division 1	1–1
1912	Notts County	H	League Division 1	0–0
1929	Aston Villa	A	League Division 1	3–2
1935	Wolves	A	League Division 1	1–3
1946	Derby County	A	League Division 1	4–1

Jack Balmer, a week after scoring a hat-trick, scored all four goals in this victory.

1957	Ipswich Town	A	League Division 2	1–3
1960	Southampton	H	League Cup 3rd round	1–2
1963	Fulham	H	League Division 1	2–0
1974	Everton	A	League Division 1	0–0

Phil Neal made his first team debut after signing for the club some six years earlier.

1985 West Bromwich Albion H   League Division 1   4–1

With the Reds on a roll, West Bromwich Albion looked as though they knew they were on to a hiding even during the kick in before the game. The only amazing fact was that they went in at half-time at 1–1, when it could have been at least 5–1 to the Reds. Garth Crooks scored in the 36th minute with the visitors only shot of the game before Nicol scored just on the stroke of half-time after good work from Walsh. Kenny's team talk at half-time was probably keep on playing the same way and the goals will come, and that is exactly what happened. Still charging forward Molby scored, before Lawrenson running what seemed like the length of the pitch to score the third and Walsh deservedly scoring a goal himself, which was his eighth in six games, he was still trying to prove a point while on the transfer list. The result was even sweeter with news that Manchester United had dropped another point, which meant that the gap was now down to five points, and the championship race was still alive, contrary to what the rest of the country thought.

| 1986 | Sheffield Wednesday | H | League Division 1 | 1–1 |

1994 Steve McManaman came on as substitute for England in their 1–0 victory over Nigeria to start his international career.

| 1996 | Leeds United | A | Premier League | 2–0 |

NOVEMBER 17TH

| 1894 | Everton | H | League Division 1 | 2–2 |

Everton's first-ever visit to Anfield in a League game. Hannah and Ross, with a last-minute equaliser, scored the goals.

1896 Harry Chambers was born in Northumberland.

1900	Sheffield Wednesday	A	League Division 1	2–3
1906	Newcastle United	A	League Division 1	0–2
1923	Aston Villa	A	League Division 1	0–0
1928	Bolton Wanderers	H	League Division 1	3–0
1934	Leicester City	H	League Division 1	5–1
1951	Stoke City	A	League Division 1	2–1
1956	Lincoln City	H	League Division 2	4–0
1962	Leyton Orient	H	League Division 1	5–0
1965	Blackburn Rovers	H	League Division 1	5–2
1973	Ipswich Town	H	League Division 1	4–2
1979	Tottenham Hotspur	H	League Division 1	2–1

1982 Sammy Lee scored on his debut for England in the 3–0 win over Greece in Salonika, during the European Championship qualifier.

| 1990 | Coventry City | A | League Division 1 | 1–0 |
| 1991 | West Ham United | A | League Division 1 | 0–0 |

NOVEMBER 18TH

1893	Notts County	H	League Division 2	2–1
1899	Aston Villa	H	League Division 1	3–3
1905	Preston North End	H	League Division 1	1–1
1911	Manchester United	H	League Division 1	3–2
1922	Aston Villa	H	League Division 1	3–0
1933	Derby County	A	League Division 1	1–3
1950	Arsenal	H	League Division 1	1–3
1961	Huddersfield Town	A	League Division 2	2–1
1967	Sunderland	A	League Division 1	1–1
1972	Newcastle United	H	League Division 1	3–2
1984	Newcastle United	A	League Division 1	2–0
1995	Everton	H	Premier League	1–2
1997	Grimsby Town	H	League Cup 4th Round	3–0

Michael Owen scored his first hat-trick for the club. It's safe to say there will be many more to come.

NOVEMBER 19TH

1892	Northwich Victoria	A	FA Cup Qualifying round	1–2
1898	Bury	A	League Division 1	0–3
1904	Gainsborough Town	A	League Division 2	2–1
1910	Notts County	A	League Division 1	0–1
1921	Middlesbrough	H	League Division 1	4–0
1927	Middlesbrough	A	League Division 1	1–1
1932	Derby County	H	League Division 1	6–1
1938	Brentford	A	League Division 1	1–2
1949	Aston Villa	H	League Division 1	2–1
1955	Leeds United	A	League Division 2	2–4
1960	Charlton Athletic	A	League Division 2	3–1

1965   Gary Ablett was born in Liverpool. Gary was to play over 100 games for the club before moving to Everton in 1992. Later joined Birmingham City for £390,000 in 1996.

| 1966 | Leeds United | H | League Division 1 | 5–0 |

1975   Joey Jones won his first cap for Wales in the 1–0 win over Austria at Wrexham. He went on to win over 70 caps for his country.

| 1977 | Bristol City | H | League Division 1 | 1–1 |

John Toshack played his final game for the club in which he set up the goal for Kenny Dalglish. Toshack arrived from Cardiff in 1970. He formed an ideal foil for Kevin Keegan and created many goals for his fellow striker and was the perfect foil. He played in a total of 236 games in his seven-year spell scoring 95 goals. He won 3 Championship medals, 2 UEFA Cup winners' medals and the FAC cup in 1974. He moved to Swansea as player–manager and guided them from the Fourth division straight to the First. He later moved to Europe where he managed as well.

1983	Stoke City	H	League Division 1	1–0
1986	Coventry City	A	Littlewoods Cup 4th Round	0–0
1988	Queens Park Rangers	A	League Division 1	1–0
1989	Millwall	A	League Division 1	2–1

NOVEMBER 20TH

1897	Wolves	H	League Division 1	1–0
1909	Preston North End	H	League Division 1	2–0
1920	Newcastle United	A	League Division 1	0–2
1926	West Bromwich Albion	H	League Division 1	2–1
1937	Huddersfield Town	H	League Division 1	0–1
1948	Charlton Athletic	H	League Division 1	1–1
1954	Nottingham Forest	H	League Division 2	1–0

1961   Dave Watson born in Liverpool. He first signed professional forms with Liverpool in 1979 but was sold to Norwich City for £100,000 without having played for the first team in 1980. After helping the Canaries to the League Cup in 1985 he returned to Merseyside in 1986, costing Everton £900,000.

| 1965 | Stoke City | A | League Division 1 | 0–0 |
| 1971 | Coventry City | A | League Division 1 | 2–0 |

1976	Arsenal	A	League Division 1	1–1
1982	Notts County	A	League Division 1	2–1
1991	Port Vale	A	League Cup 3rd round replay	4–1
1996	Everton	H	Premier League	1–1

NOVEMBER 21ST

1876	Jack Cox was born in Blackpool. Cox played for Blackpool before moving to Liverpool in 1898.			
1896	Everton	H	League Division 1	0–0
1903	Newcastle United	H	League Division 1	1–0
1908	Middlesbrough	A	League Division 1	0–1
1914	Sheffield United	A	League Division 1	1–2
1925	Birmingham City	A	League Division 1	0–2
1931	Manchester City	H	League Division 1	4–3

Cyril Done scored with the last kick of the game for his second and Liverpool's fourth goal to secure the win.

1936	Manchester United	A	League Division 1	5–2

Fred Howe scored a hat-trick. His first was in the last minute of the first half and his second coming in injury time of the second. Any time you score five against Manchester United is worth savouring.

1953	Arsenal	H	League Division 1	1–2
1959	Leyton Orient	H	League Division 2	4–3

Despite trailing for most of the game Fred Morris scored the winner for Liverpool just 10 minutes from the end.

1964	Stoke City	A	League Division 1	1–1
1970	Everton	H	League Division 1	3–2

Three goals in the last twenty minutes earned Liverpool another derby victory in a pulsating second half which produced all five goals.

1973	Sunderland	A	League Cup 3rd round	2–0
1981	West Bromwich Albion	A	League Division 1	1–1
1987	Norwich City	H	League Division 1	0–0
1993	Newcastle United	A	Premier League	0–3

NOVEMBER 22ND

1902	Derby County	A	League Division 1	1–2
1913	Newcastle United	H	League Division 1	0–0
1919	Preston North End	A	League Division 1	1–2
1924	Leeds United	H	League Division 1	1–0
1930	Portsmouth	A	League Division 1	0–4
1944	Bob Graham was born in Motherwell. He joined Liverpool straight from school in 1960 as an apprentice, where he was to stay for 12 years.			
1947	Blackburn Rovers	H	League Division 1	2–1
1952	Derby County	A	League Division 1	2–3

Ronnie Moran made his debut for the club.

1958	Bristol Rovers	H	League Division 2	2–1
1969	Leeds United	A	League Division 1	1–1
1972	Leeds United	A	League Cup 4th round replay	1–0

1975	Coventry City	H	League Division 1	1–1
1976	Northampton Town	A	Friendly	2–2
1977	SV Hamburg	A	European Super Cup	1–1
1980	Aston Villa	H	League Division 1	2–1
1983	Fulham	H	League Cup 3rd round replay	1–1
1997	Barnsley	H	Premier League	0–1

NOVEMBER 23RD

1895	Darwen	H	League Division 2	0–0
1901	Newcastle United	A	League Division 1	0–1
1907	Preston North End	H	League Division 1	1–2
1912	Manchester United	A	League Division 1	1–3
1929	Leeds United	H	League Division 1	1–0
1935	Derby County	H	League Division 1	0–0
1946	Arsenal	H	League Division 1	4–2

Jack Balmer became the only player to have scored hat-tricks (or more) on three successive Saturdays. Two weeks earlier he scored all three in 3–0 home win over Portsmouth, followed that with all four in the 4–1 win at Derby the following week and in this game he netted three in the 4–2 win over Arsenal.

1957	Blackburn Rovers	H	League Division 2	2–0
1963	Manchester United	A	League Division 1	1–0
1974	West Ham United	H	League Division 1	1–1
1982	Shamrock Rovers	A	Friendly	1–1
1985	Birmingham City	A	League Division 1	2–0

With Manchester United firmly in their sights, the team were beginning to find their rhythm and had looked pretty ominous in recent matches and this continued in another hopelessly one-sided affair at St Andrews. It was only the brilliance of young goalkeeper David Seaman in the Birmingham goal that kept the scoreline respectable for the home side. The front two of Rush and Walsh continued their fine form of previous weeks and scored a goal apiece to set up victory after just 20 minutes. The news that Manchester United had been thrashed at Filbert Street brought Liverpool within two points of the leaders.

1986	Everton	A	League Division 1	0–0
1988	Arsenal	N	League Cup 3rd round 2nd replay	2–1
1991	Wimbledon	A	League Division 1	0–0
1992	Queens Park Rangers	A	Premier League	1–0
1996	Wimbledon	H	Premier League	1–1

NOVEMBER 24TH

1894	Sunderland	A	League Division 1	2–3
1900	Newcastle United	A	League Division 1	1–1
1906	Aston Villa	H	League Division 1	5–2
1923	Aston Villa	H	League Division 1	0–1
1928	Sheffield Wednesday	A	League Division 1	2–3
1934	Derby County	A	League Division 1	2–1
1951	Manchester United	H	League Division 1	0–0
1956	Swansea Town	A	League Division 2	1–1

1962	Birmingham City	A	League Division 1	2–0
1973	Queens Park Rangers	A	League Division 1	2–2
1979	Arsenal	A	League Division 1	0–0
1984	Ipswich Town	H	League Division 1	2–0
1987	Watford	H	League Division 1	4–0
1990	Manchester City	H	League Division 1	2–2

NOVEMBER 25TH

1893	Newcastle United	A	League Division 2	0–0
1899	Wolves	H	League Division 1	1–1
1905	Newcastle United	A	League Division 1	3–2
1911	Preston North End	H	League Division 1	0–1
1922	Aston Villa	A	League Division 1	1–0
1925	Huddersfield Town	A	League Division 1	0–0
1933	West Bromwich Albion	H	League Division 1	1–1

Alan Arnell was born in Chichester. Alan was an excellent schoolboy player who represented his county on many occasions whilst he was on the books for Worthing FC before moving to Liverpool as an amateur in 1953 and turning professional in March 1954.

1947   Steve Heighway was born in Dublin.

1950	Burnley	A	League Division 1	1–1
1961	Swansea Town	H	League Division 2	5–0
1964	Anderlecht	H	European Cup 2nd round 1st leg	3–0
1967	Wolves	H	League Division 1	2–1
1972	Tottenham Hotspur	A	League Division 1	2–1
1980	Wolves	A	League Division 1	1–4
1995	Middlesbrough	A	Premier League	1–2

NOVEMBER 26TH

1892	Rossendale United	A	Lancashire League	2–0
1898	Nottingham Forest	A	League Division 1	3–0
1910	Manchester United	H	League Division 1	3–2

1915   Cyril Sidlow was born in Colwyn Bay. He arrived at Anfield just after the War after Liverpool paid Wolves £4000 for his goalkeeping services

1921	Middlesbrough	A	League Division 1	1–3
1927	Huddersfield Town	H	League Division 1	4–2
1932	Blackpool	A	League Division 1	1–4
1938	Blackpool	H	League Division 1	1–0
1949	Wolves	A	League Division 1	1–1
1955	Fulham	H	League Division 2	7–0
1960	Sheffield United	H	League Division 2	4–2
1966	West Bromwich Albion	A	League Division 1	1–2
1969	Vitoria Setubal	H	European Fairs Cup 2nd round 2nd leg	3–2
1975	Slask Wroclaw	A	UEFA Cup 3rd round 1st leg	2–1
1977	Leicester City	A	League Division 1	4–0
1983	Ipswich Town	A	League Division 1	1–1
1985	Manchester United	H	League Cup 4th Round	2–1

1986	Coventry City	H	Littlewoods Cup 4th round replay	3–1
1988	Wimbledon	H	League Division 1	1–1
1989	Arsenal	H	League Division 1	2–1
1994	Tottenham Hotspur	H	Premier League	1–1

NOVEMBER 27TH

1897	Nottingham Forest	A	League Division 1	3–2
1909	Notts County	A	League Division 1	1–3
1920	Newcastle United	H	League Division 1	0–1
1926	Bury	A	League Division 1	2–0
1937	Blackpool	A	League Division 1	1–0
1942	Peter Thompson was born in Carlisle. Peter signed from Preston in 1963 for £37,000.
1948	Stoke City	A	League Division 1	0–3
1954	Leeds United	A	League Division 2	2–2
1957	Rotherham United	H	League Division 2	2–0
1965	Burnley	H	League Division 1	2–1
1971	West Ham United	H	League Division 1	1–0
1973	Hull City	A	League Cup 4th Round	0–0
1976	Bristol City	H	League Division 1	2–1
1982	Tottenham Hotspur	H	League Division 1	3–0
1990	Don Hutchinson was signed from Hartlepool for £175,000.
1991	Swaravaski Tirol	A	UEFA Cup 3rd round 1st leg	2–0
1996	Arsenal	H	League Cup 4th Round	4–2

NOVEMBER 28TH

1896	Nottingham Forest	A	League Division 1	0–2
1903	Aston Villa	A	League Division 1	1–2
1908	Manchester City	H	League Division 1	1–3
1914	Aston Villa	H	League Division 1	3–6
1925	Bury	H	League Division 1	0–1
1931	Arsenal	A	League Division 1	0–6

A humiliating performance at the hands of Arsenal for whom Jack Lambert scored a second-half hat-trick.

1936	Derby County	H	League Division 1	3–3
1953	Cardiff City	A	League Division 1	1–3
1959	Huddersfield Town	A	League Division 2	0–1
1964	Tottenham Hotspur	H	League Division 1	1–1
1967	Ferencvaros	A	European Fairs Cup 3rd round 1st leg	0–1
1970	Arsenal	A	League Division 1	0–2
1981	Southampton	H	League Division 1	0–1
1987	Tottenham Hotspur	A	League Division 1	2–0
1992	Crystal Palace	H	Premier League	5–0
1993	Aston Villa	H	Premier League	2–1
1995	Newcastle United	H	Coca-Cola Cup 4th round	0–1

NOVEMBER 29TH

| 1902 | Sheffield United | A | League Division 1 | 0–2 |

1913	Tottenham Hotspur	H	League Division 1	2–1
1919	Preston North End	H	League Division 1	1–2
1924	Birmingham City	A	League Division 1	2–5
1930	Sheffield United	H	League Division 1	6–1

Gordon Hodgson helped himself to another hat-trick. He was to go on and score 36 goals in 40 games during the season.

1947	Manchester City	A	League Division 1	0–2
1952	Blackpool	H	League Division 1	2–2
1958	Ipswich Town	A	League Division 2	0–2
1969	Arsenal	H	League Division 1	0–1
1972	Dynamo Berlin	A	UEFA Cup 3rd round 1st leg	0–0
1975	Norwich City	H	League Division 1	1–3
1977	Coventry City	H	League Cup 4th Round	2–2
1980	Sunderland	A	League Division 1	4–2
1983	Fulham	A	League Cup 3rd round 2nd replay	1–0
1986	Coventry City	H	League Division 1	2–0
1989	Sheffield Wednesday	A	League Division 1	0–2

NOVEMBER 30TH

1895	Leicester Fosse	A	League Division 2	0–2
1901	Aston Villa	H	League Division 1	1–0
1912	Aston Villa	H	League Division 1	2–0
1929	Sheffield Wednesday	A	League Division 1	1–2
1935	Portsmouth	A	League Division 1	1–2
1946	Blackpool	A	League Division 1	2–3
1954	Watford	A	Friendly	2–3
1957	Sheffield United	A	League Division 2	1–1
1960	Nantes	H	Friendly	5–1
1963	Burnley	H	League Division 1	2–0

1970 Phil Babb was born in London. Phil started his career with Bradford City before moving to Coventry in a £500,000 deal in the summer of 1992. After a very impressive two years Roy Evans splashed out nearly £4 million for Babb who was to form a three man defence with Neil Ruddock and another new signing, John Scales.

1974	Coventry City	A	League Division 1	1–1
1982	Norwich City	H	League Cup 4th Round	2–0
1985	Chelsea	H	League Division 1	1–1

Chelsea arrived at Anfield knowing that the previous 18 visiting teams had all left empty handed. They were under the charge of new manager John Hollins and thus were determined to prove themselves to him. With a below-par performance by Liverpool they thoroughly deserved their point, and were probably unlucky not to take all three. Liverpool were awarded a fortunate penalty gratefully accepted by Molby in the 85th minute after referee Neil Ashley spotted an infringement in the penalty area, something the 38,482-strong crowd had missed. Justice was done, however, when Pat Nevin scored a very late equaliser after Bruce Grobbelaar had gone on one of his goalmouth expeditions, while seemingly forgetting about the ball. It was not all bad news as Watford scored a late equaliser at Old Trafford to keep the gap at the top of the league to two points.

1988	West Ham United	A	League Cup 4th Round	1–4
1991	Norwich City	H	League Division 1	2–1
1994	Blackburn Rovers	A	League Cup 4th Round	1–3
1997	Arsenal	A	Premier League	1–0

DECEMBER 1ST

1894	Wolves	H	League Division 1	3–3
1900	Sheffield United	H	League Division 1	1–2
1906	Derby County	A	League Division 1	1–0
1923	Sheffield United	A	League Division 1	1–1
1928	Derby County	H	League Division 1	3–0
1934	Aston Villa	H	League Division 1	3–1
1951	Tottenham Hotspur	A	League Division 1	3–2
1956	Sheffield United	H	League Division 2	5–1
1962	Fulham	H	League Division 1	2–1
1965	Standard Liege	H	European Cup-Winners' Cup 1st round 1st leg	3–1
1973	West Ham United	H	League Division 1	1–0
1979	Middlesbrough	H	League Division 1	4–0
1981	Arsenal	A	League Cup 4th Round	0–0
1984	Chelsea	A	League Division 1	1–3

Jan Molby scored his first goal for the club.

| 1992 | Crystal Palace | H | League Cup 4th Round | 1–1 |
| 1993 | Wimbledon | H | League Cup 4th Round | 1–1 |

DECEMBER 2ND

1893	Ardwick	H	League Division 2	3–0
1899	Burnley	A	League Division 1	1–2
1905	Aston Villa	H	League Division 1	3–0
1911	Aston Villa	A	League Division 1	0–5
1922	Newcastle United	H	League Division 1	0–2
1933	Arsenal	A	League Division 1	1–2
1950	Chelsea	H	League Division 1	1–0
1961	Southampton	A	League Division 2	0–2
1967	Fulham	A	League Division 1	1–1
1972	Birmingham City	H	League Division 1	4–3
1975	Arsenal	H	League Division 1	2–2
1978	Arsenal	A	League Division 1	0–1
1980	Birmingham City	H	League Cup 5th round	3–1
1989	Manchester City	A	League Division 1	4–1
1990	Arsenal	A	League Division 1	0–3
1995	Southampton	H	Premier League	1–1
1996	Tottenham Hotspur	A	Premier League	2–0

DECEMBER 3RD

1892	Fleetwood Rovers	H	Lancashire League	7–0
1898	Bolton Wanderers	H	League Division 1	2–0
1904	Bolton Wanderers	A	League Division 2	0–2

1910	Oldham Athletic	A	League Division 1	1–3
1921	Aston Villa	A	League Division 1	1–1
1927	Newcastle United	A	League Division 1	1–1
1932	Sunderland	H	League Division 1	3–3
1938	Derby County	A	League Division 1	2–2
1949	Portsmouth	H	League Division 1	2–2
1955	Port Vale	A	League Division 2	1–1
1966	Sheffield United	H	League Division 1	1–0
1968	Southampton	H	League Division 1	1–0
1977	West Ham United	H	League Division 1	2–0
1983	Birmingham City	H	League Division 1	1–0
1985	Tottenham Hotspur	H	Screen Sport Super Cup 2nd round 1st leg	2–0
1991	Peterborough United	A	League Cup 4th Round	0–1
1994	Coventry City	A	Premier League	1–1

DECEMBER 4TH

1900 Rev Jimmy Jackson was born in Newcastle. He started his professional career in Scotland with Queen's Park before moving on to Aberdeen where he enjoyed four good years before coming south to Liverpool in the May of 1925.

1909	Newcastle United	H	League Division 1	6–5

From the very first minute when Newcastle took the lead, Liverpool were always going to be chasing what appeared to be a lost cause. This seemed to be the case when at half-time they went into the dressing-rooms trailing 2–5. Ronald Orr grabbed a pair in the second half with Robinson getting another, making the game all square at 5–5. Unbelievably Arthur Goddard grabbed the winner in the closing minutes to cap a famous victory that many of the 20,000 crowd will not forget for a very long time. Tom Watson the manager was reported to have stayed in his office during the second half only appearing on the touchline when he heard that Liverpool had equalised. Some 90 years later this fixture still provides similar scorelines.

1920	Burnley	H	League Division 1	0–0
1926	Birmingham City	H	League Division 1	2–1
1937	Derby County	H	League Division 1	3–4
1948	Burnley	H	League Division 1	1–1
1954	Middlesbrough	H	League Division 2	3–1
1965	Chelsea	A	League Division 1	1–0
1971	Ipswich Town	A	League Division 1	0–0
1972	Tottenham Hotspur	H	League Cup 5th round	1–1
1973	Hull City	H	League Cup 4th round replay	3–1
1976	Ipswich Town	A	League Division 1	0–1
1978	Anderlecht	A	European Super Cup	1–3
1982	Norwich City	A	League Division 1	0–1
1984	Coventry City	H	League Division 1	3–1
1988	Arsenal	A	League Division 1	1–1
1993	Sheffield Wednesday	A	Premier League	1–3

DECEMBER 5TH

1908	Sheffield Wednesday	A	League Division 1	3–2

1914	Manchester City	A	League Division 1	1–1
1925	Blackburn Rovers	A	League Division 1	1–1
1931	Birmingham City	H	League Division 1	4–3
1936	Wolves	A	League Division 1	0–2
1949	AIK Stockholm	H	Friendly	4–2
1953	Blackpool	H	League Division 1	5–2

Alan Arnell made his League debut.

1959	Ipswich Town	H	League Division 2	3–1
1964	Burnley	A	League Division 1	5–1
1970	Leeds United	H	League Division 1	1–1
1979	Norwich City	A	League Cup 5th round	3–1
1981	Nottingham Forest	A	League Division 1	2–0

DECEMBER 6TH

1902	Grimsby Town	H	League Division 1	9–2
1913	Aston Villa	A	League Division 1	1–2
1919	Middlesbrough	A	League Division 1	2–3
1924	West Bromwich Albion	H	League Division 1	1–1
1930	Sunderland	A	League Division 1	5–6
1947	Aston Villa	H	League Division 1	3–3
1958	Swansea Town	H	League Division 2	4–0
1969	Everton	A	League Division 1	3–0
1972	Tottenham Hotspur	A	League Cup 5th round replay	1–3
1975	Burnley	A	League Division 1	0–0
1977	SV Hamburg	H	European Super Cup	6–0
1980	Tottenham Hotspur	H	League Division 1	2–1
1986	Watford	A	League Division 1	0–2
1987	Chelsea	H	League Division 1	2–1
1994	Celtic	H	Friendly	6–0
1997	Manchester United	H	Premier League	1–3

DECEMBER 7TH

1895	Loughborough Town	H	League Division 2	1–0
1901	Sheffield United	A	League Division 1	1–2
1907	Aston Villa	H	League Division 1	5–0
1912	Sunderland	A	League Division 1	0–7
1929	Burnley	H	League Division 1	1–3
1935	Preston North End	H	League Division 1	2–1
1946	Wolves	H	League Division 1	1–5
1957	West Ham United	H	League Division 2	1–1
1963	Arsenal	A	League Division 1	1–1
1966	Ajax	A	European Cup 1st round 1st leg	1–5
1968	West Ham United	H	League Division 1	2–0
1974	Derby County	H	League Division 1	2–2
1985	Aston Villa	H	League Division 1	3–0

Liverpool continued where they left off against Chelsea in their last game and seemed as if they were finding it hard to get going despite the best of starts when cult hero

Molby scored in the first two minutes with a spectacular free kick. The second half was a lot better with Liverpool regaining the confidence that had taken them on a long winning run since their last defeat on the plastic pitch of QPR. It was fitting that Walsh who had now scored 12 goals in the last 12 games and Johnston the best players on the park scored both the goals in the second half.

| 1991 | Southampton | A | League Division 1 | 1–1 |

Jamie Redknapp scored on his first-team debut for the club.

| 1992 | Everton | A | Premier League | 1–2 |
| 1996 | Sheffield Wednesday | H | Premier League | 0–1 |

DECEMBER 8TH

1894	Sheffield United	A	League Division 1	2–2
1900	Manchester City	A	League Division 1	4–3
1906	Bristol City	A	League Division 1	1–3
1923	Sheffield United	H	League Division 1	2–3
1928	Sunderland	A	League Division 1	1–2
1934	Chelsea	A	League Division 1	1–4
1951	Preston North End	H	League Division 1	2–2

Terry McDermott was born in Kirkby. Terry started as an apprentice with Bury before he moved to Newcastle in 1973 for £22,000. He moved to Anfield in the winter of 1974 for £170,000 where he was to spend eight very successful years.

| 1956 | Nottingham Forest | A | League Division 2 | 0–1 |

| 1960 | | | | |

Craig Johnston was born in Johannesburg. Craig paid his way from Australia to try and break into British football and he earned himself a contract at Middlesbrough before hitting the big time with his move to Liverpool in April 1981 for £575,000.

1962	Sheffield Wednesday	A	League Division 1	2–0
1973	Everton	A	League Division 1	1–0
1979	Aston Villa	A	League Division 1	3–1
1981	Arsenal	H	League Cup 4th round replay	3–0

A tight game that had to be decided in extra time where Liverpool scored three quick goals to go forward into the next round. Ray Kennedy played his last game for Liverpool before his move to Swansea a few weeks later. Ironically it was against his former club Arsenal were he won the 'Double'. To add to his honours with Arsenal whilst at Liverpool he won three European Cup winners' medals, five League Championships, one UEFA cup winners' medal and a League Cup winners' medal.

| 1993 | Queens Park Rangers | H | Premier League | 3–2 |

DECEMBER 9TH

1893	Walsall Town Swifts	H	League Division 2	3–0
1899	Preston North End	H	League Division 1	1–0
1905	Wolves	H	League Division 1	4–0
1911	Newcastle United	H	League Division 1	0–1
1922	Newcastle United	A	League Division 1	1–0
1933	Sheffield Wednesday	H	League Division 1	1–3
1950	Portsmouth	A	League Division 1	3–1
1961	Plymouth Argyle	H	League Division 2	2–1

1967	Leeds United	H	League Division 1	2–0
1970	Hibernian	A	European Fairs Cup 3rd round 1st leg	1–0
1972	West Bromwich Albion	A	League Division 1	1–1
1978	Nottingham Forest	H	League Division 1	2–0
1984	Independiente	Tokyo	World Club Championship	0–1

For the second time Liverpool failed to beat their South American opponents in this competition. On both occasions they have now played in it they have failed to score.

1986	Celtic	Dubai	Friendly	1–1
1989	Aston Villa	H	League Division 1	1–1
1995	Bolton	A	Premier League	1–0

DECEMBER 10TH

1898	Derby County	A	League Division 1	0–1
1910	Bury	A	League Division 1	0–3
1921	Aston Villa	H	League Division 1	2–0
1927	Birmingham City	H	League Division 1	2–3
1932	Birmingham City	A	League Division 1	0–3
1938	Grimsby Town	H	League Division 1	2–2
1949	Huddersfield Town	A	League Division 1	2–3
1955	Burnley	H	League Division 2	1–1
1960	Swansea Town	H	League Division 2	4–0
1966	Manchester United	A	League Division 1	2–2
1975	Slask Wroclaw	H	UEFA Cup 3rd round 2nd leg	3–0
1977	Norwich City	A	League Division 1	1–2
1983	Coventry City	A	League Division 1	0–4

DECEMBER 11TH

1897	Wolves	A	League Division 1	1–2
1909	Middlesbrough	H	League Division 1	0–0
1920	Burnley	A	League Division 1	0–1
1926	Tottenham Hotspur	A	League Division 1	2–1
1937	Bolton Wanderers	A	League Division 1	0–0

1942   Alf Arrowsmith was born in Manchester. Alf was signed from Ashton United in August of 1960 for just over £1000. He spent over eight years at Anfield before being sold to Bury in 1968 for £25,000. Whilst his appearances were limited he scored a respectable 24 goals in 50 games for the club, most of the appearances came in the Championship winning season of 1963/4.

| 1948 | Preston North End | A | League Division 1 | 2–3 |
| 1954 | Birmingham City | A | League Division 2 | 1–9 |

This abysmal performance equalled the club's worst-ever defeat in the League.

1961   Steve Nicol was born in Irvine. Steve joined Ayr United straight from the Juniors and quickly made an impression. He played 90 games for Ayr before joining Liverpool in 1981.

| 1965 | Arsenal | H | League Division 1 | 4–2 |

1969   Stig-Inge Bjornebye was born in Elvcrum, Norway.

| 1971 | Derby County | H | League Division 1 | 3–2 |
| 1976 | Queens Park Rangers | H | League Division 1 | 3–1 |

1982	Watford	H	League Division 1	3–1
1988	Everton	H	League Division 1	1–1
1991	Swaravaski Tirol	H	UEFA Cup 3rd round 2nd leg	4–0

Dean Saunders scored a hat-trick.

1993	Swindon Town	H	Premier League	2–2
1994	Crystal Palace	H	Premier League	0–0

1996 John Scales was sold to Tottenham for £2.6 million. John had never really cemented his place at the club despite making over 80 appearances in his two years at the club. He won a League Cup winners' medal in 1995 before returning south, where injury has once again halted his career for a lengthy period.

DECEMBER 12TH

1896	Bury	H	League Division 1	3–1
1903	Wolves	H	League Division 1	1–2
1908	Bury	A	League Division 1	1–2
1914	Bradford	A	League Division 1	0–1
1925	Cardiff City	H	League Division 1	0–2
1931	Portsmouth	A	League Division 1	0–2
1936	Sunderland	H	League Division 1	4–0
1953	Portsmouth	A	League Division 1	1–5
1959	Bristol Rovers	A	League Division 2	2–0
1964	Arsenal	A	League Division 1	0–0
1970	West Ham United	A	League Division 1	2–1
1977	St Mirren	A	Friendly	1–1
1978	Werder Bremen	A	Friendly	1–1
1987	Southampton	A	League Division 1	2–2

DECEMBER 13TH

1902	Aston Villa	A	League Division 1	2–1
1913	Middlesbrough	H	League Division 1	2–1
1919	Middlesbrough	H	League Division 1	1–0
1924	Tottenham Hotspur	A	League Division 1	1–1
1930	Arsenal	H	League Division 1	1–1
1947	Wolves	A	League Division 1	2–1
1952	Manchester United	H	League Division 1	1–2
1958	Scunthorpe United	A	League Division 2	2–1
1969	Manchester United	H	League Division 1	1–4
1972	Dynamo Berlin	H	UEFA Cup 3rd round 2nd leg	3–1
1975	Tottenham Hotspur	A	League Division 1	4–0
1980	Ipswich Town	A	League Division 1	1–1
1981	Flamengo	Tokyo	World Club Championship	0–3

Liverpool's first attempt at winning the trophy ended in failure.

1991	Nottingham Forest	H	League Division 1	2–0
1992	Blackburn Rovers	H	Premier League	2–1
1997	Crystal Palace	A	Premier League	3–0

DECEMBER 14TH

1895	Darwen	A	League Division 2	4–0
1901	Nottingham Forest	H	League Division 1	0–2
1907	Newcastle United	H	League Division 1	1–5
1912	Bolton Wanderers	A	League Division 1	1–1
1929	Sunderland	A	League Division 1	3–2
1935	Brentford	A	League Division 1	2–1
1946	Sunderland	A	League Division 1	4–1
1957	Barnsley	A	League Division 2	1–2
1963	Blackburn Rovers	H	League Division 1	1–2
1966	Ajax	H	European Cup 1st round 2nd leg	2–2
1968	Manchester United	A	League Division 1	0–1
1974	Luton Town	H	League Division 1	2–0
1979	Michael Owen was born.			
1985	Arsenal	A	League Division 1	0–2

A repeat of the opening day's fixture saw Liverpool go to London to face an Arsenal team that had been inconsistent throughout the season. The Gunners also had a mini injury crisis and were forced to play unknown youngster Niall Quinn, a 6ft 4in centre half (who played alongside Tony Adams in the youth team) converted into a centre forward to help their cause. Two silly mistakes in the first half gave the Gunners a 2-0 lead which was to prove decisive as Liverpool were unable to break down a resolute and effective defence. Charlie Nicholas scored the first after just five minutes and Bruce failed to hold a speculative effort from Davis 20 minutes later and the young debutant scored with the rebound. At exactly halfway through the campaign Liverpool were five points behind leaders Manchester United who had won at Aston Villa.

1986	Chelsea	H	League Division 1	3–0
1993	Wimbledon	A	League Cup 4th round replay	2–2
1996	Middlesbrough	H	Premier League	5–1

Robbie Fowler scored four of the goals in this victory. Robbie's second goal after 28 minutes was his 100th for the club in just 165 games. He therefore beat Ian Rush's record by one game.

DECEMBER 15TH

1881	Alf West was born in Nottingham.			
1894	Small Heath	H	League Division 1	3–1
1900	Bury	H	League Division 1	1–0
1906	Notts County	H	League Division 1	5–1
1923	Cardiff City	H	League Division 1	0–2
1924	Cardiff City	A	League Division 1	3–1
1928	Blackburn Rovers	H	League Division 1	1–1
1934	Tottenham Hotspur	H	League Division 1	4–1
1951	Portsmouth	A	League Division 1	3–1
1956	Huddersfield Town	A	League Division 2	3–0
1962	Blackpool	A	League Division 1	2–1
1965	Standard Liege	A	European Cup-Winners' Cup 1st round 2nd leg	2–1
1973	Norwich City	A	League Division 1	1–1
1976	Aston Villa	A	League Division 1	1–5

One of the most astonishing first half-displays of football Villa Park has ever witnessed saw League champions Liverpool blitzed five goals to one. Andy Gray and John Deehan both scored twice and Brian Little once as Villa tore in to a side destined to win both the First Division and European Cup and reach the final of the FA Cup in the same season. On the evidence of their first half display, it was Villa who looked more like European champions and a crowd of 42,851 roared their approval. Villa were unable to maintain the form into the second half, primarily because the Liverpool team were given a roasting at half-time by their manager and recovered their composure, if not their pride, in the second half. Still, the 5–1 win Villa recorded sent shock waves across English football that evening!

1979	Crystal Palace	H	League Division 1	3–0
1984	Aston Villa	A	League Division 1	0–0
1990	Sheffield United	H	League Division 1	2–0

Steve McManaman made his senior debut for the club.

DECEMBER 16TH

1899	Nottingham Forest	A	League Division 1	0–1
1905	Sheffield United	A	League Division 1	2–1
1911	Sheffield United	A	League Division 1	1–3
1922	Nottingham Forest	H	League Division 1	2–1
1933	Manchester City	A	League Division 1	1–2
1950	Wolves	H	League Division 1	1–4
1961	Bristol Rovers	H	League Division 2	2–0
1964	Anderlecht	A	European Cup 2nd round 2nd leg	1–0

Roger Hunt scored in the 90th minute to maintain Liverpool's 100% record in their first season in European competition.

1967	Manchester City	H	League Division 1	1–1
1972	Ipswich Town	A	League Division 1	1–1
1978	Bristol City	A	League Division 1	0–1
1986	Shrewsbury Town	A	Friendly	2–0
1989	Chelsea	A	League Division 1	5–2
1992	Crystal Palace	A	League Cup 4th round replay	1–2

DECEMBER 17TH

1892	Blackpool	H	Lancashire League	0–2
1898	West Bromwich Albion	H	League Division 1	2–2
1904	Bristol City	H	League Division 2	3–1
1910	Sheffield United	H	League Division 1	2–0

James Bradley played what was to be his last game for the club. Bradley who made his debut at the age of 17 hardly missed a game in his five years in the team and was an integral part of the Championship-winning team in 1906. He played a total of 184 games, scoring eight goals.

1921	Manchester United	H	League Division 1	2–1
1927	Tottenham Hotspur	A	League Division 1	1–3
1932	West Bromwich Albion	H	League Division 1	2–0
1938	Sunderland	A	League Division 1	3–2
1949	Sunderland	A	League Division 1	2–3

1955	Nottingham Forest	H	League Division 2	5–2
1960	Leeds United	A	League Division 2	2–2
1977	Queens Park Rangers	H	League Division 1	1–0
1983	Notts County	H	League Division 1	5–0
1988	Norwich City	H	League Division 1	0–1
1995	Manchester United	H	Premier League	2–0
1996	Nottingham Forest	H	Premier League	4–2

DECEMBER 18TH

1897	Blackburn Rovers	H	League Division 1	0–1
1909	Aston Villa	A	League Division 1	1–3
1920	Aston Villa	H	League Division 1	4–1
1926	West Ham United	H	League Division 1	0–0
1937	Arsenal	H	League Division 1	2–0
1948	Aston Villa	H	League Division 1	1–1
1954	Doncaster Rovers	A	League Division 2	1–4
1965	Newcastle United	A	League Division 1	0–0
1971	Tottenham Hotspur	H	League Division 1	0–0
1976	West Ham United	A	League Division 1	0–2
1982	Aston Villa	A	League Division 1	4–2
1991	Tottenham Hotspur	A	League Division 1	2–1

Michael Thomas made his debut for the club shortly after his £1.5 million transfer from Arsenal. Whilst the home crowd abused him throughout the game Thomas showed his quality by ignoring the crowd and producing a fine display, even if the rest of the team didn't.

1992 Stig-Inge Bjornebye was signed from Norwegian champions Rosenborg for £600,000. The Norwegian international has now played over 60 games for his country and was a regular member of the World Cup team in France 98.

1993	Tottenham Hotspur	A	Premier League	3–3
1994	Chelsea	A	Premier League	0–0

DECEMBER 19TH

1896	Derby County	A	League Division 1	2–2
1903	Bury	A	League Division 1	2–2
1908	Sheffield United	H	League Division 1	2–1
1914	Oldham Athletic	H	League Division 1	1–2
1925	Sheffield United	A	League Division 1	1–3
1931	Derby County	H	League Division 1	1–1
1936	Huddersfield Town	A	League Division 1	0–4
1953	Manchester United	A	League Division 1	1–5
1959	Cardiff City	H	League Division 2	0–4

Bill Shankly's first game in charge of the club as manager, obviously he had a few words to say after this game, as the rest is history!

1964	Blackburn Rovers	H	League Division 1	3–2
1970	Huddersfield Town	A	League Division 1	0–0
1973	Wolves	A	League Cup 5th round	0–1
1978	Anderlecht	H	European Super Cup	2–1

| 1987 | Sheffield Wednesday | H | League Division 1 | 1–0 |
| 1992 | Coventry City | A | Premier League | 1–5 |

DECEMBER 20TH

1902	Nottingham Forest	H	League Division 1	2–1
1913	Sheffield United	A	League Division 1	1–0
1919	Everton	A	League Division 1	0–0
1924	Bolton Wanderers	H	League Division 1	0–0
1930	Birmingham City	A	League Division 1	0–2
1947	Preston North End	A	League Division 1	3–3
1952	Preston North End	H	League Division 1	2–2
1958	Grimsby Town	A	League Division 2	3–2
1975	Queens Park Rangers	H	League Division 1	2–0
1977	Coventry City	A	League Cup 4th round replay	2–0
1980	Wolves	H	League Division 1	1–0
1982	Khartoum XI	A	Friendly	1–1
1983	Birmingham City	A	League Cup 4th Round	1–1
1986	Charlton Athletic	A	League Division 1	0–0

Gary Ablett made his league debut. After coming through the youth ranks Gary spent a short time on loan at Derby County and Hull City who in October 1986 tried to buy him for a ridiculously low figure which was turned down by the club.

| 1991 | Manchester City | H | League Division 1 | 2–2 |
| 1997 | Coventry City | H | Premier League | 1–0 |

DECEMBER 21ST

1895	Lincoln City	A	League Division 2	1–0
1907	Middlesbrough	A	League Division 1	1–3
1912	Sheffield United	H	League Division 1	2–2
1927	John Smith was born in Birkenhead.			
1929	Arsenal	H	League Division 1	1–0
1935	Sheffield Wednesday	H	League Division 1	1–0
1946	Aston Villa	H	League Division 1	4–1
1957	Bristol Rovers	H	League Division 2	4–3
1963	Blackpool	A	League Division 1	1–0
1968	Tottenham Hotspur	H	League Division 1	1–0
1974	Birmingham City	A	League Division 1	1–3
1984	Queens Park Rangers	A	League Division 1	2–0
1985	Newcastle United	H	League Division 1	1–1

After a very lacklustre performance against Arsenal in the previous game, Newcastle – who had just made it into the top half of the table – arrived at Anfield and started the game like it was a cup final. In the first minute a young Paul Gascoigne burst through to be hacked from behind by Lawrenson to prevent a certain goal and a penalty was awarded, however the linesman had his flag raised and the offside was given instead. Ironically the name of this linesman was a Mr Everton. Peter Beardsley who was to be a menace all afternoon deservedly put Newcastle ahead in the 22nd minute with a typical sweet finish over Grobbelaar, who had no chance. Ian Rush, who had a rare run of matches, not scoring in his last five games, missed a sitter by firing straight at the keeper and it looked like it was going to be another bad day. However, Steve Nicol restored the status quo when he scored a terrific solo effort in the 35th minute. The second half was evenly matched with Gascoigne and Beardsley always threatening and even the emergence of King Kenny couldn't decide this enthralling encounter. Arsenal, however, after inflicting a 2–0 defeat on Liverpool the week before returned the compliment by winning 1–0 at Old Trafford thanks to a Charlie Nicholas goal. The lead was now down to just four points.

| 1994 | Everton | A | Premier League | 0–2 |

DECEMBER 22ND

1900	Nottingham Forest	A	League Division 1	0–0
1906	Sheffield United	A	League Division 1	0–1
1923	Cardiff City	A	League Division 1	0–2
1928	Manchester City	A	League Division 1	3–2
1934	Sunderland	A	League Division 1	3–2
1951	Chelsea	H	League Division 1	1–1
1956	Bury	H	League Division 2	2–0
1962	Blackburn Rovers	H	League Division 1	3–1
1970	Hibernian	H	European Fairs Cup 3rd round 2nd leg	2–0

Steve Heighway and Phil Boersma scored the goals that put the club through to the quarter-final where they played Bayern Munich.

1973	Manchester United	H	League Division 1	2–0
1979	Derby County	A	League Division 1	3–1
1981	Rangers	A	Friendly	2–0
1983	Birmingham City	H	League Cup 4th round replay	3–0

The lowest crowd of the season, and for many a year at Anfield, of just over 11,000 saw two goals from Ian Rush see Liverpool through to the next round. Bad weather and the fact it was just three days before Christmas may've had something to do with the poor attendance.

| 1990 | Southampton | H | League Division 1 | 3–2 |

DECEMBER 23RD

1899	Glossop	H	League Division 1	5–2
1905	Notts County	H	League Division 1	2–0
1911	Oldham Athletic	H	League Division 1	1–0
1922	Nottingham Forest	A	League Division 1	3–1
1933	Newcastle United	H	League Division 1	1–2
1950	Sunderland	A	League Division 1	1–2
1961	Leeds United	A	League Division 2	0–1
1967	Newcastle United	A	League Division 1	1–1
1972	Coventry City	H	League Division 1	2–0
1989	Manchester United	H	League Division 1	0–0
1995	Arsenal	H	Premier League	3–1

One year after Robbie Fowler scored the fastest-ever hat-trick in the Premiership he scored another, but not in such quick time.

| 1996 | Newcastle United | A | Premier League | 1–1 |

DECEMBER 24TH

1892	South Shore	A	Lancashire League	1–0
1898	Blackburn Rovers	A	League Division 1	3–1
1904	Manchester United	A	League Division 2	1–3
1910	Aston Villa	A	League Division 1	1–1
1921	Manchester United	A	League Division 1	0–0
1927	Manchester United	H	League Division 1	2–0
1932	Sheffield Wednesday	A	League Division 1	0–3
1938	Chelsea	A	League Division 1	1–4
1949	Everton	H	League Division 1	3–1

Two goals from Joe Fagan and one from Kevin Baron ensured the red half of Merseyside had a good Christmas Day as Everton were stuffed at Anfield!

1955	Hull City	A	League Division 2	2–1
1966	Chelsea	A	League Division 1	2–1

DECEMBER 25TH

1894	Bolton Wanderers	A	League Division 1	0–1
1896	Aston Villa	H	League Division 1	3–3
1897	Bolton Wanderers	A	League Division 1	2–0
1899	Derby County	A	League Division 1	2–3

Harry Bradshaw died aged 26. Harry who was part of the Liverpool Division 2 Championship-winning teams of 1894 and 1896 played 138 games and scored 54 goals in his time at the club. He later moved down south to Tottenham and Thames Ironworks (West Ham) before illness tragically ended his life at such a young age.

1900	Derby County	H	League Division 1	0–0
1902	Bolton Wanderers	H	League Division 1	5–1
1903	Derby County	A	League Division 1	0–2
1905	Bolton Wanderers	H	League Division 1	2–2
1906	Manchester United	A	League Division 1	0–0
1907	Chelsea	H	League Division 1	1–4
1908	Aston Villa	A	League Division 1	1–1
1909	Bolton Wanderers	H	League Division 1	3–0
1911	Bolton Wanderers	H	League Division 1	1–0
1913	Manchester City	H	League Division 1	4–2
1914	Bolton Wanderers	A	League Division 1	1–0
1919	Sunderland	H	League Division 1	3–2
1920	Chelsea	A	League Division 1	1–1
1922	Oldham Athletic	A	League Division 1	2–0
1923	Newcastle United	H	League Division 1	0–1
1924	Notts County	A	League Division 1	2–1
1925	Newcastle United	H	League Division 1	6–3

Harry Chambers helped himself to a hat-trick in this Christmas feast at Anfield.

1926	Burnley	A	League Division 1	0–4
1928	Burnley	A	League Division 1	2–3
1929	Sheffield United	A	League Division 1	0–4
1930	Grimsby Town	A	League Division 1	0–0
1931	Sheffield Wednesday	H	League Division 1	3–1

1933	Portsmouth	H	League Division 1	2–2
1935	Arsenal	H	League Division 1	0–1
1936	West Bromwich Albion	A	League Division 1	1–3
1946	Stoke City	A	League Division 1	1–2
1947	Arsenal	H	League Division 1	1–3
1948	Manchester United	A	League Division 1	0–0
1950	Blackpool	A	League Division 1	0–3
1951	Blackpool	H	League Division 1	1–1
1952	Burnley	A	League Division 1	0–2
1953	West Bromwich Albion	A	League Division 1	2–5

On the same day that the club were humiliated at home by West Bromwich Albion John Evans and Frank Lock arrived at the club after Don Walsh spent £20,000 on both players.

1954	Ipswich Town	H	League Division 2	6–2

Billy Liddell scored four of the goals.

1956	Leyton Orient	H	League Division 2	1–0
1957	Grimsby Town	A	League Division 2	1–3

Antonio Rowley will be remembered as the last player to score for Liverpool on a Christmas Day.

1984	John Balmer died aged 68.

DECEMBER 26TH

1896	Burnley	A	League Division 1	1–4
1898	West Bromwich Albion	A	League Division 1	1–0
1901	Sunderland	H	League Division 1	0–1
1903	Blackburn Rovers	H	League Division 1	1–2

Arthur Riley was born in Transvaal. Another of the South African influx at Anfield arrived in August 1925.

1904	Barnsley	H	League Division 2	2–1
1905	Stoke City	A	League Division 1	1–2
1906	Bolton Wanderers	H	League Division 1	0–2
1908	Nottingham Forest	H	League Division 1	1–1
1910	Sunderland	H	League Division 1	1–2
1912	Newcastle United	H	League Division 1	2–1
1913	Manchester City	A	League Division 1	0–1
1914	Manchester United	H	League Division 1	1–1
1919	Manchester United	A	League Division 1	0–0
1921	Newcastle United	H	League Division 1	1–0
1922	Oldham Athletic	H	League Division 1	2–1
1923	Newcastle United	A	League Division 1	1–2
1924	Notts County	H	League Division 1	1–0
1925	Newcastle United	A	League Division 1	0–3
1928	Burnley	H	League Division 1	8–0

Gordon Hodgson scored a hat-trick, Jimmy Clarke and Dicky Edmed scoring twice each. This is the only time Liverpool has recorded an 8–0 victory in a League match.

1929	Sheffield United	H	League Division 1	2–0
1930	Grimsby Town	H	League Division 1	1–1
1931	Sheffield Wednesday	A	League Division 1	1–1

1932	Chelsea	H	League Division 1	3–0
1933	Portsmouth	A	League Division 1	0–1
1934	Middlesbrough	H	League Division 1	2–2
1935	Arsenal	A	League Division 1	2–1
1936	Stoke City	A	League Division 1	1–1
1938	Stoke City	A	League Division 1	1–3
1946	Stoke City	H	League Division 1	2–0
1949	Chelsea	A	League Division 1	1–1
1950	Blackpool	H	League Division 1	1–0
1951	Blackpool	A	League Division 1	0–2
1952	Burnley	H	League Division 1	1–1
1953	West Bromwich Albion	H	League Division 1	0–0

After the heavy defeat the day before against the same opposition a much improved performance avoided another heavy defeat. The highlight of the day was when the announcement of the teams was made and Frank Lock was at No 3 and John Evans at No 8. With the lack of newspapers etc over the holiday period the majority of the crowd didn't know the pair were bought the day before.

1955	Stoke City	H	League Division 2	2–2
1956	Leyton Orient	A	League Division 2	4–0
1957	Grimsby Town	H	League Division 2	3–2
1958	Rotherham United	A	League Division 2	1–0
1959	Charlton Athletic	A	League Division 2	0–3
1960	Rotherham United	H	League Division 2	2–1
1961	Rotherham United	A	League Division 2	0–1
1963	Stoke City	H	League Division 1	6–1
1964	Sunderland	A	League Division 1	3–2
1966	Chelsea	H	League Division 1	2–1
1967	Coventry City	A	League Division 1	1–1
1968	Burnley	H	League Division 1	1–1
1969	Burnley	A	League Division 1	5–1
1970	Stoke City	H	League Division 1	0–0
1972	Sheffield United	A	League Division 1	3–0
1973	Burnley	A	League Division 1	1–2
1974	Manchester City	H	League Division 1	4–1
1975	Stoke City	A	League Division 1	1–1
1977	Nottingham Forest	A	League Division 1	1–1
1978	Manchester United	A	League Division 1	3–0
1979	Manchester United	H	League Division 1	2–0
1980	Manchester United	A	League Division 1	0–0
1981	Manchester City	H	League Division 1	1–3
1983	West Bromwich Albion	A	League Division 1	2–1
1984	Leicester City	H	League Division 1	1–2
1985	Manchester City	A	League Division 1	0–1

Howling wind and rain greeted this Boxing Day fixture and it certainly affected the players, who found it very hard to get into their stride. To make it even more difficult Manchester City played the entire game with 10 men behind the ball at every opportunity. They did have one effort in the game and it resulted in a headed goal for defender Clive Wilson. Everton revived the Xmas spirit by smashing Manchester United at Goodison 3–1 to keep the lead down to four points, however, West Ham after a good run themselves had joined Liverpool on 45 points.

1986	Manchester United	H	League Division 1	0–1
1987	Oxford United	A	League Division 1	3–0
1988	Derby County	A	League Division 1	1–0
1989	Sheffield Wednesday	H	League Division 1	2–1
1990	Queens Park Rangers	A	League Division 1	1–1
1991	Queens Park Rangers	A	League Division 1	0–0
1993	Sheffield United	A	Premier League	0–0
1994	Leicester City	A	Premier League	2–1
1996	Leicester City	H	Premier League	1–1
1997	Leeds United	H	Premier League	3–1

DECEMBER 27TH

1897	Sunderland	H	League Division 1	0–2
1898	Nottingham Forest	A	League Division 1	1–1
1902	Bury	A	League Division 1	1–3
1909	Arsenal	A	League Division 1	1–1
1910	Everton	A	League Division 1	1–0
1913	Blackburn Rovers	H	League Division 1	3–3
1919	Everton	H	League Division 1	3–1
1920	Chelsea	H	League Division 1	2–1
1921	Huddersfield Town	H	League Division 1	2–0
1926	Burnley	H	League Division 1	2–2
1927	Arsenal	H	League Division 1	0–2
1930	Blackburn Rovers	A	League Division 1	3–3
1932	Chelsea	A	League Division 1	2–0
1937	Birmingham City	A	League Division 1	2–2
1938	Stoke City	H	League Division 1	1–0
1947	Arsenal	A	League Division 1	2–1
1948	Manchester United	H	League Division 1	0–2
1949	Chelsea	H	League Division 1	2–2
1954	Ipswich Town	A	League Division 2	0–2

Ipswich gained revenge for their humiliating result two days earlier.

1955	Stoke City	A	League Division 2	2–3
1958	Rotherham United	H	League Division 2	4–0
1960	Rotherham United	A	League Division 2	0–1
1965	Leeds United	H	League Division 1	0–1
1971	West Bromwich Albion	A	League Division 1	0–1
1975	Manchester City	H	League Division 1	1–0
1976	Stoke City	H	League Division 1	4–0
1977	Wolves	H	League Division 1	1–0
1980	Leeds United	H	League Division 1	0–0
1982	Manchester City	H	League Division 1	5–2

Kenny Dalglish scored a hat trick.

1983	Leicester City	H	League Division 1	2–2

| 1986 | Sheffield Wednesday | A | League Division 1 | 1–0 |

1901	Blackburn Rovers	H	League Division 1	1–0
1903	Wolves	A	League Division 1	2–4
1907	Sheffield United	H	League Division 1	3–0
1909	Sheffield United	A	League Division 1	2–4
1912	Arsenal	A	League Division 1	1–1
1926	Bolton Wanderers	H	League Division 1	1–2
1929	Middlesbrough	H	League Division 1	5–2
1935	Chelsea	H	League Division 1	2–3

South African Gordon Hodgson played his last game for the club before his £3000 transfer to Aston Villa. Gordon who made his debut in 1926 played 378 games scoring 240 goals. For over 30 years he held the club goalscoring record before being overtaken by Roger Hunt. He managed to win three caps for England during his time at Anfield. Will always be remembered as a Liverpool legend.

1946	Sheffield United	H	League Division 1	1–2
1957	Cardiff City	A	League Division 2	1–6
1959	Charlton Athletic	H	League Division 2	2–0
1964	Sunderland	H	League Division 1	0–0
1965	Leeds United	A	League Division 1	1–0
1982	Sunderland	A	League Division 1	0–0
1985	Nottingham Forest	A	League Division 1	1–1

In freezing conditions on a pitch that at best described as unsafe, it was always going to be a difficult game for Liverpool. However, they stuck at their task in atrocious circumstances and despite going behind to a Neil Webb strike always looked the more likely to score. It wasn't until the second half though when McDonald completed a nice move involving five players to calmly place the ball in the corner. It was fitting though that it was left to Bruce to provide the moment of the game, he acrobatically saved a penalty from Peter Davenport in the 65th minute to earn a draw.

1987	Newcastle United	H	League Division 1	4–0
1991	Everton	A	League Division 1	1–1
1992	Manchester City	H	Premier League	1–1
1993	Wimbledon	H	Premier League	1–1
1994	Manchester City	H	Premier League	2–0
1997	Newcastle United	A	Premier League	2–1

1894	Small Heath	A	League Division 1	0–3
1897	Sheffield United	A	League Division 1	2–1
1900	Blackburn Rovers	A	League Division 1	1–3
1923	West Ham United	H	League Division 1	2–0
1928	Bury	A	League Division 1	2–2
1934	Blackburn Rovers	A	League Division 1	2–0
1936	West Bromwich Albion	H	League Division 1	1–2
1951	Huddersfield Town	A	League Division 1	2–1
1956	Grimsby Town	A	League Division 2	0–0

1973	Chelsea	A	League Division 1	1–0
1976	Manchester City	A	League Division 1	1–1
1979	West Bromwich Albion	A	League Division 1	2–0
1984	Luton Town	H	League Division 1	1–0
1996	Southampton	A	Premier League	1–0

John Barnes scored the only goal of the game which meant Liverpool finished the year in top position in the table. Unfortunately they were not able to hold on to the positon.

DECEMBER 30TH

1893	Grimsby Town	H	League Division 2	2–0
1899	Stoke City	H	League Division 1	0–0
1905	Arsenal	H	League Division 1	3–0
1911	Arsenal	H	League Division 1	4–1

Two goals each from John Bovill and Jack Parkinson helped finish off the year in style. The new year didn't follow suit as it saw Liverpool go 13 games without a win and narrowly avoid relegation.

1922	Chelsea	A	League Division 1	0–0
1933	Wolves	H	League Division 1	1–1
1967	Coventry City	H	League Division 1	1–0
1972	Crystal Palace	H	League Division 1	1–0
1988	John Jeffers was sold to Port Vale for £30,000.			
1989	Charlton Athletic	H	League Division 1	1–0
1990	Crystal Palace	A	League Division 1	0–1
1995	Chelsea	A	Premier League	2–2

DECEMBER 31ST

1892	Heywood Central	A	Lancashire League	2–1
1898	Sheffield Wednesday	A	League Division 1	3–0
1904	Glossop	A	League Division 2	2–0
1910	Bradford City	A	League Division 1	3–1
1921	Bradford City	A	League Division 1	0–0
1927	Sheffield United	H	League Division 1	2–1
1932	Wolves	A	League Division 1	1–3
1938	Preston North End	H	League Division 1	4–1

The last game to be played on New Year's Eve before the outbreak of the War the following year. Phil Taylor scored two goals, with Joe Fagan and Jack Balmer getting the other goals.

1949	Arsenal	H	League Division 1	2–0
1955	Blackburn Rovers	H	League Division 2	1–2
1960	Middlesbrough	H	League Division 2	3–4
1966	Everton	H	League Division 1	0–0
1977	Newcastle United	A	League Division 1	2–0
1983	Nottingham Forest	A	League Division 1	1–0

Ian Rush finished off the year as he started it by scoring the only goal of the game.

| 1994 | Leeds United | A | Premier League | 2–0 |